TELLING
THE TRUTH

Other books
by Marvin Olasky

*Renewing American Compassion: Toward a Personal
and Spiritual War on Poverty* (1996)

*Fighting for Liberty and Virtue: Political and Cultural
Wars in Eighteenth-Century America* (1995)

Loving Your Neighbor, coauthor (1995)

Philanthropically Correct (1993)

*Abortion Rites: A Social History of Abortion
in America* (1992, 1995)

The Tragedy of American Compassion (1992, 1995)

Patterns of Corporate Philanthropy, coauthor
(1991, 1992)

*Central Ideas in the Development of American
Journalism* (1991)

More Than Kindness, coauthor (1990)

The Press and Abortion, 1838-1988 (1988)

Freedom, Justice, and Hope, coauthor (1988)

Prodigal Press (1988)

Patterns of Corporate Philanthropy (1987)

Turning Point, coauthor (1987)

*Corporate Public Relations: A New Historical
Perspective* (1987)

TELLING THE TRUTH

How to Revitalize Christian Journalism

MARVIN OLASKY

CROSSWAY BOOKS • WHEATON, ILLINOIS
A DIVISION OF GOOD NEWS PUBLISHERS

Telling the Truth

Copyright © 1996 by Marvin Olasky

Published by Crossway Books
a division of Good News Publishers
1300 Crescent Street
Wheaton, Illinois 60187

Art Direction/Design: Mark Schramm

First printing, 1996

Printed in the United States of America

ISBN 0-89107-885-1

Library of Congress Cataloging-in-Publication Data
Olasky, Marvin N.
    Telling the truth : how to revitalize Christian journalism /
    Marvin Olasky.
        p.   cm.
    ISBN 0-89107-885-1
    1. Journalism, Religious—United States.   2. Christian literature—
    —Publication and distribution—United States.   3. Press, Protestan—
    —United States   4. Evangelism—United States.   I. Title.
    PN4888.R4043   1996
    070.4'492—dc20   95-42467

05	04	03	02	01	00	99	98	97	96
15	14	13	12	11	10	9	8	7	6	5	4	3	2	1

DEDICATION

For Joel Belz, Nickolas S. Eicher,
and Katherine Eicher

TABLE OF CONTENTS

ACKNOWLEDGMENTS

My greatest acknowledgment, as always, is to Jesus Christ, who not only yanked me off the fast road to perdition two decades ago but has continued to present gifts ever since: dear wife Susan, most excellent children Pete, David, Daniel, and Benjamin, and opportunities for writing and adventure. I have frequently sinned in not praying as I should, but He has constantly been not only faithful but more than faithful: He has given what I could never have asked for, because my imagination concerning the warmth of marriage and the enjoyment of children was too small.

I also acknowledge the servants of Christ who are found in abundance at Crossway Books. Faithfulness in Christian publishing means facing down theological temptations and putting up with economic constraints; Crossway personnel such as Lane Dennis, Len Goss, and Steve Hawkins pass the test.

A third round of appreciation goes to the Lynde and Harry Bradley Foundation, which provided funding for this work, and to the fine *World* writers whom I quote in the pages that follow: Among them are Joe Maxwell, Roy Maynard, and Mindy Belz. Many others at *World*, including those in the graphics and business areas, also deserve recognition, but this book is dedicated to two *World* people specifically and to one other. If, as E. B. White noted, it is hard to find someone who is both a good friend and a good writer, it is triply hard to find friend, writer, and teacher all rolled into one—but that is what publisher Joel Belz is. Nick Eicher is a friend and a superb managing editor, *World's* most valuable player, and a joy to work with week after week.

The third person in the dedication, Nick's daughter Katherine, never had the opportunity to write, or even talk; she died in the summer of 1995 of a genetic disorder after living for only four months. Even during that time, though, her life and the faith of her parents touched many other lives. I never met Katherine, but her role in God's providence is such that although there are many people I look forward to interviewing in heaven, she is the one of all those now dead whom I look forward to hugging.

The Sad State of Christian Journalism

A t every mail delivery the tide rolls in. At my post as editor of *World* I see more of the flotsam and jetsam of Christian journalism than I ever imagined existed. The postman brings some Christian publications flush with public relations pieces and propaganda. He brings others filled with "objective" articles beloved by those journalism professors who lack a sense of objective truth and see a story that balances ungodly subjectivities as the highest form of service.

Eight years ago, in a book called *Prodigal Press*, I described how American secular journalism is the wayward son of Christianity. Now, after some additional experience in editing, journalism teaching, and service as a judge in Evangelical Press Association contests, I need to acknowledge that much of modern evangelical journalism also has gone astray. Many newspapers have little news. Many publications that deem themselves Christian are neither hot nor cold, but tepid. Thoughtful readers thus spit them out.

Too often some of the most prominent publications provide not more but LESS: Lukewarm Evangelical Substance and Style. Too often evangelical publications, instead of exhibiting the journalistic excitement of the hunt, are content to print public-relations releases and carry on their business in a joyless manner that makes them resemble a proctologist's press. Too often they fall from a proper seriousness of purpose into solemnity, so that readers who page through them do so out of duty rather than pleasure. And many in search of news do not bother.

One form of Christian journalism has had an enormous spurt in recent years; one form has not. Christian talk radio is on a roll; quality Christian news publications are hard to find, and none of the conventional explanations tells why.

• Contrary to some modern myths, the problems of Christian print journalism have not arisen because readership of newspapers and magazines is declining. True, the percentage of American adults who read a daily newspaper each day has declined significantly over the past thirty years, but the number of nondaily newspapers has soared: Since the mid-1960s total circulation of weekly newspapers has almost doubled, from thirty to fifty-five million. Big circulation gains during the 1990s at conservative public affairs magazines such as *National Review* and *The American Spectator* have also shown that if the right stories are printed and marketed, readers will come.

• The argument that news publications aimed at a particular segment of the population cannot survive and thrive also does not hold. Specialty news publications that are of high interest to advertisers, such as *Golf Digest*, have prospered, but other news carriers aimed at particular ethnic, ideological, or religious niches—blacks, Hispanics, New Agers, singles, the elderly, parents, homosexuals, Catholics, Jews, and so on—have also done well.

• Nor can Christian publishers argue reasonably that their audience is not sufficiently print-oriented to keep press hope alive. The *Washington Post*, in referring to evangelicals as unintelligent and easily led, implied also that they were poorly read, but that is true neither historically or—at least in relation to the general population—currently. It is true that weak worship at some churches has contributed to not only lightness of belief but a decreased willingness to read tough-minded analyses of current events. Fluff generates fluff, yet non-Christians who face parallel social tendencies have still managed to develop quality news analysis.

• Nor can it reasonably be said that evangelicals have no need for quality publications. Now as in the past, Christians under attack desperately need good magazines and newspapers, just as colonists under attack before the American Revolution needed committees of correspondence. For example, it will be hard to replace the welfare state with a truly compassionate system based in religious and private charities if effective groups face antagonistic coverage by those committed to increasing centralized power.

• The success of Christian radio talk shows has not eliminated the need for words on paper. Articles provide readily reproducible affirmation of heroes and in-depth criticism of villains in a way that tapes cannot. At the least, Christian publications can hold powerful liberal newspapers and magazines accountable in a way that now-you-hear-them, now-you-don't broadcasts cannot.

The need is great—and yet, instead of having quality publications, evangelicals are for the most part put to shame. Some of the slimiest publications in terms of morality are far more attractive in style than biblically solid but journalistically stolid local Christian newspapers. In central Texas, for example, a side-by-side graphics and writing comparison of the Bible-believing *Texas Messenger* and the Scripture-spurning *Texas Triangle*, a homosexual monthly, shows that the *Messenger*'s mediocre writing and layout do not glorify God. In city after city throughout America, publications that exhibit moral depravity often show technical superiority.

None of the big economic reasons—the "macro" explanations, to borrow a term from the economists—explain why the *Triangle* is more journalistically readable than the *Messenger*, and why similarly sad comparisons can be made across the country. It therefore becomes necessary to look at the "micro"—particular editorial decisions and especially the writing. Strong photos and graphic elements add enormous value to a publication, but good writing is at the heart of most successful newspapers and magazines, and that is what this book will emphasize.

The rarity of good Christian news publications represents both a crisis of entrepreneurship and a faltering of applied faith. Many aspiring Christian journalists know the Bible but do not know how to apply biblical wisdom to problems of writing and editing. Those who hope to build God's kingdom through journalism need more than good intentions and more than a secular journalism-school education: They need to see how to hold every thought, and every part of their editing and reporting process, captive to Christ.

Judging from their publications, many editors do not know how to develop stories that pile up specific detail gained through journalistic pavement pounding. They fill their pages with warmed-over sermons rather than realistic stories of successful independent schools or corrupted churches and thereby miss an opportunity to teach boldness. They do not go after stories that could expose the aggressiveness of liberal culture and thereby miss an opportunity to alert and organize people as the committees of correspondence did just before the American Revolution. Those publications that do speak up often communicate in a tone so screeching as to be useless in coalition-building.

Sadly, vision without apprenticeship is common. Over the past eight years I have received numerous telephone calls from Christians who "have a vision" for publishing a national newspaper (or some such large project) and are looking for advice. I am obnoxious enough to ask questions about journalistic training: Rarely have those with good intentions paid their dues as reporters or copy editors. I ask about management expertise: Rarely have those with that particular vision put together or even heard of a publication business plan. I am usually forced to suggest to my eager callers that they take two aspirin—one labeled journalistic experience, one labeled business knowledge—and call me in the morning (a morning about five years hence).

That bedside manner does not make me popular, since most callers typically look not for cautionary words but for approval of their plans. The good news is that most of those who have the vision but are inadequately prepared do not have money to throw away on a prematurely begun endeavor. The bad news is that establishing a thriving Christian magazine or newspaper is hard under the best of circumstances. If editors and writers do not have a solid understanding of the principles of biblical journalism and their practical applications, the likelihood of success quickly falls to slim or none. In journalism as in life, God graces us with miracles—but to *expect* a miracle, when we are not using our talents intelligently, is presumption.

Is the struggle for strong Christian journalism worth it? The scheduling of concurrent sessions at a Wheaton College conference eight years ago caused me great consternation: The great theological writer J. I. Packer was scheduled to speak in one room, and I was placed in the next. I knew that Mr. Packer's words would be more valuable than mine, and I wondered whether attendees would—or should—come to a session on ephemeral journalism, when they could hear a fine lecture on eternal verities.

Providentially, I was staying in a dorm room that shared a bathroom with another dorm room. Before walking over to my lecture, as I brushed my teeth in the bathroom, who should come in from the other door to brush his teeth but the estimable theologian himself? Mr. Packer showed God's grace in his kindness: When I stammeringly expressed my sense that I was, in comparison to him, talking trivia, and noted that if I were not speaking I would be sitting in the theology room, not the journalism hall, Mr. Packer said in his resonant British accent, "Nonsense. Think of what revitalizing journalism would do for the cause of Christ in America! It is the most needed sort of pre-evangelism, it is training in Christian worldview, it is an aid to sanctification, and you need to teach people how to do it."

Since then, although I have spent time writing about fighting poverty and abortion and doing many other things, I have always thought that revitalizing Christian journalism was essential. I have also understood, however, that the race is worth running only if our goal is God's glory and not our own. Our prayer should be Paul's to the Galatians: "May I never boast except in the cross of our Lord Jesus Christ" (6:14 NIV).

Along those lines, this book emphasizes the need for those who manage journalistic enterprises to have a well-developed Christian worldview and the ability to apply it. Much of the book focuses on the how-to of writing, with a particular emphasis on what feature-writing reporters need to think through. I have also included material on the great cloud of Christian journalistic witnesses—those reporters and editors of the past who showed us how much can be achieved with the faith that produces courage—along with two chapters from my earlier book, *Prodigal Press*: "The Decline of American Journalism" and "A Christian Journalism Revival?".

There is great opportunity today for those who have that faith and are willing to move beyond the conventional journalistic practices of this secular century. This book is written so much with such pioneers in mind that I have sometimes gone outside my standard, third-person writing and addressed the reader directly: "you." Some literary elegance is lost in the process, but my goal is to challenge readers directly, in the hope that some will become writers. If even fifty new, talented, biblically directed journalists were to emerge in America during the next few years, the revitalization of Christian journalism would be well under way.

CHAPTER ONE

Biblical Objectivity

B efore you begin publishing a newspaper or magazine, you should be able to describe coherently your publication's theological, political, and cultural perspective. Merely saying that your publication is Christian is not enough: Liberal denominations have so devalued verbal theological precision that the glorious word *Christian* can mean little more than, "We hope to be nice."

A better place to start is with J. I. Packer's succinct definition of biblical faith: "God saves sinners." Our holy God saves; man is totally incapable of saving himself; neither government nor any other institution can save us. Our righteous God saves through his sovereign grace, not because of anything we do but out of love for those He calls and covers over with Christ's blood. Our compassionate God saves sinners; we are not essentially good and brought down by a flawed social environment. We are sinners.

You may differ from other Christian journalists on some doctrinal matters, but there is no point in being a Bible-based editor or reporter unless you agree that sinful man needs Christ as Savior and also as Lord. Christian publications lose their punch unless the journalists in charge understand that the Bible is useful not only for salvation but also for application to all aspects of current events as well. Bible-based magazines and newspapers, like individual Christians, should be in the top right-hand quadrant of the adjacent graph (Figure 1), witnessing to

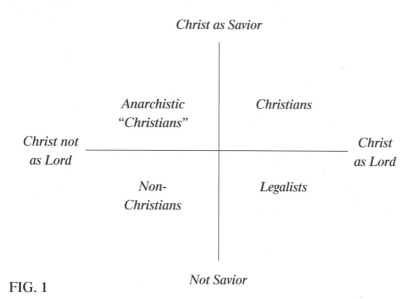

Christ as Savior

Anarchistic   *Christians*
"Christians"

Christ not   *Christ*
as Lord   *as Lord*

Non-   *Legalists*
Christians

Not Savior

FIG. 1

God's saving power but also to ways in which transformed sinners can take Christ-centered dominion over parts of God's creation.

Some people and publications, however, are at top left, praising Christ as Savior but trusting in worldly rather than biblical wisdom to live their lives and cover the news; they emphasize moments of justification but pay less attention to years of perseverance. Others emphasize the Lord's rules but not his saving grace and thus practice a disciplined but joyless Christianity that rapidly becomes legalistic (the bottom-right quadrant). And non-Christians, of course, are in the lower-left quadrant, just saying no to Christ as either Savior or Lord.

This book is addressed to those who are or want to be in the top-right quadrant, and to all of you I speak emphatically: If you are serious about putting out a theologically sound publication, you should also be committed to the final authority of the Bible as the inerrant written Word of God.

Some hard-edged reporters might contend that ideas do not have practical consequences, but biblical commitment or lack of it will radically affect your publication's posture in every area. Some evangelicals have tended to become otherworldly, and others in recent years have compromised with secular liberalism, the dominant cultural trend of recent decades. Courageous Christian journalists, however, need a biblical understanding of this world; only then can their analysis go far beyond the conventional wisdom.

Furthermore, sound theology has consequences in political philosophy: An understanding of sin and a willingness to battle government-supported sin will place you, in the current American political spectrum, right of center. Some Christians are political liberals, but they should realize that the liberal emphasis in twentieth-century America has been on liberation from traditional institutions—family, church, business—in the belief that these institutions are oppressive. They should also see that liberals repeatedly have used governmental power to batter the walls of those institutions: Some of the battering has been unintentional, but the assault is increasingly deliberate. They should see that liberal culture, which emphasizes government rather than family and stresses subjectivity (as in the freedom to choose abortion) rather than objective truth, is becoming the established religion, one that Christians should oppose.

An understanding of sin will even lead you to become what could be called a "biblical conservative." The word *conservative*, of course, carries a heavy burden. Many blacks during past decades have associated it with racism, and the Social Darwinist variety of conservatism—humanity evolves economically through survival of the financially fittest and elimination of the poor—has turned its back on the needy. Nevertheless, conservatives generally believe that limitations on human progress come out of human nature, not external forces. Furthermore, conservatives who fight for limited government may privately defend sin, but they do not use governmental force to push others to sin.

Although non-Christian conservatives do not understand the origins and true nature of sin, they see its consequences and are unlikely to buy government-surplus stain removers that in practice grind the evil deeper into the social fabric. The next four-quadrant graph (Figure 2) distinguishes from left to right those who emphasize unbounded human potential and those who understand the limitations of sinful man, and from top to bottom a reliance on the Bible versus a first turning to man's wisdom.

You must grasp the depth of sin's ravages if you are to understand

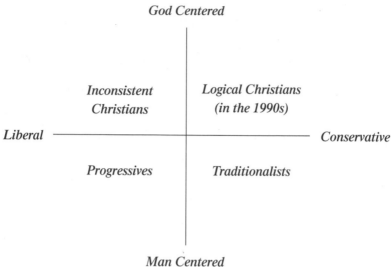

FIG. 2

the full need for Christ's sacrifice: If man is essentially good, Jesus did not have to die. At the same time, an understanding that God saves sinners will push you toward biblical compassion, which means *suffering with* those in need and offering a Christ-based challenge to sinful practices. (True compassion is very different from the liberal, social universalist variety that assumes natural goodness and thus offers merely a pat on the back and coins in the pocket.)

A stress on biblical compassion also separates Christians from those secular conservatives who twist the biblical understanding of man's limitations into scorn for tender mercies. Those differences can be expressed graphically in a way that also depicts the position of Marxists who take liberal ideas of man's goodness and, hoping to speed up the move to utopia, exalt ruthlessness.

The secular left and the secular right are both wrong, but at least those who emphasize private rather than governmental action are less likely to seize power and spread mass misery, as Figure 3 suggests.

My hope is that you will develop or support a biblically conservative publication that combines a stress on man's sinfulness with a concern for others that is based in God's holy compassion. I hope that you will criticize liberal evangelicals but not see them as the chief opponents; rather,

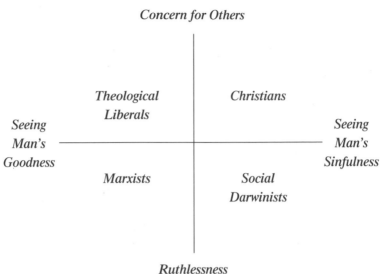

FIG. 3

you should concentrate on the aggression of secular liberals and help to turn back that aggression by forming coalitions with secular conservatives on issues such as governmental control of welfare, education, and health care.

In short, you can be most useful if you fight a limited war against secular liberal culture, which is the dominant social, political, and philosophical force in America today. Your goal should not be the creation of a new Israel or the winning of total victory, for we know that God has placed us in Babylon, and that Christian triumph will come only when Christ returns. Your goal should be faithful perseverance in the containment of evil. Other Christians may have different objectives, in part because there are differing understandings as to whether evangelicals should oppose liberalism, in part because some of our brothers hope to create a new Israel out of American society. Figure 4 notes agreements and differences.

My proposal is that we fight a limited war. We cannot destroy sin—Christ will take care of that when He comes again—but through God's grace we can contain it, and regain lost ground when possible. All Christians try to contain sin through prayer, through building strong churches and strong families, and through worshipping and taking action in many differ-

Babylon

Personal Peace and Affluence	***Cultural Conflict***
1. pluralist by philosophy	1. pluralist by providence
2. spiritual emphasis only	2. battling with confidence (kingdom both already here and not yet)
3. warm fuzzies	3. no illusions of total earthly victory (e.g. abortion)
	4. goal: faithful perseverance

Peace ————————————————————————— *War*

Progressivism	***Total Conflict***
1. universalist re-education redistribution will bring universal harmony	1. tolerationists are enemies
2. goal: peaceable kingdom with man as king	2. goal: Israel reestablished
3. coalitions with those who favor governmental centralization	3. victory will come if only we are firm

FIG. 4   *Israel*

ent ways. Some Christians are called to particular strategies of containment; for example, some work politically, and others establish crisis pregnancy centers, adoption agencies, or biblically based homeless shelters. Your particular calling may be to work journalistically; our weapons are not guns but biblical ideas prayerfully applied to public issues.

How will you—or any of us—know the right applications? Only by realizing that this is the world that the Lord has made, and that only He understands it fully. The Christian journalistic goal, then, is true objectivity: presentation of the God's-eye view. We acknowledge our inability to do that, since we are sinners with fallen wills and very limited understanding. Nevertheless, we do not give up. The Koran calls Allah "inscrutable," but the Bible shows that God reveals his thoughts to man. Much remains hidden, as Job learned, and much we see darkly, as the apostle Paul pointed out. Still, we do have some sight, and when we study the Bible to see what God says about issues, we can come closer to that God's-eye view.

The opportunity to approach true objectivity also depends on the nature of the issue. White-water rafters speak of six classes of rapids: class-one rapids are easy enough for a novice to navigate, and class-six rapids whisper death. The issues that journalists report are rapids; providentially, the Bible is clear enough so that many of them fall into class one or two. Here are the classes and examples:

Class one: explicit biblical embrace or condemnation. The Bible condemns homosexuality so clearly that only the most shameless of those who twist Scripture can try to assert the practice's biblical acceptability. Biblical objectivity means showing the evil of homosexuality; balancing such stories by giving equal time to gay activists is ungodly journalism. Similarly, in an article showing the sad consequences of heterosexual adultery there is no need to quote proadultery sources.

Class two: clearly implicit biblical position. Even though there is no explicit biblical injunction to place children in Christian or home schools, the emphasis on providing a godly education under parental supervision is clear. Biblical objectivity means supporting the establishment and improvement of Bible-based education, and criticizing government schools, in the understanding that turning education over to "professionals" who have no regard for God is an abdication of biblical parental responsibility.

Class three: partisans of both sides quote Scripture but careful study allows biblical conclusions. On poverty-fighting issues, partisans from the left talk of God's "preferential option" for the poor, but the biblical understanding of justice means giving the poor full legal rights and not treating them as more worthy than the rich by virtue of their class position. Since even widows are not automatically entitled to aid, broad entitlement programs are suspect. Biblically, provision of material help should be coupled with the provision of spiritual lessons; the poor should be given the opportunity to glean but challenged to work.

Class four: biblical understanding backed by historical experience. Even though there is no indisputable biblical commandment that strictly limits government, chapter 8 of 1 Samuel describes the dangers of human kingship, and it is clearly bad theology to see government as savior in areas such as health care. The historical record over the centuries is clear, and in recent American experience we have particular reason to be suspicious of the person who says, "I'm from the government and I'm here to help you."

Class five: biblical sense of human nature. On class-five issues there is no clear biblical mandate and no clear historical trail, but certain understandings of human nature can be brought to bear. For example, those who believe that peace is natural emphasize negotiations and dis-armament. A biblical understanding of sin, however, leads to some tough questions: What if war is the natural habit of sinful, post-Fall man? What if some leaders see war as a useful way to gain more power in the belief that they can achieve victory without overwhelming losses? History is full of mistaken calculations of that sort—dictators have a tendency to overrate their own power—but they may still plunge ahead unless restrained by the obvious power of their adversaries. Objectivity in such a situation emphasizes discernment rather than credulity: If we do not assume a benign human nature concerning warfare, we need to plan for military preparedness and raise the cost of war to potential aggressors.

Class six: Navigable only by experts, who might themselves be over-turned. On a class-six issue there is no clear biblical position, no histor-ical trail for the discerning to apply, and not much else to mark our path. On an issue of this kind—NAFTA is a good example—you should bal-ance views and perspectives.

This six-fold definition suggests a framework for biblical objectiv-ity that will enable you to push hard but avoid twisting Scripture. When you take a very strong biblical stand on a class-one or class-two issue, you will be objective. When you take a more balanced position on a class-five or class-six issue by citing the views and approaches of a vari-ety of informed sources, you also are being biblically objective, because we cannot be sure on an issue when the Bible is not clear. Objectivity is faithful reflection of the biblical view, as best we can discern it through God's Word. When there is no view that we can discern, then we cast about for wisdom where we can find it.

It is important to keep in mind throughout this process that many rapids are class one or two. One of the great contributions of the Protestant Reformation was its emphasis on the perspicuity (literally, the "see-through-ableness") of Scripture. All Christians are commanded to search the Scriptures (John 5:39, Acts 17:11, 2 Tim. 3:15–17). It is bad to mistake hard rapids for easy ones, but experienced Christian journalists who read the Bible faithfully can have confidence in their ability to paddle aggres-sively through most rapids without being thrown into freezing water.

Accuracy and fairness are always essential for journalists; fear is not. There is no need to approach every issue as if it were a class six. At the same time, arrogance is ungodly and also unproductive: If a Christian journalist pulls a Bible verse out of context in order to tell readers that God commands a specific action in relation to Bosnia or Korea, he generates sneers among those disposed to think that all biblical application is of the here-a-verse, there-a-verse variety. There is nothing wrong with cautiously approaching a truly dangerous section of the river.

In summary, biblical objectivity—commitment to proclaiming God's objective truth as far as we know it—has different applications on different kinds of questions. Biblical objectivity does not fall into relativism or situational ethics, however, because its sole ethic is to reflect biblical positions. In that way its philosophical base is diametrically opposed to the prevailing liberal theory of objectivity, which assumes that there is no true truth on any issue and that every issue must thus be approached as if it were a class six. Christ did not die for us so that we would be captives of fear.

Liberal theory emphasizes the balancing of subjectivities: Specific detail A, which points a reader in one direction, should be balanced by specific detail B, which points the reader in another. A prosomething statement by Person X is followed by an antisomething statement from Person Y. In practice, this objectivity has limitations: Reporters have never felt the need to balance anticancer statements with procancer statements. In recent practice, secular-liberal reporters have seen pro-life concerns or homophobia as cancerous, and many other Christian beliefs as similarly harmful. But you should be aware that many reporters still publicly maintain their so-called objectivity.

The balancing act in recent years has become farcical: Many reporters privately acknowledge that they put their hands on the scales, but try to do so in subtle ways unnoticed by readers. Christian journalists, in situations where the Bible shows us the right path (and it does so most of the time), should reject both the theory and the farce. Biblically, there is no neutrality: We are either God centered or man centered.

Christian reporters should give equal space to a variety of perspectives only when the Bible is unclear. Editors who see leftist evangelicals as misled should still give them a chance to respond to questions—but a solidly Christian news publication should not be balanced. Its goal should be provocative and evocative, colorful and gripping, Bible-based news analysis.

The kind of approach suggested here—even novices can aggressively hit those class-one and class-two rapids, and more experienced reporters can shoot through class threes and fours as well—is also liberating for Christian reporters, who should not have to pretend: Readers deserve to know the whole story and the perspective from which it is being told, and writers do their best work when they are allowed to tell what they know and believe.

Again, it is vital to distinguish between journalism and propaganda. In navigating tricky rapids, Christian journalists should try not to ignore boulderlike facts that may be shocking enough to force a change in course: Through crisis God teaches us. Later chapters will also note the need to avoid propagandizing, but the crucial need always for Christians is discernment, the ability to apply the Bible to specific situations as they arise, and for humility when it comes to the tougher problems, as Figure 5 suggests:

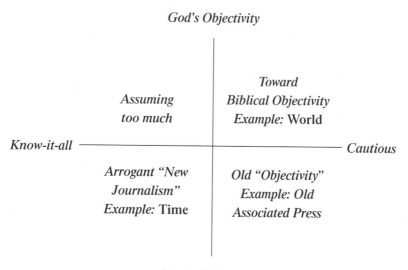

God's Objectivity

	Toward
Assuming	*Biblical Objectivity*
too much	*Example:* World

Know-it-all ——————————————————— *Cautious*

Arrogant "New	*Old "Objectivity"*
Journalism"	*Example: Old*
Example: Time	*Associated Press*

Man's Subjectivity

FIG. 5   *(in practice, worship of man's idols)*

In practice at *World,* I roughly categorize probable stories by rapids class, with the proviso that the classification may change as we gain more insight. For example, a *World* analysis of anti-addiction organizations began with the assumption that tough Bible-based programs could succeed, and governmental programs that by law exclude God would fail.

(This would not be a class-one story because the Bible does not say explicitly that secular antidrug programs will have low success rates. It might be a class two in that "the fear of the Lord is the beginning of wisdom"; but I had looked into other programs in the past and had seen the difference that Christ makes, so I was proceeding on a biblical sense backed up by history.)

Often assumptions prove inaccurate, but in this case the evidence backed them up. Here are excerpts from the story, "A Government Cure for Sin," that resulted:

> Mogan eases his lanky 6-feet-3-inch frame under staple-suspended wiring that would have brought an adrenaline rush to any building inspector; he steps through doorways that seem to be shedding paint and structural integrity each time his heavy footfalls shake the dubious wooden floors.
>
> "Just in here," Mogan says, ducking another electrical cord and flashing a smile at a Hispanic man peeling potatoes at the sink. "Here: the tile. Look at the workmanship."
>
> About half of one wall of a nightmare kitchen in a decaying, discolored three-story house is tiled. Mogan is right; the tile is straight, unchipped, clearly the work of someone who cares. At second glance, the wiring isn't so bad, either. It hangs from the ceiling, but no bare metal shows. The floors are old and achy, but they're swept clean.
>
> Mogan, a 43-year-old former drug dealer, returns to boasting about the tile work. The man who did it, he says, is one of "us." Mogan explained, "He was an addict for years, then he came to Victory Outreach," an inner-city ministry founded by and for addicts who have turned to Christ and rejected their old lifestyles.
>
> Like the tile work, Victory Outreach's drug rehabilitation program in Houston's dismal Third Ward back streets is unexpected order amid chaos. Through the sounds of sirens and blaring horns from the nearby interstate, through the vocal posturing of politicians promising drug rehabilitation for all who need it, Mogan speaks softly about what works—and why the government's preferred methods of rehabilitation don't.
>
> "It's not a disease," he says of addiction. "It's something you do to yourself, it's an action you take. It's sin."

Following the descriptive lead came a look at the disjunction of Washington theory and street practice. First came the official story.

President Clinton traveled to a Maryland prison on Feb. 9 to announce his new strategy in the war on drugs. Citing his cocaine-abusing brother and his alcoholic stepfather, the president told prisoners he wants to spend $13.2 billion beginning Oct. 1 to fight this "threat to the stability of our society and the economic future of our country."

Law enforcement would be beefed up by $271 million, but interdiction efforts, now de-emphasized, would be cut by $94.3 million. Treatment would be boosted from $826.5 million to $5.4 billion. Of that, new government treatment programs costing $355 million would treat 140,000 "hard-core" drug abusers.

Then the streetwise reality:

Pastor Mike Hernandez inspected on Feb. 14 a possible new recovery house and reflected on the president's plan, wondering what kind of treatment Clinton was talking about.

"I understand what [the government] wants to do, but all the money in the world isn't going to buy them one rehabilitation," Hernandez says. "In fact, the more money that is there, the more harm. I call them the dogs of war—the people who put together these drug-treatment programs. They'll see the money, they'll start a program and find some addicts, and then you have five doctors and three lawyers getting the government to pay them. It costs them nothing [emotionally] because they have no love for the addicts, and because they have no love, they have no success."

After presenting the disjunction, reporter Roy Maynard brought in additional evidence.

The debate is on. Clinton showed his desire to move away from a war on drugs and cling more tightly to the concept of drug addiction as a disease: "I know treatment works." But the track record of government programs has been, Hernandez knows, simply dismal. For example, the *Minneapolis Star Tribune* published a stinging evaluation last year of Minnesota's government programs, which are widely copied and commended.

"The $100 million-a-year Minnesota treatment industry claims a recovery rate of 60 to 70 percent," the newspaper reported. But "findings show that the short-term abstention rate is certainly less than 50 percent. And observations from halfway houses and drug and alcohol abusers themselves indicate that the true, long-term success rate may be closer to 30 percent, even as little as 10 percent."

Maynard then took on a pet government-funded program.

> And although it's a drug prevention—as opposed to drug rehabilitation—program, Drug Abuse Resistance Education (better known by its acronym, DARE) is by far the largest antidrug effort in the nation, with $700 million per year being spent to send police officers into fifth-grade classrooms across the nation. It, too, is a failure, according to a slew of studies.
>
> Although there's a good chance that some of the 5 million children who go through the 17-week DARE program each year will develop warm feelings about police officers by actually meeting one, a 1991 Kentucky study showed "no statistically significant differences between experimental groups and control groups in the percentage of new users. . . ." according to William Coulson, a California psychologist who has defected from the DARE camp.
>
> DARE's emphasis on self-esteem—and the belief that low self-esteem leads to drug abuse—is flawed, Coulson adds. Kids "don't need to be told they're wonderful," he says. "They need to be given direction."

Maynard further examined the government's "disease model" and then presented more testimony from the streets.

> Mike Hernandez, himself a former drug dealer who now pastors Victory Outreach's Houston chapter, agrees. "If it was a disease, then science could find a cure," Hernandez says. "But science can't. What science has come up with—for example, methadone, which I was on even when I was still taking heroin—has failed. This hasn't. That's because we're letting God do the work, letting God do the healing." . . .
>
> "I wasn't thinking about anything like my environment or peer pressure when I took a drug," Hernandez says. "I just wanted the drug. I knew it was going to feel good. I did it because I wanted to have everything—and I guess to some people, it would look like I did. I had my drugs, I had money from dealing drugs, I had my wife, I had my girlfriends, I had my gang around me. But I also had a void. I knew something was missing. I was trying to fill that void with drugs, with sex, with alcohol, but it wasn't working. What worked was when my wife was about to leave me and I knew I was at the bottom. That's when I found out about Victory Outreach, and I told my wife I was going in to detox for a couple of weeks, then come home. But I never came home. Instead, she came in with me, and we've been in for 14 years."

Here, then, was a picture of a shoestring program that works—and, unsurprisingly, it ran afoul of government authorities.

> In Santa Paula, California, a Victory Outreach chapter bought a farm and incorporated organic farming into its daily regimen of prayer, Bible study, and hard work. More than two dozen men were working the farm and Pastor Bob Herrera converted the barn into a dormitory. County health officials threatened the group with criminal charges for what it termed an illegal conversion. Herrera and his supporters worked to correct that; they eventually moved the men into an old hotel, which Victory Outreach members now manage.

The story's conclusion then brought us back to its beginning.

> Mogan, the 43-year-old former addict, is visibly proud of the fading, 1940s-era house, although he knows Houston city officials would nail the door shut if they were to ever venture out into that part of the 3rd Ward. When the house was given to the ministry a few months ago, Mogan slept on the rotting wooden floors each night to keep out the crack users, dealers, and prostitutes. It will take thousands of dollars to repair and remodel the house, but Mogan isn't intimidated by the job. The house is now livable—barely.
>
> A group from a Houston Presbyterian church stopped by the other day, Mogan says, and offered to pay for materials to fix the windows, which are at best drafty, but more often simply broken. The bedrooms have tight, Spartan bunk beds. . . .
>
> When asked what the neighbors thought when more than a dozen drug addicts moved in, Mogan laughs.
>
> "They're not worried about us attracting a bad element," Mogan says. "They are the bad element. Next door to us, that's a crack house. The apartments on the other side are drug-infested. This is a gang area. For them, we're a step up. Also, they know they might need us here someday."

Christian journalists who can pound the pavement to pick up specific detail concerning antidrug programs and approach them biblically are needed not only someday, but right now.

CHAPTER TWO

Directed Reporting

Opposition to the world's definition of *objectivity* does not mean that you should have in your publication more opinion writing of the kind that dominates newspaper editorial pages.* Your news and feature stories should have some implicit Christocentric content, which can come out in a variety of ways: by showing how man without God is a beast, by showing how Christians can make a difference by putting biblical precepts into practice, by showing the difference between the fraudulent pretensions of some Christians and the real thing, by exposing anti-Christian leaders and programs, by showing how individuals can glorify God even in Babylon, by showing how Christians enjoy what God has given. . . . But your stories should do this by *showing*.

---

*The editorial page has a sociological origin—reporters wanted to confine publishers to a small part of the publication so that they could run free through the rest—but also a theological base: Nineteenth-century journalists fell into the pietistic pattern of having secular (news) and sacred (editorial) pages. And yet, all news is God's news, showing how he has acted in the world, and abandoning most of the newspaper to a theoretical neutrality places an enormous burden on the opinion section that remains: It is as if we hired ten persons to carry a trunk packed with gold and nine of them sat around.

Many Christian publications (as well as their secular counterparts) love to tell. Some tell bombastically: "Christians are coming forward and standing-up to be *counted* to return America to Christian principles!" Some tell angrily: "Well, we finally made the 'Big Time!' Just as the Union of the Soviet Socialist Republic [sic] fades into the sunset, Comrade Clinton steps into the picture." But such material talks down to the reader because it does not show. God tells us to taste and eat, to see whether it is good, and that is what we should also do for our readers. We should give them sensational facts and understated prose—aromatic food, not just a descriptive menu—and then allow them to taste and eat.

Later on we will go into the means of doing this in detail, but for now it is vital to stress that in what I call *directed reporting*, both parts—biblical *direction* and detailed *reporting*—are essential. A *directed-reporting* article is factually accurate and based on solid research, but it has a clear point of view and an emphasis on showing rather than telling.

The search in directed reporting is always for specific detail. For example, to show that a law pushed by Louisiana governor Edwin Edwards to allow gambling machines at major Louisiana truck stops was also opening the door to gambling in places off the beaten path, give a specific example.

> When a Caddo Parish store owner eight miles from Interstate 20 on a two-lane state highway decided he wanted part of the action, he applied to be certified as a truck stop. Neighbors objected, but he insisted that some loggers stop at his place. Besides, he got the governor to write a letter to the state police, which set up a special section to regulate the video machines at truck stops. And he included the required picture of his establishment—a photo of Edwards campaigning on the property.

In a similar vein, do not tell us that a Christian football player is big; give us his height in feet and inches, his weight in pounds; show him filling up an elevator or dancing with his girlfriend. Do not tell us that a candidate from the feared religious right is energetic: Show him running to meetings or racing around with his children. Do not tell us that a school-board curriculum is messing up children: Show us a child frustrated at not being able to read, a girl putting a condom on a banana, a boy joking about God; give us specific detail about the number and type of complaints from parents. Do not tell us that a teenager has good manners: Show us how he knew which of six forks to use, that he opened doors for elderly folks, that he wrote thank-you notes before the sun went down.

Directed reporting—the combination of a biblical worldview and precise, tough-minded reporting—is atypical within Christian journalism for two reasons. First, it is time-intensive: It is much easier to pontificate about the decline of the Cuban economy than to go to Cuba, interview people there about tight rationing, and report that:

> to get even those limited rations, Cubans stand interminably in line. "For four hours I waited for this!" one grandmother fumed to us as she stalked into her home late one afternoon. She raised a small plastic bag which held two tiny rolls and three small bars of soap.

Second, among those able and willing to do a good job from the field, there is sometimes a reluctance to merge opinion and reporting, even though the opinion in directed reported comes through the selection of specific detail, and it has long been recognized that all reporters inevitably select. Biblical objectivity, however, does not emphasize *personal* opinion: The goal is perspective that is grounded in a biblical worldview. If there is insufficient biblical rationale for a story theme, out it should go.

A Christian publication, in short, should teach, but it should teach effectively by showing rather than telling. Directed reporting is designed to show readers the salient facts in Bible-based contextualization, and allow them to agree or disagree with the conclusions reached. It differs from reporting that picks up here a fact, there a fact, because it is directed within a biblical framework; it does not dither. It also differs from theoretical writing that does not have a base in pavement-pounding reporting. Figure 6 clarifies this.

There is a simple way to check a story that you write or edit: Go through your article and circle each concrete detail, each specific example, each defining quotation. Then put a line through each generality and each nonspecific adjective or adverb. Here is an example of one article published in a local Christian newspaper that, besides containing obnoxious puffery, failed the circle-line test (try applying it yourself):

> If you missed the Right to Life First Annual Fundraising banquet on October 9th, you missed history in the making. The Hyatt was pro-

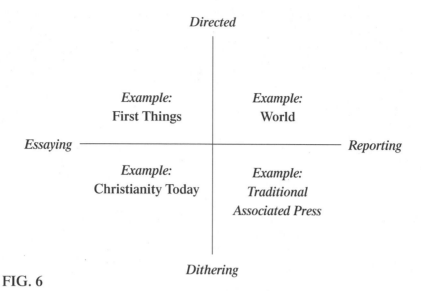

FIG. 6

life headquarters for the evening, with hundreds filling the huge banquet room.

As guests came from far and near, it was obvious from the start, this night belonged to the pro-life movement. Everywhere you turned there was this wonderful feeling of victory.

As the festivities began, X [name removed to protect the innocent] dazzled the large audience with her wit and charm. Known for her dedication and sensitivity for the right to life, she generated an air of success for all present.

State Representative Y showed why he was elected to the state legislature with his boyish smile and soft humor.

And then of course there was Z! This woman stuns any crowd with her ability to reach into the heart of an audience.

To say the banquet was a success is of course an understatement. It was wonderful to say the least. . . .

This material is embarrassing, to say the least. Try to avoid telling readers that something is awful or wonderful, and even try to avoid quoting people who say that. Try to be the eyes and ears and pores of readers, and then have fun making the metaphorical connections that readers will enjoy.

It was the last full day before the official arrival of spring when Kenneth Ryskamp's hearings before the Senate Judiciary Committee began. Outside the Dirksen Building the day was blustery—so windy, in fact, that the National Park Service closed the Washington Monument two hours early as a precaution. A spokesman for the agency suggested that such high velocity blowing could propel children away from their parents.

Inside the paneled hearing room the air was hot. The federal judge from Miami was finally getting a chance to appear on behalf of his nomination to the circuit court of appeals. . . . Auxiliary fixtures were mounted around the walls to illumine the senators and those testifying before them for the television cameras. A gaggle of still photographers was there at the beginning to record the event. . . .

Description of that sort is both literal and metaphorical: high velocity blowing inside and outside, with geese close at hand. Through description, the writer humorously conveyed a sobering thought about judiciary committee hearings.

In thinking through each article, you will need to ask not only whether it will inform readers, but also whether it will have the action necessary for a story to come alive. You will want to know whether there are interesting personalities to be described, or whether the subject is a played-out mine. The thinking process involves how to give broad appeal to what might be a narrow story, and how to convey the essence of a broad story by looking at a microcosm.

The challenge lies in combining uniqueness and universality. Human-interest stories—learning how a particular individual puts into practice biblical principles, or lives apart from God and reaps the consequences—are valuable in this regard. Your publication can avoid ridicule and sarcasm but still have fun with the absurdities and inconsistencies of those who hate God. You should remember to entertain as well as crusade: Since we are to glorify God and enjoy him forever, journalists can begin doing that right now by showing God's glory and providing readers with enjoyment.

Once you have your overall perspective figured out, you must then execute—and that means determining a coverage strategy. The first decision to be made is not how to write about particular issues and questions, but which topics to cover: The world is vast, resources are limited, and choices must be made; even a local publication has more shoveled onto its plate than it can consume. That statement is obvious in one regard, but some editors simply say, "We'll cover the news." (Or, in the *New York Times'* famous line, "All the news that is fit to print.")

The trouble with broad, bland statements is that news does not just happen: Some stories are obligatory for publications to report, but more often editors have considerable discretionary choice over which occurrences to cover. Even editors who stress their objectivity generally acknowledge the inevitability of agenda setting: not telling readers what to think, but instructing them in what to think about. An influential evangelical publication, whether it admits it or not, is also an agenda setter and not just a transcriber of events.

Increasingly, leading news magazines are going further, and telling readers exactly what to think. *Newsweek*, for example, ended an article about an emergency operation aboard an airplane by sermonizing that:

> our lives depend, moment by moment, on a series of tiny miracles. Physicists say that the universe had to surmount vast odds to exist at all; if certain physical constants had been even very slightly different, we would still be waiting for the Big Bang. No one stops to think about that, ordinarily, until an event like this one brings it into focus. Thousands of planes take off every day *without* a surgeon on board. But there was a surgeon on Flight 32.

Furthermore, unless your publication has a very large staff and a travel budget as large as the world, you will need to plan ahead for purposes of coverage and attempt to anticipate the news. This is not always possible, for in a frequently unpredictable world some assignments always need to be reactive. But if you read a wide variety of publications, attempt to detect social trends, and follow the legislative and court calendars, your publication can be on top of information concerning topics that will become hot—and when they do, you will be ready with timely stories. Figure 7 shows how to position yourself in this respect:

Staying ahead will be easier if you become a Christian contrarian, proceeding on the principle that the conventional wisdom revealed in *Time* or *Newsweek* is backward: If they are campaigning for x, it is likely that x is wrong and others will see so. For example, if the top-down leaders are glamorizing homosexual activists, biblically oriented people will be opposing them. Editors can learn much by listening to the bottom-up

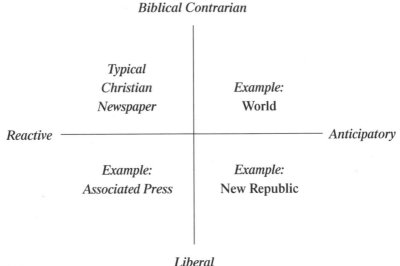

FIG. 7

concerns of Christian and conservative activists who are preparing to derail the secular liberal express.

You should also keep a running projection of when certain stories may appear—but be ready to change plans as new issues emerge or old ones proceed more quickly or slowly than projected. Update your projections every month or so, but hold on to your old ones so you can review whether your publication's planning system is working. What follows is part of a listing from June 1994 of stories that *World* anticipated for the second half of that year:

ANTICIPATORY STORIES, JULY–DECEMBER 1994

Lengths: cover stories are 3,000 words; profiles, 1,000 words; inside stories, generally 750 words (one page), sometimes 1,500 words (two pages).

Black Conservatives

Black church-based enterprise*
Minority politics conference, September 30*
Profiles: Elizabeth Wright, Nona Brazier, Reuben Greenberg, Bob Woodson

* = prospective covers

Growth of black Christian schools, with Atlanta school as face*

Culture Wars

Homosexual culture, following June 27 Stonewall anniversary*
Woodstock aftershocks, following August 13–14 event
No little people, no little places—small victories in culture wars*

Poverty

Comparing federal, Mormon, and Christian welfare systems*
Hardline on homelessness
Christian Community Development Association*
Immigration—border crossings*

Politics

Term limits, based on Supreme Court challenge, and problems
   for Tom Foley in his district*
Profiles: Mike Huckabee, Ron Lewis
Huffington campaign*
Fall campaign wrap-up*

Education

Survey of Christian schools*
Educational movement: Classical Christian schools*
Debate: A Year at Covenant College
Education Watch: Test scores, new history standards, school choice
   in Europe
Profile: Philip Johnson

Pro-life

Norplant vs. abstinence, based on Mall rally in late July, with looks
   at Promise Keepers and Best Friends program*
Profiles: Ken Conner, adoptive families
Euthanasia letter

Media

National Empowerment Television
Comparing Christian and general booksellers conventions
Environmental media association awards and Gorbachev

* = prospective covers

International

Freedom in eastern Europe
Haiti flip-flops
North Korea
Burkina Faso letter
Nigeria letter

As can be seen, *World* covered not only obviously hot issues such as abortion, education, and homosexuality but also picked out other areas of the culture and attempted to familiarize readers with developments of which they might have been unaware. Other Christian publications should also try to provide a biblically conservative alternative in areas that have been captured by secular liberals and their allies among evangelicals.

For example, many Christian publications that are edited by, and predominantly read by, white evangelicals have not given blacks much coverage—and readers thus have not been helped to realize that most blacks share their predominantly conservative values on social issues. If a Christian publication commits itself to more coverage of blacks but takes its cues from the major media, it will pay attention largely to those who have been anointed by white liberals and radicals.

The knee-jerk tendency for Christian publications wishing to reach out to blacks has been: Interview the Jesse Jacksons. There is a more thoughtful approach, however. The black conservative movement, often arising out of black evangelical churches, is now growing rapidly, despite the hostility it faces from the civil-rights establishment. As the NAACP is seen more and more as an ideological interest group, new black organizations are arising to oppose it. Several black conservative magazines, including *National Minority Politics*, *Destiny*, and *Issues and Views*, have emerged recently.

The evangelical tendency to imitate secular trends in music and publishing, generally about ten years late, often has been noted and even lampooned. Christian magazines can interview the usual liberal suspects and make blacks seem like alien creatures to most white evangelicals—"it's a black thing, you wouldn't understand." The alternative, though, is for once to get ahead of the curve by profiling emerging black conservative leaders, and in doing so show readers that family-oriented people of both races have similar political and cultural goals.

World in May 1994 decided to follow that more adventurous path. The first fruit of the new approach was a June 4 cover story— "Emancipation: Black Political Leaders Cast Off Liberal Ideology"— that pointed out the new trend and gave it a face, that of Houston congressional candidate Beverly Clark:

> When Beverly Clark sat on the Houston City Council, she was considered a bright new leader in the black community. Her initiatives—including one that established a daytime curfew for teens— were hailed as boons to black neighborhoods besieged by a rise in youth crime in early 1991. During her two-year term as a council member, she blasted liberal philosophies that put early-release parolees back on the streets in minority neighborhoods and failed to steer young blacks away from crime. Those philosophies weren't in keeping with what most blacks believe, she contended, and had helped sink the community in a morass of unimportant issues and self-defeating lifestyles.
>
> "Our liberal views have gotten us in trouble," she said in 1991. "We have to get back to the old conservative views."
>
> But when she ran for an open congressional seat in Houston, her rejection of lock-step liberalism came back to haunt her. . . .

World then ran other stories about the political changes as well as profiles of Bible-based black conservatives. When Christian publications deal with racial issues, and in doing so challenge readers to go beyond the nostrums of the left, editors are not preaching to the choir; they are pushing the choir to sing better. That should be a goal of your publication.

As long as you provide good reporting, your articles can offer direct challenges to readers without alienating them. For example, one *World* cover story discussed transracial adoption by reporting the challenges that particular families have faced and the satisfaction they have gained. The article contained specific detail about the process, the opposition of many social workers to transracial adoption, and the apathy of many white Christians. It also included questions.

> If a society is judged by how it handles its children, as pro-lifers often say, then what about adoption? And what about transracial

adoption? Ultimately, are American Christians—black and white—walking the pro-life walk, or just talking the anti-abortion talk?

Some readers who become angry with you will cancel subscriptions, but if you print their angry letters and are doing a good job generally, new subscribers will hasten to take their place. Besides, it is exciting to find stories that lend themselves to lively reporting and the opportunity to propose practical alternatives. If you are active rather than reactive in deciding what to cover and when to crusade, you can show how Christians extend the good news outward.

> Terri Cooney, 48, and her husband Jim, 54, were just providing foster care for infant Nathan. They already had two children—both white—one by birth and another by adoption. But as the months went by, their attachment to Nathan grew deeper. The fact that he was black and they white mattered less and less.
>
> For a full 18 months, Nathan stayed in their home as social workers sought to resolve legal issues with the child's birthparents. Nathan's delay had to do with locating an absent father to seek consent for adoption; but it isn't uncommon for black children in America to endure such lengthy delays in processing, most often while a black family is being sought to take the child.
>
> By the time everything was straightened out, Bethany Christian Services was concerned about taking Nathan out of an already stable family environment.
>
> "Would you be willing to adopt?" Bethany asked the Cooneys.
>
> They said yes, and have since adopted five more black and biracial children. Their decision was made after much prayer and was based on believing "God wanted us to do this." Terri says, "We felt it wouldn't be a bed of roses. We weren't foolish."

Try also to be active rather than reactive in examining evil, based on your understanding of the sinfulness of man (all of us) and the holiness of God. For example, instead of merely decrying homosexuality, why not send a reporter into one particular heart of darkness?

> There was little leather visible in the Phoenix, a small, dark bar in San Francisco's Castro district. A few blocks down were the real "leather bars," such as the Eagle and the Barracks, but the Phoenix seemed to be for men intent on drinking away inhibitions, trading raunchy innuendo, and working up the nerve for an evening's outing.

These weren't the militant gays seen in the videos circulated by Christian groups; these were homosexuals in their own district, in a city they won in a fair fight; gays in their most secure environs and yet in their most vulnerable, insecure state. Now began "the nightly search," as one homosexual would term it later that evening.

This article in *World* then went up close and personal with people most evangelicals do not meet.

Denny and Michael were arguing about how deep into the Castro district they should go before driving down to San Jose for a Gay Pride celebration. June 27 marked the 25th anniversary of the Stonewall riots, the accepted birth of the homosexual rights movement, so in nearly every sizable city activities were scheduled on that day and during the preceding week. Rallies were also held in the heart of the country's smaller towns, such as Missoula, Montana, and Tyler, Texas. But it is in San Francisco that homosexuals have moved beyond Stonewall and have established a gay fortress.

Denny, a mid-30s man wearing a Levi's jacket without the arms, was flashing a hard, frowning look at Michael, a little younger and wearing a 1993 Gay Pride T-shirt. The bartender took sides in their argument: "I don't know why you're in a rush to go to San Jose. You'll be bored to tears there."

It was clear that Denny and Michael were regulars, so when asked about the Castro district they seemed delighted to help—and that ended their spat. "Your first time here? To San Francisco?" asked Michael. "There are some things you just can't miss. This place, well, they water down the drinks."

He smiled playfully at the bartender, who feinted with his rolled-up bar towel.

"You need the tour, honey," Denny said. "Come on. You'll be my reason for staying. It'll be better than San Jose—even if this hag keeps bitching." Michael answered that with a wave of his hand. Denny finished his rum-and-coke, then asked if Michael was coming.

"Of course I am," Michael said. "You have the car keys. And I'm not bitching. Come, let's show him our city. . . ."

Then came a tour of the homosexuals' city, along with a portrayal of their brave and beleaguered opposition:

Pastor Chuck McIlhenny agrees—it's "their city." Beginning 25 years ago—or by some estimations, since World War II—San

Francisco has been the model, the experiment, and the proving ground for the gay agenda. For the last 20 years, McIlhenny has watched the city fall, despite the efforts of a tiny band of evangelicals. McIlhenny and his church, an Orthodox Presbyterian congregation, have been the victims of firebombing, assault, vandalism, a lawsuit, and almost constant threats.

The story went on from there to show the battles; overall, the story was strong in its description and characterization, and also provided some comic relief through the sad antics of Michael and Denny.

Try also to find serious stories that anticipate the news but lend themselves to humor. For example, it became clear at the beginning of 1994 that the Clinton administration would propose a welfare-reform package in a few-months' time, but that it would stop, start, and weave back and forth. A story combining three elements—a bit of humor, some critical reporting, and presentation of a biblical alternative to secular liberal programming—became possible.

The story began with a nursery rhyme: "The Grand old Duke of York; / He had 10,000 men; / He marched them up a hill; / Then marched them down again." It then detailed the administration's retreats on "ending welfare as we know" it, and pointed out that "relying on Clinton's 'New Democrat' rhetoric is risky business, Moynihan and others are learning, especially when it comes to reform."

Crucially, the writer did not just settle for criticism, but went on to describe a biblical alternative.

> If Clinton, "the man from Hope," were to look for a model for how welfare should work, he could do worse than to examine Dallas's Voice of Hope Ministries, founded by Kathy Dudley. Mrs. Dudley developed the principles by which she runs Voice of Hope not in a Washington think tank or during a White House all-nighter; she learned them growing up poor in rural Appalachia.
>
> "You've got to have programs of development, not dependency," she says. "If you have programs that don't have any sort of accountability and requirements for personal participation, they're not going to work."
>
> Voice of Hope, based in a poor, black area of West Dallas, has all the usual trappings of a government-run "community development" welfare program: job training, a health clinic, home rehabilitation and construction, a thrift store, and clean-up campaigns.

But Voice of Hope emphasizes the Bible and parental involvement. Children who attend Bible classes also begin job training at the age of nine. Teenagers and their parents are offered classes to learn computer skills, music, math, bookkeeping, and art. In 11 years, the ministry has grown to a $700,000-per-year endeavor that will change the lives of 140 families in West Dallas this year. That budget is met by contributions, not tax dollars.

The program emphasizes personal change through prayer and hard work, not giveaways.

Those changes won't all be comfortable for their clients, Mrs. Dudley says.

"The intensity of the way we work with our families is very high," she notes. "We work with a family for six months in our housing program, helping them to set up a budget, helping them to start a savings account. We help them overcome credit problems, write letters to creditors. We don't do it for them; we do it alongside them. The key is to build people, not just houses."

The ministry also concentrates on rebuilding families.

"An example is our youth programs [at Voice of Hope]," Mrs. Dudley says. "There's no financial cost to the families for the after-school tutoring and job-training programs. You might say that's charity, but it's not. There are definite requirements that the families must meet. It's not in dollars; that's what the poor don't have. What they do have is time, so we require that parents come and participate and commit to volunteering some of their time. If they don't do that, then their kids don't participate. That's something the government absolutely wouldn't do—they're afraid they'd have a political battle on their hands."

World escalated its welfare, and welfare-alternative, coverage in 1995, as Congress took up welfare reform. For example, correspondent Amy Sherman visited Rosedale Park Baptist Church in Detroit's inner city to hear Pastor Hamon Cross Jr. tell those who have been sucked into dependency, "I gotta hurt ya before I can help ya." The church offers free counseling services, but clients must pledge to study specific Scriptures that bear on their problems, to discuss them in counseling sessions, and to hear and take notes on a good sermon each week. The goal is transformation, not just training.

In Michigan, to get a more accurate portrait than that offered by liberal social workers, *World* interviewed Mary Jackson, a cheerfully maternal, middle-aged black woman who eleven years ago deliberately moved into the Smith Homes, a rough inner-city project, in order to help youngsters there. She runs a weekly Bible-club program for about three dozen children and is frank about the problems of "lazy" project residents who have been on welfare for years and have a "deeply embedded" entitlement mentality: "They just want to stay in their own little worlds. . . . They think somebody owes them something."

World showed how some AFDC recipients are heroically trying to turn their lives around in very difficult circumstances, but it was also honest and important to quote Ms. Jackson's irritation with welfare mothers who refused to pay $50 for their children to attend a week-long summer camp: "It's not like they don't have any money. They can afford to get their hair and nails done and wear leather coats that working people can't afford." Michigan welfare reform will succeed only when the moms that Ms. Jackson sees begin treasuring their children above their nails.

Similarly, managing editor Nick Eicher's welfare alternatives reporting from Missouri went much deeper than the conventional wailing about "what will happen to the children" if significant welfare reform kicks in. He spent time not with Children's Defense Fund press releases but with Jerry Hayes, who heads the Sunshine Mission in St. Louis and has set up an MBA program—Mind, Body, and Attitude—for kids likely to fall prey to the street culture of irresponsibility.

Hayes personally understands the difference between that culture and an opportunity culture: As a child he lived part of the time in a government housing project with his mother, and part of the time with a great aunt who made it a priority to quiz him each day on Bible verses and teach him the value of hard work and thrift. He understands that the cultures cannot readily be merged; they have antithetical values, and a person needs more than a government training program to move from one to another.

Coverage of that sort was part of the overall goal of showing, through solidly analytical reporting, the vitality of biblical principles, the usefulness of a biblical worldview, and the emptiness of the current dominant culture, which is secular liberalism. Story planning for the first several months of 1995 reflected interest in attempts by congressional conservatives to dismantle governmental bulwarks of that culture. (In the following partial listing, *C* stands for cover story (3–4 pages), *I* for inside story (1–2 pages), *S* for a series of inside stories, and *P* for profile.)

Battles Against Secular Liberalism in Politics

S Washington policy analysis
CP Presidential candidate profiles
S Contract with America scorecard
P J. C. Watts
P Trent Lott
I Term limits under Republicans
I Social Security: The crazy grandma in the basement
I How to cut government subsidies to farms
C Middle-class and corporate welfare
I Budget savings through privatization
I Racial redistricting in La., Miss., and beyond.
I Future Party Switchers, Republican to Democratic

Battles Against Liberal Aggression in Education

S Education Watch
   Promoting parental choice
   Private vouchers
   Battle among home schoolers
C Black Christian school in Atlanta
P Polly Williams
I Why go to college? Return of the trade school?
I Home school curriculum materials
I Franchising Christian schools

War for the Family (Includes Abortion)

I Contract-with-America effects on families
I Contract with the American family?
C Silence of the Shepherds
I Golden Venture imprisonment
I School lunch programs
C Boarder Babies
S Adoption update
S LifeWatch:

Fed spending on safe sex
Adoption updates
Breast cancer and abortion—continuing coverage

Thinking through stories such as those listed above will be one of your major tasks if you become a Bible-based editor. You will plan coverage within a broad vision of what you hope your publication will accomplish. You need to make sure that your magazine has a distinct identity—within the country, if it is a national magazine, or within the community if it is local.

Remember: Your goal is to glorify God, and then turn word into flesh by walking the talk and helping others to do so also. You will need to decide on the correct mix of the familiar and the surprising, in order to innovate at a speed that will fascinate and not alienate the bulk of your publication's readers who relish the predictable but desire an escape from boredom. At the same time you must be an advocate for your writers, working to establish a friendly environment for creativity within a biblical framework.

CHAPTER THREE

A Great Cloud Of Journalistic Witnesses

Y
ou may get so wrapped up in day-to-day pursuits that you forget long-term goals. The best antidote for distorting impulses is daily Bible-reading. A lesser antidote is some knowledge of the great cloud of journalistic witnesses. Like the heroes of faith told about in Hebrews 11, our Christian journalistic predecessors sacrificed much to gain the opportunity to pursue biblically directed journalism. Christian writers and editor-journalists in the sixteenth, seventeenth, and eighteenth centuries gave up their freedom and sometimes even their lives to win for us, their theological posterity, the right to publish God-glorifying and hard-hitting articles.

Throughout this book, which emphasizes so much the immediate task, we'll be stepping back every third chapter to take a broader perspective.* Let us start about two thousand years ago, when Christ's emphasis on trusting the Father in heaven contrasted so sharply with

---

*For a scholarly examination of journalism history and full footnotes concerning the individuals and publications mentioned in this book, see my book *Central Ideas in the Development of American Journalism* (Hillsdale, N.J.: Lawrence Erlbaum Associates, 1991). Chapters 3, 6, 9, and 12 of *Telling the Truth* include about one-fourth of the material in *Central Ideas*.

Rome's *official story* of governmental power and wisdom. Caesar's message was, "If you obey, we will take care of you." Published news was what authorities wanted people to know. The *Acta Diurna*, a handwritten news sheet posted in the Roman Forum and copied by scribes for transmission throughout the empire, emphasized governmental decrees but also gained readership by posting gladiatorial results and news of other popular events. Julius Caesar used the *Acta* to attack some of his opponents in the Roman senate—but there could be no criticism of Caesar. (Had there been independent journalism, he might have survived the Ides of March.)

The Bible, with its emphasis on truth-telling—Luke (1:3–4 NIV) wrote that he personally had "carefully investigated everything from the beginning" so that Theophilus would "know the certainty of the things you have been taught"—was unique in ancient times. New Testament writers comforted the afflicted and afflicted the comfortable. Once the Catholic Church entered its bureaucratic phase, however, it showed no sympathy for independent truth-telling. In medieval times ballads and poems that mocked rulers could be passed on orally from person to person, but all the news considered fit to write down and copy reflected the desires of earthly rulers.

The tiny and fairly barbaric part of the world where English was spoken was no exception to the general rule. In 1275, the statute of Westminster I outlawed "tales whereby discord or occasion of discord or slander may grow between the king and his people or the great men of the realm." You might think that church leaders would advocate Bible-reading, but anything that could inspire such discord—including the Bible, which stated laws of God under which every man and woman, whether king or commoner, had to live—was banned from common use. After John Wycliffe translated the Bible into English during the late-fourteenth century, a church synod forbade Scripture translation. Wycliffe's books were burned in 1410 and 1412; his bones were dug up and burned in 1428.

The technological opportunity for a big change came in the mid-1400s, with the development of movable type in the Mainz workshop of Johann Gutenberg. Innovation creates possibility; worldviews determine whether, and how quickly, inventions are used. Demand from monasteries and kings or commercial leaders for big Latin Bibles was growing, and at first printed volumes merely met that demand: The Bibles were usually for show rather than tell. Printing created potential for change, but as long as priests discouraged Bible-reading and governments jailed or killed independent printers, journalism that was dependent on God but independent from state or state church pressures had little opportunity to flourish.

Early post-Gutenberg developments in England showed the limited effect of the technological revolution by itself. Printing began there in 1476 when William Caxton, given royal encouragement and grant of privileges upon good behavior, set up a press in Westminster. Others followed, but were careful to avoid publishing works that might irritate king or prelates. Regulations limited the number of printers and apprentices. Royal patents created printing monopolies. Importation, printing, and distribution of threatening books—such as English translations of the Bible—were prohibited. In this policy England remained in line with other state-church countries during the early 1500s—but then came the providential sound of a hammer on a door, and the beginning of a theological onslaught (aided by journalistic means) that changed Europe.

The effect of Martin Luther's theses and his subsequent publications is well known, but one aspect often is missed: Luther's primary impact was not as a producer of treatises, but as a very popular writer of vigorous prose that concerned not only theological issues but their social and political ramifications. Between 1517 and 1530 Luther's thirty publications probably sold well over three hundred thousand copies, an astounding total at a time when illiteracy was rampant and printing still an infant.

Luther and other Reformation leaders emphasized the importance of Bible-reading; Christians were to find out for themselves what God was saying. Literacy rates began to skyrocket everywhere that the Reformation took root, while remaining low wherever it was fought off. Luther not only praised the translation of the Bible into vernacular languages but also made a masterful one himself. In preparing his German translation, Luther so understood the need for specific detail to glorify God and attract readers that when he wanted to picture the precious stones and coins mentioned in the Bible, he first examined German court jewels and numismatic collections. Similarly, when Luther needed to describe Old Testament sacrifices, he visited slaughterhouses and gained information from butchers.

Furthermore, Luther understood that it was important to present bad news as well as good. Luther's Reformed theological understanding led him to write, "God's favor is so communicated in the form of wrath that it seems farthest when it is at hand. Man must first cry out that there is no health in him. He must be consumed with horror. . . . In this disturbance salvation begins. When a man believes himself to be utterly lost, light breaks. Peace comes in the word of Christ through faith." Reformation leaders believed that people would seek the good news only after they became fully aware of bad news: Man needs to become aware of his own corruption in order to change through God's grace, and if you help make readers aware of sin you do them a service.

In England, Henry VIII broke from Rome not to battle sin but to try to advance his own. The bishops that he appointed became little more than political arms of the state, used to stamp out religious dissent, which was seen as a threat to social order. When Catholics opposed to unlimited governmental authority, such as Thomas More, refused to endorse Henry's whims, he beheaded them. Henry added new antipress legislation almost as often as he added new wives. In 1534, his "Proclamation for Seditious Books" ordered that no one should print any English book without a license from the king's councils or those persons appointed by the king as licensers. His "Proclamation of 1538" left the press with only one master: the king.

Parliament's regulatory law of 1542-43 was totalitarian: "Nothing shall be taught or maintained contrary to the King's instructions." The law stated:

> There shall be no annotations or preambles in Bibles or New Testaments in English. The Bible shall not be read in English in any church. No women or artificers, prentices, journeymen, servingmen of the degree of yeomen or under, husbandmen, nor labourers, shall read the New Testament in English. . . . if any spiritual person preach, teach, or maintain anything contrary to the King's instructions or determinations, made or to be made, and shall be thereof convict, he shall for his first offense recant, for his second abjure and bear a fagot, and for his third shall be adjudged an heretick, and be burned.

Henry VIII's structure of government and society was simple: The state, with its official church, was at the center, giving orders to other social institutions. But in the thought of Reformation leaders such as John Calvin, the kingdom of God could not be equated with state interests. Instead, the Reformers believed that God reigns everywhere and man can serve God directly in every area of life—in government, journalism, education, business, or whatever. Reformed thinkers placed God's laws above those of the state or any other institution.

The Reformers did not advocate extremist intransigence or easy disobedience of governmental authority. Scotland's John Knox, for instance, appealed for moderation and compromise whenever truly fundamental issues were not at stake. But under the Reformed doctrine, for the first time, journalists could be more than purveyors of public relations. They had their own independent authority and could appeal to biblical principle when officials tried to shackle them. The Bible had to be carefully followed, and the interpretations of those who had studied it at length were not to be negligently disregarded, but the Bible was clear enough on most matters for ordinary individuals to read it themselves and see its truths for themselves.

During the reign of Mary Tudor, "Bloody Mary," from 1553 to 1558, government confrontation with those who based their lives on *sola scriptura*—the Bible only—reached its zenith. One of the first Protestants to go to the stake was John Hooper, publicly burned at Gloucester on February 9, 1555. He was joined by about seventy-five men and women who were burned as heretics that year, and many more during the following two years. Soon, reports of those burnings spread illegally throughout England: Ballads and other publications—one was called *Sacke full of Newes*—attacked the queen and praised the heroism of the martyrs.

The sixteenth-century journalist who made the greatest impression on several generations of English men and women originally had no desire to report on current events. John Foxe, born in 1516, was an excellent student. He became a fellow at Oxford, but was converted to the Reformed faith and had to give up his stipend if he wanted to go beyond doing public relations for the king. In 1548, Foxe began writing a scholarly history of Christian martyrdom, but it turned journalistic in 1553 when Mary became queen. Facing death in 1554 Foxe left England and began earning a poor living as a proofreader with a Swiss printer, but he continued to collect historical material about past persecutions and testimony about current ones.

Foxe published two volumes in Latin during the 1550s but switched to English for his journalistic output, with the goal of telling the martyrs' stories in a readable manner. He was able to return to England with the ascension of Elizabeth to the throne in 1558 and then spend five more years interviewing, collecting materials, and writing, before publishing the sensational account that became known as *Foxe's Book of Martyrs*. To make sure everything was accurate, he worked seven years more before putting out in 1570 an expanded, second edition that contained woodcuts portraying burnings and whippings; later, large-scale editions increased the number of illustrations.

Foxe was following Luke's biblical tradition of careful investigation and interviewing of eyewitnesses. Foxe vividly wrote of how John Hooper, tied to a stake, prayed for a short time. Then the fire was lit, but the green wood was slow to burn. Hooper was shown a box and told it contained his pardon if he would give in: "Away with it!" he cried. As the fire reached Hooper's legs a gust of wind blew it out. A second fire then slowly burned up Hooper's legs, but went out with Hooper's upper body still intact.

Using specific detail, Foxe wrote of how the fire was rekindled, and soon Hooper was heard to say repeatedly, "Lord Jesus, have mercy upon me; Lord Jesus, have mercy upon me; Lord Jesus, receive my spirit!" Hooper's lips continued to move even when his throat was so scorched that no sound could come from it: Even "when he was black in the mouth, and his tongue swollen, that he could not speak, yet his lips went till they were shrunk to the gums." Finally, one of Hooper's arms fell off, and the other, with "fat, water, and blood" dripping out at the ends of the fingers, stuck to what remained of his chest. At that point Hooper bowed his head forward and died.

Foxe also described the deaths of Hugh Latimer and Nicholas Ridley. Ridley, chained over another of those slow-burning fires, was in agony, but Latimer seemed to be dying with amazing ease—Foxe wrote that he appeared to be bathing his hands and face in the fire. Latimer's last words to his suffering friend were, "Be of good comfort, Master Ridley, [so that] we shall this day light such a candle, by God's grace, in England, as I trust shall never be put out."

Foxe's third famous report concerned the death of Thomas Cranmer, archbishop of Canterbury and leader of the English Protestants. Imprisoned for months without support of friends, Cranmer received daily ideological hammering from theological adversaries. After watching Ridley die, he wrote out a recantation and apology in return for pardon. When Cranmer was told later that he had allegedly led so many people astray that he would have to burn anyway, his courage returned and he resolved to go out boldly. He declared in one final statement that his recantation was "written with my hand contrary to the truth which is in my heart, and written for fear of death." He offered a pledge: "As my hand hath offended, writing contrary to my heart, therefore my hand shall first be punished; for when I come to the fire, it shall be first burned." Foxe wrote of how Cranmer made good on that promise; sent to the stake, he placed his right hand firmly in the fire and held it steadily there until it appeared like a coal to observers. Soon, Cranmer's entire body was burned.

Foxe's book became very popular not only because of its combination of theological fervor and grisly detail, but through its use of colorful Bible-based imagery. For example, Foxe's report on the impending death of John Hooper described how light overcame darkness as Hooper was led through London to Newgate prison.

> Officers had ordered all candles along the way be put out; perhaps, being burdened with an evil conscience, they thought darkness to be a most fit season for such a business. But notwithstanding this device, the people having some foreknowledge of his coming, many of them came forth of their doors with lights, and saluted him; praising God for his constancy in the true doctrine which he had taught them. . . .

Foxe's stress on accuracy was maintained by Miles Coverdale, who wrote in 1564 that "it doth us good to read and heare, not the lying legendes . . . triflyng toyes & forged fables of corrupted writers: but such true, holy . . . epistles & letters, as do set forth unto us ye blessed behaviour of gods deare servantes." (Think of the forged fables that today's "spin doctors" provide.) For a time it appeared that a free press, with careful fact-checking, might arise—but Queen Elizabeth, while allowing direct criticism of her predecessor, Mary, cracked down on anyone who objected to her reign or to the domination of the established Anglican religion.

In 1570, Elizabeth's proclamation offered a reward to those who informed against anyone writing or dispersing books in opposition to the queen or nobles. The secret tribunal known as the Star Chamber did not hesitate to prosecute and persecute Puritan rebels, including Hugh Singleton, Robert Waldegrave, John Stroud, and John Hodgkins. Puritans as an organized journalistic group first went public in 1572 with *An Admonition to Parliament*, a sixty-page attack on state churches; *Admonition* authors John Field and Thomas Wilcocks spent a year in prison.

Other pamphlets soon appeared. John Stubbes, an English Puritan who in 1579 wrote a pamphlet respectfully criticizing Queen Elizabeth, was punished by having his right hand "cut off by the blow of a Butcher's knife." A contemporary account tells of his amazing response: "John Stubbes, so soone as his right hand was off, put off his hat with the left, and cryed aloud, God save the Queene." Stubbes, under such duress, set the pattern of respecting those in authority over us, while exposing their unbiblical actions.

Among the best-read Puritan products at the end of the sixteenth century were pamphlets published in 1588 and 1589 and called the Martin Marprelate tracts; these tracts humorously satirized and ridiculed the heavy-handed theological treatises put out by defenders of the established church. The tracts, printed by John Hodgkins on a press that was dismantled repeatedly and moved around by cart, irritated king and court so much that a massive search for its producers began. Hodgkins escaped harm until he was unloading his press one day in the town of Warrington before curious onlookers. A few small pieces of metal type fell from one of the boxes. A bystander picked up a letter and showed it to an official, who understood the significance of the discovery and summoned constables. Arrested and repeatedly tortured, Hodgkins refused to admit guilt and implicate others.

The bravery of Hodgkins, like that of Martin Luther, John Hooper, John Stubbes, and many others, could not be ignored; persecution of the Puritans, instead of stamping them out, led to new conversions. When James I became king of England in 1603 and Puritans presented petitions for religious and press freedom, he threatened to "harry them out of the land, or else do worse." James, arguing that he was "above the law by his absolute power," and that "it is presumptuous and high contempt in a subject to dispute what a king can do, or say that a king cannot do this or that," advised subjects to "rest in that which is the king's revealed word in his law." But that is something that Puritan writers, committed as they were to following God's law whatever the costs, would not do.

Puritan doctrines won increasing acceptance particularly in English towns; opposition to James and his successor, Charles I, increased. When one Puritan critic, Alexander Leighton, wrote and published a pamphlet in 1630 entitled *An Appeal to Parliament*, Charles and his court were outraged. Leighton insisted that Scripture was above everything, including kings, so that subjects could remain loyal while evaluating their kings against biblical standards; Leighton said his goal was to correct existing problems "for the honour of the king, the quiet of the people, and the peace of the church." The Star Chamber saw the situation differently, terming Leighton's work "seditious and scandalous." On November 16, 1630, Leighton was whipped at Westminster, and had one of his ears cut off, his nose slit, and one side of his face branded. One week later the mutilation was repeated on the other side.

The penalty did not stop other Puritans. John Bastwick, Henry Burton, and William Prynne were hauled into the Star Chamber in 1637 and charged with seditious libel for writing pamphlets that criticized royal actions. Each man was sentenced to huge fines, perpetual imprisonment without access to writing materials, and the loss of their ears. The royal authorities, believing that they had the populace on their side, proclaimed a public holiday highlighted by the public mutilations. But when the three men were allowed to make public statements, according to the custom of the day, as the officials waited with knives, they were cheered. Prynne was actually arrested and maimed twice; when he was released from prison and allowed to return to London, he was greeted by a crowd of ten thousand.

Barbarous attempts to control the press prompted even more determined opposition; as a *Boston Gazette* essayist would note over a century later, the English civil war had as its "original, true and real Cause" suppression of the press, and "had not Prynn lost his Ears, K. Charles would have never lost his Head." The verbal battle of Parliament versus crown, and Puritans versus Anglicans, led to war during the 1640s. The changed political environment led to a journalistic surge, as a Puritan-dominated Parliament, remembering past oppression, abolished in 1641 the torture-prone Star Chamber. The result, according to a parliamentary committee in 1643, was that many printers "have taken upon them to set up sundry private Printing Presses in corners, and to print, vend, publish and disperse Books, pamphlets and papers. . . . ."

Some of these publications were regular newspapers with high standards. Samuel Pecke's weekly, *A Perfect Diurnall,* began with these words: "You may henceforth expect from this relator to be informed only of such things as are of credit. . . ." Pecke did not make up things. Although clearly a Puritan partisan, he truthfully reported royalist military victories, and twice covered wrongful conduct by Parliamentary soldiers. He also gave opponents space to express their views: When Archbishop Laud was executed for murder, Pecke included a transcript of the archbishop's speech from the scaffold.

Similarly, when John Dillingham began his newspaper, *The Parliament Scout,* in 1643, he pledged "to tell the truth" and not to "vapour and say such a one was routed, defeated," when there actually had been no battle. Dillingham wrote of plundering by Cromwell's soldiers, the bravery of some captured Royalists, and the need for better medical treatment of the wounded on both sides. He did what we should do today: Support the side fighting for biblical values, but tell the truth about our own vices and our opponents' virtues.

Some Puritan leaders did not like criticism any more than the king's officials did, but most were committed to the idea of biblical rather than personal authority, and of letting individuals read for themselves. One Puritan leader and friend of John Milton, Samuel Hartlib, reflected general hopes when he predicted in 1641 that "the art of Printing will so spread knowledge that the common people, knowing their own rights and liberties, will not be governed by way of oppression."

Parliament in 1643 did pass a law that restricted sales of pamphlets and newsbooks, but it received little enforcement and much criticism. Puritan pamphleteer William Walwyn noted that licensing might restrict some evil publications but would also "stopt the mouthes of good men, who must either not write at all, or no more than is suitable to the judgments or interests of the Licensers." Another Puritan, Henry Robinson, proposed that theological and political combat should "be fought out upon eaven ground, on equal termes, neither side must expect to have greater liberty of speech, writing, Printing, or whatsoever else, than the other."

The most famous response to the new law was penned by Milton himself. Licensing, he wrote, brought back memories of Bloody Mary, she of "the most unchristian council and the most tyrannous inquisition that ever inquired," and was inconsistent with the "mild, free and human government" that the Puritans said they would provide. Milton's most famous words in his *Areopagetica* were:

> Though all the winds of doctrine were let loose to play upon the earth, so truth be in the field, we do injuriously by licensing and prohibiting to misdoubt her strength. Let her and falsehood grapple; who ever knew truth put to the worse, in a free and open encounter.

Milton had faith in God's invisible hand over journalism; he asked, "For who knows not that truth is strong, next to the Almighty? She needs no policies, nor stratagems, nor licensings to make victorious; those are shifts and the defenses that error uses against her power."

The greatest journalistic talent of seventeenth-century England emerged during this mid-1640s period of relative freedom. Marchamont Nedham was born in 1620 in a small town near Oxford. He studied Greek, Latin, and history as a child, received a bachelor's degree from Oxford University in 1637, and spent the next six years as a schoolteacher, law clerk, and dabbler in medicine. During those six years, Nedham underwent a theological and political transformation that led him to side with the Puritans. When King Charles established in 1643 his own weekly newspaper, the *Mercurius Aulicus*, Nedham was hired to help out with a competing newspaper from the Parliamentary side, *Mercurius Britanicus*. Within a year Nedham was in charge and doing almost all of the writing for a newspaper that was eight pages long and typographically clean enough to make possible headache-free reading of it three centuries later.

Nedham's writing was sensational and colorful; rather than theorizing or preaching, he provided specific detail about the vices of Royalists. Lord Ratcliffe, for example, was "bathing in luxury, and swimming in the fat of the land, and cramming his Hens and Capons with Almonds and Raisins," and Lord Porter was "that Exchequer of Flesh, which hath a whole Subsidie in his small guts and his panch, and hath bestowed the Sessments, and taxes of the State in sawces." Nedham saw himself turning darkness into light by exposing corruption; when Nedham reviewed his work as editor, he wrote:

> I have by an excellent and powerful Providence led the people through the labyrinths of the enemies Plots . . . King could not keepe an evil Councellour, but I must needs speake of him. The Queene could not bring in Popery, but I must needs tell all the world of it. . . . I undisguised the Declarations, and Protestations, and Masqueries of the Court.

Nedham, while thoroughly partisan, desired accuracy and criticized the propagandistic tendencies of Royalist newspaper editor John Birkenhead.

> Oh! what Prodigious Service hath he done, he could tell of Battailes and victories, when there was not so much as an Alarme or skirmish, he could change Pistolls into Demi-Cannons, and Carbines into Culverings, and Squadrons and Troopes into Regiments and Brigades, he could rally routed Armies and put them into a better condition when they were beaten then before.

Unlike Birkenhead, Nedham commented on his own side's difficulties: "The King is too nimble for us in horse, and his designers ride, while ours go on foot, and we lacquey beside him, and usually fall short of his Army, and we shall scarce be able to encounter him, unless he please to turn back and fight with us." Furthermore, he made theological points through laying up specific detail, rather than by preaching: "Prince Rupert abides in Westchester . . . the young man is lately grown so devout, that he cannot keep the Lord's day without a Bull baiting, or Beare baiting."

Nedham rarely drew attention to himself, but in one issue he explained that "I took up my pen for disabusing his Majesty, and for disbishoping, and dispoping his good subjects." Exposure was his goal: He wanted to take off the "vailes and disguises which the Scribes and Pharisees at Oxford had put upon a treasonable and popish Cause." He enjoyed his effectiveness: "I have served a Parliament and Reformation hitherto in unmaking and unhooding incendiaries of all sorts. . . . Everyone can point out the evil Counsellours now." But, in a question-and-answer note (an early version of "Dear Abby") at the end of each issue of *Mercurius Britanicus*, he regularly cautioned against arrogance: When asked, "What are we to do or expect now in this time when our forces are so considerable?" Nedham answered, "Not to trust nor looke too much upon them, but through them to a Diviner power, lest we suffer as we did before."

Nedham had many ups and downs over the next two decades, as the Puritan revolution soured and the monarchy returned in 1660. In May 1662, the new, Royalist-dominated Parliament passed a bill enacting a new, stringent censorship system. No more, said Parliament, would

> evil disposed persons [sell] heretical, schismatical, blasphemous, seditious and treasonable books, pamphlets and papers . . . endangering the peace of these kingdoms, and raising a disaffection to his most excellent Majesty and his government.

Nedham retired from journalism and turned to the practice of medicine. A tight censorship eliminated regular news coverage unless it helped to propel the official news. For Puritan journalists, life was even harder than it had been before the revolution. For example, John Twyn in 1663 was convicted of sedition for printing a book arguing that citizens should call to account a king whose decrees violated biblical law. After Twyn refused to provide the name of the book's author, his "privy-members" were cut off before his eyes, and he was then beheaded. Twyn's body was cut into four pieces, and each was nailed to a different gate of the city as a warning to other printers or writers.

If you are a biblically directed journalist today, you do not have to fear punishment similar to Twyn's. You may be fired, but only occupationally—and, if Twyn could know the risk and still write directly, what excuse do you have for dithering?

CHAPTER FOUR

Field Reporting and Interviewing

The sacrifices of John Twyn and others started the process of making the world safe for biblically directed reporting. You should partake of that liberty by being out in the field, not sitting in the office. Many writers like to be thumb suckers, sitting in air-conditioned comfort, worshipping their own muse, and then writing brainy thoughts. The desperate need of Christian publications is for pavement pounders, those who will walk down mean streets to get the specific detail that distinguishes reporting from essay writing.

Hanging around news sites is vital: "You can learn a lot just by watching," Yogi Berra is reported to have said. For example, to write a story about homelessness, you should eat with homeless folks at a shelter; you might do so both as a reporter and dressed as a homeless person. To write about the impact of federal environmental laws on workers in the timber industry, visit the home of a logger who lost his job: "Mrs. Lynch home-schools her children in a modest sky-blue house with a For Sale sign in the small front yard." Wherever you go, sit and listen.

Remember as you do so the importance of biblical direction. The theme of the Bible is, as noted in chapter one, God saves sinners. The overall theme of your reporting should be that there is a God, there is salvation, there are sinners. Bible-based bits of reporting have a theme derived from those great themes. Since we as reporters are fallen sinners, we will often find in the course of reporting that the specific themes we came up with at first are wrong. Nevertheless, every reporting excursion should start with a theme, or thesis, because, as you spend time looking around, you need a sense of what to look at most closely.

You may find that your original theme was wrong, but you should always have one—be prepared to revise it—or else the tendency is to dither. With a theme in mind, keep looking for ways to tell a lot with a little. Train yourself to observe and record the details that help to characterize a person, a meeting, and so forth. For example, to give an impression of a conservative congressman who will not give in to liberal, government-expanding political pressure, note that:

> Henry Hyde's office also has room for the two bulldog bookends of twentieth-century British politics, Winston Churchill and Margaret Thatcher, and a portrait of Thomas More, the sixteenth-century English lord chancellor. . . . Hyde has a bust of More as well: "He gave his life for a principle."

When you are thinking of skipping that last interview, keep in mind the sacrifices of those like More and the Puritan journalists; they had different theologies but a similar opposition to totalitarian government, and they got to work early and stayed late. You should get to the site of an interviewee ten minutes ahead of time, and then redeem the minutes by observing; if possible, you should stick around after the main event also. When covering a meeting, you should stay afterward and elicit reactions. (The most important hours for a baseball reporter are not those during a game but those before and after when he talks with players in the clubhouse.)

Some stories can be written well from afar, but being there makes the difference in specificity of detail. For example, a *World* article about a Virginia Republican convention began by giving a sense of *convention*, i.e., lots of people crowded together.

> Just four elevators were available to hoist Virginia Republican convention delegates 18 floors to the Christian Coalition hospitality suite atop the Richmond Marriott. The night before the 14,000-plus delegates selected Oliver North as their candidate for the U.S.

Senate, a mighty throng made the pilgrimage to suite 1809 to drink a glass of punch or a bottle of Miller Sharp's nonalcoholic brew and schmooze with like-minded Christian conservatives. Merely to board one of the elevators could take up to 15 minutes; then there was the slow, shoulder-to-shoulder, belly-to-back ride that seemed to stop at every floor. Once the elevator reached the top, delegates and journalists moved like huddled masses to get near one of the doors. In more ways than one, the Christian Coalition's two-room suite was a bulging, big tent.

That opening played on the Coalition's desires for expansion; another bit of specific detail showed the tendency of Virginia's Republican Party generally.

Thousands [of Virginians] first became active in the party last year, on the coattails of home-school activist and lieutenant-governor candidate Mike Farris. Evidence that the state's GOP understands the needs of the big-family Christian delegates was posted on several of the doors leading to seats at the Richmond Coliseum: Notices read, "Nursing mother's station, 20-U."

Then came interviews with delegates, with visual as well as aural details provided.

Delegate Tom Ruzic of Newport News was one of those who asked hard, issue-related questions. Wearing a home-made sticker that read, "I am the Religious Right," Ruzic explained that North left him unsatisfied. "Nobody gave me a good reason to vote for Oliver North. He was just a 'great American,' a blood-and-guts, kick-butt hero," the Deerpark Baptist Church member said. "But what were the specifics that he was going to do? Nobody ever told me."

Collect, collect, collect. You will want more in your notebook than you can use. Make notes to remind you of sights and sounds. You will find that "writing blocks" almost always occur because you do not have good material. Some people try to write around holes in their research, and some get away with it for a while, but the common denominator of good stories is tenacious research. Writers who do not have adequate material often try to make up for that lack by adding rhetoric; they end up with heat but no light. It is far better for writers to use a computer screen that occasionally flashes this motto: "Sensational Facts, Understated Prose."

You also need to know enough about a story to find a face with which to personify it. Reader interest is highly correlated with the human interest of stories: More people like to read about people than issues. Strong articles allow readers to identify themselves with characters in a story and project themselves into the situations described. For example, it is easy to write a theoretical story about school vouchers, but the question becomes real to otherwise-uninvolved readers when you find a face.

> Thelma Hunter watched her granddaughter J'Keisha's behavior and school work decline. J'Keisha, who lives with her grandmother, hadn't had any behavior problems at her suburban kindergarten north of Austin. But when Mrs. Hunter and J'Keisha moved to the poor east side of Austin, they found her first grade to be a different story. "It was really bad," Mrs. Hunter says. "Kids were fighting. She saw a kid beat unconscious there, and no one stopped it. And J'Keisha's behavior was not real good there." She knew she had to get her granddaughter out.
>
> Mrs. Hunter tried to transfer J'Keisha to another school, but in Austin that proved impossible. That's when she read an article in the local newspaper about a private voucher plan that was working in San Antonio. "If only we had something like that in Austin," she said.

You need to search for material with strong narrative and descriptive opportunities. Good narrative demands characters plus action: words and sentences have to show movement, and readers need to see action. Talking heads are deadly, and lack of characterization also cramps stories. As William Randolph Hearst accurately pointed out, "People are interested in the fundamentals—love, romance, adventure, tragedy, mystery." You will need to practice journalistic fundamentalism, and that means describing briefly the characters introduced into a story: Physical and occupational characteristics are easy, mannerisms and ways of thinking are better.

Figure 8 suggests a good positioning.

Introducing character and action at the right pace is an art. Like the good storyteller who does not list the plot details at the beginning of his story, you should not recite facts without drama. You should introduce

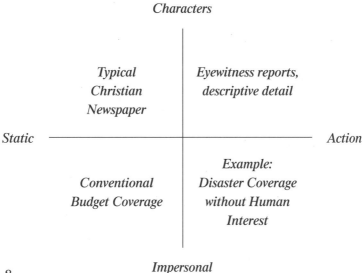

FIG. 8

characters who are forced to confront problems in realistic ways, and do so at a pace that places readers on a slope with a gradual ascent. For example, this first paragraph introduced one side in a culture war.

> There is a Petri dish down in the warm, close-to-the-earth culture of south Mississippi. It is called Ovett, population 300. For more than one hundred years, Ovett citizens have lived in a largely Christ-influenced culture. It has had its problems, but none the prevailing ethic hasn't appropriately spoken to. Many residents are from the "free state of Jones," a name given the county after many of its citizens refused to fight for either side in the Civil War.

The second paragraph introduced the other set of characters, and the story was off and running.

> About seven months ago, however, a new challenge entered the community. A social activist lesbian couple—Brenda and Wanda Henson (who consider themselves married)—have come to town intent on creating a lesbian-feminist retreat center from which, in part, to educate the area according to their convictions. Christian res-

idents say the Hensons represent a cultural threat that must be contained, if not completely expelled.

Good stories often show conflict between individuals, between individuals and physical obstacles, between our natural tendencies and the slow sanctification brought about by the Holy Spirit. You need to show the conflict, and not merely string together heated quotations. Here is how a draft of one article began:

> "The Clinton presidency is the most antifamily administration in history," commented Bob Morrison, education policy analyst of the Family Research Council. "In all earnestness, it is breathtaking." Kay Cole James, the executive vice president of FRC, agreed. James A. Smith, the director of government relations for the Southern Baptist Convention's Christian Life Commission, told *World* that the President has been pursuing a "truly radical, anti-biblical, immoral agenda."

Those all are good statements, but a story that goes on in that vein, slinging quotes like hash, gets old quickly. A revised version, however, provided specific instances of antifamily policies. For example, Clinton administration proabortionists appeared to be using the IRS.

> "Tactics of delay," sighed Patricia Bainbridge, executive director of Life Decisions International, a nonprofit organization devoted to researching and revealing corporate sponsors of Planned Parenthood and other pro-abortion organizations. Though LDI applied for "501(c)(3)" tax-exempt status in December 1992, "We still do not have a ruling. It's been a matter of one minute our application is in Brooklyn, the next minute it's in Washington . . . one story after another."
>
> In the 1980s it was easy for pro-life groups to receive 501(c)(3) status, which for years was given almost automatically by the IRS to a variety of educational and philanthropic organizations. Ms. Bainbridge's earlier experience was typical: "I've gotten 501(c)(3) for pro-life organizations before. It was the simplest thing in the whole wide world. I head up a local Christian Action Council. We applied for and received our 501(c)(3) within 60 days—90 at the most."
>
> Now, however, her attempt to get the tax-exempt status for LDI has been going on almost a year with no end in sight. Ms. Bainbridge

sent *World* 12 pages of documentation. . . . IRS agents have specifically mentioned LDI's opposition to Planned Parenthood as a reason
for the delay in the ruling.

Details make a story real. Football players making a goal-line stand
hear the crowd chanting, "Defense. Defense." Calls for "detail, detail,"
should ring in your ears. Describe. Be specific. Dump vagueness. Show,
do not tell. Do not summarize scenes; recreate them. Do not say, "It was
a Christian environment"—show the readers what made it so. In Mark
Twain's words, "Don't say the old lady screamed—bring her on and let
her scream."

You are the eyes, ears, and nose of each reader. You are providing vicarious experience, going places the readers have not or could not, ranging from major-league locker rooms to radio studios. For example, one
article about a popular talk-show host began:

> Marlin Maddoux has spent his morning sifting through dozens of
> articles and editorials. They'll be fodder for his 90-minute talk show,
> *Point of View*, broadcast from a Dallas studio bordering on elegant.
> Maddoux has a staff of 25 (not counting his USA Radio
> Network's new division), three satellite uplinks, and a stealth-bomber
> shaped table with ample microphones for his guests. . . . Behind the
> glass wall, three 20-something staff members run sound and equip-
> ment checks. To ease the pre-show tension, one engineer pipes in a
> satirical spot cribbed from Rush Limbaugh's show earlier in the day.
> The engineers are unabashed Maddoux fans; they laugh at his jokes,
> react with horror to his ain't-it-awful news nuggets. By 1 p.m., the
> entire studio is focused on Maddoux. . . ."

Every generalization should be followed by specific detail to indicate
the truth of the generalization. If you say a person is witty, give an example. If you say a campaign is being run debt-free, show us how.

> Farris is running a debt-free campaign so he can with credibility
> attack the Democratic incumbent, Don Beyer, as "big-debt Don."
> Part of that effort to run a lean campaign was apparent in the
> Richmond Center, across the street from the coliseum, where all the
> campaigns had set up tables to distribute literature, campaign but-
> tons, stickers, balloons, and T-shirts. Working the Farris table was
> a homeschool family from Front Royal who run an advertising and

promotional items business. Dan and Tracie Thomas and their two
sons, Chris and Davis, assembled campaign trinkets on an as-
needed basis. Davis, the youngest of the boys, banged out four campaign buttons per minute on a hand-cranked machine. T-shirts were
emblazoned with the Farris logo upon purchase. A sign warned people to stay away from the T-shirt press: "This press is hot—and so
is Mike."

"This way," Mrs. Thomas explained, "there is no cash outlay for
the campaign." Unused materials, like T-shirts and unstamped buttons, could be returned at no cost to the campaign.

Good descriptive material should be spread throughout the story.
Sometimes it is necessary to trim it—and if the descriptive detail gets
tedious, to use a machete. There is no need to show readers insignifi-
cant or irrelevant objects; those clutter up the room. But good descriptive writing can make a biblical point better than formal editorializing.
The most effective editorial page of a typical newspaper today is its
front page.

Use all your senses, not just your ears. Some articles are not show
but show-off: The reporter is proud that he has interviewed someone
important and that he has compiled many quotations. What is missing in
the torrent of words is a word picture: mannerisms, gestures, habits, chin
strokings, and leaning back in chairs. Describe, describe, as in this continuation of the Mississippi lesbians' story.

The hamlet of Ovett appears peaceful. The center for local
activity these days is the Ovett Little General Store, a one-stop gro-
cery and general merchandise store from a pre-Wal-Mart age that
is attached to the local post office. Inside, a flock of visitors finds
bags of corn and dog food on one wall; screws, rakes, hoes, and
other hardware on another—and groceries in between. In the
store's front, townsmen—some in overalls and almost all wearing
caps—regularly sit, drinking coffee and Cokes, and eating hot
hamburgers fresh off the store's own grill.

Outside, on the west edge of town, one thin, bearded man is
rounding up stray deer dogs into the cage in the back of his pickup.
"It ain't worth fifteen cents," he says of the retreat center, then politely
excuses himself to chase dogs. On the other end of town, past the
patch of winter collard greens in one resident's yard, a group of white
Charolais cattle lie around.

Then connect location, residents, and values:

> But it is the nine churches sandwiched within the east and west sides of town that do give a lot more than fifteen cents about what is happening just three miles or so outside town. In fact, church folk from Ovett and other communities have set up the Ovett Defense Fund to gather donations for potential litigation or a buyout of the lesbians who have moved next door.
>
> Residents are concerned about their children watching lesbians publicly display their unnatural affections and promoting their views in local public schools. Kathy Stevens is a 27-year-old pregnant mother of four from Petal, near Ovett, who also serves as area representative for Concerned Women for America: "[The Hensons] have the right to own their land and they have the right to be on it and do everything they want on it," she told *World*." But when they start talking about impacting our schools, that's where I come in."

At this point remember the motto—"Sensational Facts, Understated Prose"—and do not do a rhetorical strike on homosexuality. Instead, writer Joe Maxwell doggedly dug out detail about the two particular lesbians in this story.

> Wanda Henson's antipathy for Christianity seems to have begun as a child. Now she's 39 years old and a committed, politically active lesbian; when she was still a young teenager, Wanda considered running away from home. Instead, she ended up staying for a month or two in the home of a Southern Baptist minister—William Wyser— whose family had once lived across the street from hers.
>
> "She was having trouble at home between her father and mother," Wyser, who at 68 still pastors a church near Wanda's hometown of Pascagoula, told *World.* . . .

Marriage records at the Jackson County Courthouse in Pascagoula, Miss., on the Gulf Coast, show that Wanda at age 16 married Arthur Francis Elliot on March 8, 1971. Wyser performed the ceremony. The rocky marriage produced two children. Wanda says that her husband "kept calling me queer" until she took note of it.

> About four years later, the two divorced.
>
> Eventually, Wanda, a nurse, began working at a shelter for battered women on the coast. It was there that she met Brenda Henson,

now 48 and originally from Loveland, Ohio, who moved to the coast in 1981 after her second marriage. The two-time divorcee and former alcoholic claims she was a victim of incest and spouse abuse.

Ms. Henson, a former Southern Baptist who is now a Unitarian and a practitioner of "women's spirituality" and "goddess worship," and Wanda, whom Brenda describes as a "recovering Pentecostal," fell in love.

On December 16, 1988, according to public records at the Harrison County Courthouse in Gulfport, Miss., Wanda Faye Reeves Elliot legally changed her last name to "Henson," an act Brenda says was to honor Brenda's mother.

After more background information, it's time to return to the lesbians' present pursuit:

So when 120 acres of worn, cut-over land and pig farm outside Ovett became available for $60,000, they jumped at the chance. They pooled their resources and got help from groups including the Lesbian Natural Resources organization in Minnesota, which donated $13,950. It wasn't long before the land was paid for in full and the Hensons had set up camp.

Next came a description of the camp, which the reporter reached:

over a white sand and clay road, back through gnarled, cut-over, hilly land and some grown-over old vineyards.

The road finally emerged into an opening on a hill, where two drab brown, two-story rectangular buildings sit.

Just before the buildings was a fire circle about 20 yards in diameter, marked off with a heavy thick-link chain, the kind that might be used to anchor freighter ships. On the perimeter of the circle five white poles—two to three feet high—were equidistantly positioned, each having a solar light affixed at the top. . . . Hanging from a shed was a wreath of grapevines, about two feet in diameter. Inside, a string pentagram was formed, adorned with snakeskins and bird feathers.

Then came interviews:

Brenda Henson stepped from behind a clear plastic barrier hanging from one building. "Hello," the short, round woman with stubby, thin blond hair said, extending her hand, her face seeming gentle and kind.

After a few moments of breaking the ice, Brenda led the way past an open-air room where several women offered a welcome. One had a Mohawk and combat boots; another might just as well have come from an outdoor church social.

Inside an adjoining office, while Brenda continued the interview, Wanda talked on the phone with a lesbian from Maryland. "We're beginning to get a response from all over America," Wanda told her. "I really have faith in the lesbian/gay nation. . . . We're a mighty big family."

At another point, she likened their particular situation to that of Rosa Parks' efforts in Birmingham. "We've joined [blacks] in the front seat of the bus," she said. "I think the history we are making here is real significant."

When reporter Maxwell asked about the pentagrams present in the camp, Brenda:

acknowledged that she "worships the goddess. I practice women's spirituality." Wanda abruptly hung up the phone and jumped in: "We don't want that to be printed, because what you are doing is setting us up to be attacked again."

Shortly after, Brenda acknowledged, "I believe in Mother Nature. . . . God is in everything—god or goddess, he or she, in all living things."

But the women appeared progressively irritated, and the interview ended soon after.

After more description, a summary was in order—and by this point the writer was not preaching at the reader but confirming what the reader now had seen: "The story of the lesbians and Christians of Ovett is about a clash, not only of cultures, but of fundamental religious beliefs: pagan nature and goddess worship against Christianity. . . ."

INTERVIEWING

As the Ovett story shows, interviewing for directed reporting demands planning; the interview should not just be a fishing expedition but a search for specific information and insight. You should develop a particular line of questioning, depending on the intent of the article and should also ask some general questions that allow the interviewee to open up entirely new areas of which you may be unaware. Sometimes interviews can lead you in a direction very different from that you anticipated—but you still need to anticipate.

Planning for an interview starts with thinking about what an article should include, and what you need from the interview to make a story and fill in the gaps. Write down the information needed; structure questions accordingly. Think to yourself, *The story is X, so I need Y.* Remember that your goal in interviewing is not to be a megaphone for the interviewee but to get what you need to write your story. Know what you will ask: You are in charge of the interview.

While pushing hard for specific material, retain flexibility. Be prepared to change your theme if your initial assumptions appear incorrect. Be careful not to guide the interview overly much, and do not put words into the interviewee's mouth. At the same time, guide the interview enough so that the interviewee will not neglect your theme.

With a reluctant interviewee, you may have to follow the information-eliciting techniques learned by parents: avoid questions that can be answered yes or no; encourage the recalcitrants to go further by asking, "And then? What happened next?" When stuck, ask five-W questions: "Who taught you that? What did you read that was influential? When? Where? Why?"

Whether you are interviewing a friend or a foe, follow the standard that is used for arms-control agreements: Trust, but verify. Remember that the interviewee is not God; nor is he a cockroach. If you have reason to suspect the interviewee's honesty, ask some questions to which you already know the answers, and see if he is telling the truth. If he tells you something different from what you have heard, challenge. In any event, with anyone, do not believe everything you are told.

When concluding an interview, it is useful to lay down a marker by saying that a follow-up question may be needed; ask if you can call if something else is needed. The subject will agree, and will be prepared for another contact. You also should come away from the interview with printed material, when possible. Be a pack rat: Collect copies of speeches, articles, and books.

Although the following should go without saying, remember basic manners. Reporters have such a reputation for rudeness that you can win respect by not staying overly long, by saying thank you, and by not using a person's first name unless invited to do so.

After the interview, you will want to record additional impressions immediately and then go to work trying to write a strong article by combining interview material with narrative, as in the following example.

> Michael Farris says his wife gave him the best piece of advice 10 years ago. "It's not just getting the words correct that's important," Vickie Farris said. "It's like singing a song. You have to have good words, but you also have to have a pleasing melody."
>
> Farris, an outspoken and sometimes brassy evangelical Christian leader, used his pleasing melody last week to capture the Republican nomination and win the right to seek the office of Virginia's Lieutenant Governor.

This does not mean that Farris—who became known for his work in representing Tennessee parents opposed to a public school reading series that included not only obnoxious material but also *Cinderella* and *The Wizard of Oz*—is a compromiser.

> Mike Farris' melody is uncompromisingly in harmony with his worldview. "All these politicians are saying 'I am personally opposed to abortion but.' I say, 'I am personally opposed to abortion and.' There is no dichotomy between what I personally believe and what I am going to take into action. I think a lot of people who are not necessarily coming from the same vantage point that I am like the fact that I am a straight shooter. What you see is what you get."

Having a pleasing melody does mean that Farris makes light of the opposition's scare tactics, instead of angrily attacking them.

> Farris—and court records back him up—says the case had to do with parental rights and religious freedom, not banning classics. . . . Farris zealously defended his position, but he did it with good humor and wit. One of his campaign stickers said, "I like Mike and Toto too." Videocassettes of *Cinderella* and *The Wizard of Oz* played during his hospitality party Friday night before the delegates were to vote at the party's nominating convention in Richmond. All the speeches on Saturday ended with rousing music, but Farris' speech was followed by a rendition of "Somewhere Over the Rainbow."

Another way of using interview material is to take one person's comments and let others react to them.

> Former Attorney General William Barr is an evangelical who now practices law and heads the First Freedom Coalition, a group that lobbies states to reform their prison systems. He says there are four purposes for a prison.
>
> "The first and most important is incapacitation," he explains. "We're separating the criminal from society, so he is unable to commit a crime. Second is retribution: exacting just punishment, which I think is one of the aspects of the criminal justice system that has been forgotten in this country. It needs to be reinforced that punishment serves an important purpose in and of itself. Third is deterrence. Finally, there's rehabilitation, to the extent that's possible."
>
> The small group of inmates seated in the prison chapel listen as Barr's analysis is read to them. Then they nod.
>
> "There are some people in here—predators—who should be kept in," Eugene responds. "I agree with that. But it's not as many as most people think."

Reporter Roy Maynard skillfully organized the comments so that they provided perspective on Barr's four purposes.

> Kenneth addresses retribution.
>
> "That's part of why there are prisons," he says, "but it's a part that isn't working. If it did, then crime wouldn't continue as it does in here. Where's the retribution? People can come in here and spend years at the domino table. They can work a little bit and they can go to the substance abuse counseling, but even that doesn't require much from them. . . .
>
> Rehabilitation, the men agreed, was almost non-existent.
>
> "All the humanistic rehabilitation programs in the world—the drug counseling, the job training—won't give people a sense of value for life," says Mike. "Without a redirected value system, it doesn't matter what vocational expertise people are given."
>
> "I saw something the other day," Kenneth says after a pause. "I saw a guy give his radio to someone else as he was getting out. 'Hold onto this for me,' he told him. 'I'll be back.' He'd been through all the rehabilitation programs, and he was laughing when he said he'd be back."

Some interviewees are not particularly personable, but you should avoid getting too friendly with those who are, or being influenced by the interviewee's apparent friendliness. Some interviewees will push you to talk about yourself, but do not spend valuable time in that way: Turn the questions back on the interviewee. Some journalists advise interviewers to pretend to be on the interviewee's side—but that, if you are not, is lying. Be a professional.* Do avoid off-the-record conversations. Never volunteer to go off the record; fight to stay on it, and, if necessary, explain your editor's dislike for the practice. Off-the-record conversations may be necessary when a source's health or job are in jeopardy, but remember that you are working for the readers, not carrying mail for the interviewee. Remember that you will have to tell readers the reason for going off-the-record with particular sources; a statement such as, "The source preferred to be off the record," does not wash. If necessary, indicate to the source how his comments may be used, without making a commitment.

When a source asks to go off the record, find out what he means by that: information to be used for your background only, information that can be used but not attributed at all, information that can be attributed not by name but to "a source in the xyz department," or what? Unattributed quotations that disparage a person are worthless, unless you have lots of on-the-record quotations saying similar things.

Attribution should be kept simple. For a short quotation, place the attribution at the end, on the grounds that what the speaker said is usually more important than the fact that he said it; if the opposite is true, put the attribution at the beginning. A long quotation should include an attribution in the middle, both to break it up and to let the reader know who is talking.

DISTANT INTERVIEWING

Your sense of the story determines whom you need to interview, what you need from them, and whether you can do the interview by phone.

---

*Another nannyish note: Do not be shy about asking directions to an interviewee's home or office. After directions are given, ask, "Do I need anything else to find you?"—that might elicit information about office security systems, etc. Give subject your name and telephone number, in case something happens so that the subject cannot keep the appointment.

Telephones should not be used, except in emergencies, for in-depth interviewing that attempts to get at character. In theory, interviews by phone should by used only for eliciting a comment on a particular issue or a particular item of information. But in practice, while longer stories almost always are reported on the scene, many short, breaking-news stories depend on reporting from afar—by "remote control." The key to writing such a story is persistent distant interviewing.

The problem with writing a story via telephone is that you are not in the field to observe—and yet, descriptive material and narrative telling what you have seen is vital for a story that is to have moving feet and not just talking heads. There is only one way out of the trap: You need to interview trustworthy people who can become your proxy eyes—and you need to elicit from them the type of specific detail that you could have seen had you been there. Here is how *World* used an interview with David Hooten, a missionary in Rwanda, who described how he and his wife had made it through a couple of roadblocks but saw trouble ahead:

> "I slowed down, but there was no blockade. No logs or tree stumps or rocks like they normally use to stop you—except just the people, the mob was there. I forced my way with the vehicle through them. I did not want to stop in the middle of them because I had a pretty good idea what was happening. I tried and was able to get through them. I slowed down on the other side to see if I could get a sense as to what they were doing."
>
> That pause could have cost the missionary and his wife their lives had they not been alert and able to keep going.
>
> "Sure enough," he said, "they came charging after us. One guy got a hold of the side of my door. I had my window down. He hung onto it trying to get me to stop. The rest of the crowd came at us with machetes and clubs and different implements. . . ."
>
> Hooten rammed the vehicle into gear and tore away from the crowd.

Such stories can also be told in narrative based on interviewing rather than through quotation.

> A foreshadowing of what might be in store was recently played out on the streets in Johannesburg when thousands of Inkatha supporters marching with tribal shields and spears clashed with

machine-gun-armed supporters of the African National Congress. . . . Brutal tribal fighting raged in the midst of Johannesburg's gleaming skyscrapers. When the fighting ended, 53 lay dead and nearly 200 were wounded. The aftermath of this day of carnage brought new pleas for negotiation and compromise.

Some missionaries can be very helpful as foreign correspondents, but my point is: emphasize the importance of pushing for specific detail, which goes for everyday domestic reporting as well as international coverage. For example, when interviewing a young mother who has made the transition from salaried professional to full-time mom, do not settle for a vague statement from interviewee "Jennifer" that money is tight; probe for the concrete.

Jennifer says, "I buy store brands, I compare prices. When we buy a car, we're not going to buy the Ford Explorer, which would be our vehicle of choice if we were both still working. Instead, we'll go with a less expensive four-door domestic."

Your goal, in short, is to guide the interviewee to help you write your article. You need to come away from the interview with stories, anecdotes, and specific incidents: "I don't go for Del Monte, I'll get Pathmark on some things. I buy generic dishwasher detergent, generic baby-wash—I've found that generic corn-chips are okay, too." If the interviewee makes a generalization—"the church growth movement is counterproductive"—push him to talk about what he has seen or studied. If he says someone is generous, push for an anecdote that shows generosity. Remember: Specificity is felicity. Write truck, not vehicle; write Ford truck, not truck; write Ford Ranger, not Ford truck.

Always push the interviewee for descriptive information: What exactly did you see? What did he look like? Names, dates, times, colors, locations, ages, numbers. You want specific detail that allows the reader to see. If you do not have time to visit or are not allowed into a maximum-security prison, get a description from a trustworthy guard. If you are writing about an earthquake, get graphic description from someone who was there.

You also are looking for quotations within the narrative. If a person says, "I was worried, and I was praying," ask for specifics: "What were you praying? Were you praying out loud? What did you say?" Press for lively quotations. Push the interviewee to use metaphors or similes by asking, "What was it like"? If the subject has said something substantively interesting but in a bland way, rephrase the question and see if you can get a livelier response.

The etiquette of telephone interviewing often involves calling the interviewee to set up a time for questioning. When making such a request, do not say, "I'd like an interview." Instead, say, "I'd like to ask you about x, y, and z"; specify how much time you will need. If you are able to proceed directly to the interview, the best way to start is to explain quickly what your story is about and how the subject can help.

If you are interviewing by phone, write out your important questions in advance and refer to your list. (If you are doing an in-person interview, at least have a list of questions in your head; you should also have some written in your notebook so you can refer to them toward the end of the interview and be sure you have covered the essentials.) Either way, do not recite to your interviewee a list of questions; start with one, preferably an easy one. Then, avoid questions that can be answered yes or no; do not waste time; do not promise to publish the interview or any particular answers. Listen much, speak little; you do not want your interview to contain much of your own voice.

TAPING

Reporters still debate the question of "to tape or not to tape." Tape recorders do have their disadvantages: They produce among some interviewees the wary-wording syndrome, and among others the dreaded oratorical tendency. Tape recorders can fail to work, so reporters even with tape recorders need to take some notes. Listening to and transcribing relevant parts of the interview takes a long time. (That time can be reduced if you have taken some notes during the interview so that you know when the best answers came.)

Nevertheless, recording allows you to concentrate on the subject instead of your notes; to make regular eye contact; to carry on a conversation rather than an inquisition; and to watch for body language and other nonverbal signs. Furthermore, people speak in distinctive ways that may get lost when in note taking the tendency is to translate them into your own idiom: Taping provides an accurate record of just how a person speaks.

Another practical side to taping is that not only can you check quotations, but people are also less likely to accuse you of misquotation. Tapes are also an important protection in a litigious age. Overall, you should tell your interviewees that you regularly tape, and then you should proceed to do so unless they object.* If you are not taping, you will have to develop some kind of reporter's shorthand, such as jotting down the first letter or two of each word; then, if the comment is important and you need to fill in the words while you still remember, ask a filler question so you will have time to go back. Most reporters at the least turn words such as *with* into *w*.

Whether you are taping or not, do not worry about conversational pauses, unless you are interviewing someone for radio. When the in-person interviewee is not answering your question, just stare at him; eye contact helps to elicit response. Expectant silence is also helpful.

One of the striking aspects of the work of early Reformation-era reporters is that in adverse circumstances they took down speeches, with an accuracy praised by their contemporaries—without tape recorders. With the technology and the freedom God has given us, we are without excuse if we do not do at least as well.

---

*Here is one more nannyish reminder: Put in fresh batteries and new tapes before an interview and bring extra ones, just in case. Other pieces of advice: Record a few words on a new tape, so that in case you do not depress the record button, you will hear the sound and recognize the error. Check the tape immediately after the interview; in case there has been disaster, you won't have much in the way of direct quotes, but you can summarize and describe, if you start writing immediately before the music fades.

CHAPTER FIVE

Organizing for Readability

Reporters who do not practice directed journalism often find that when they have finished their reporting and interviewing, they have a writhing mass of factoids in search of a theme. This may happen to you but it should not happen very often, because you should have been asking yourself at every step of the process: "What do I have?" Your goal—like that of the great film director John Ford—is to be "cutting in your head" even while the event is occurring or the cameras are rolling. Organization is not something to think about after you already have done your reporting: think about your expected outcome before and during reporting.

Thematically, you want to emerge from the reporting and interviewing process with your thesis—your idea of what the story is all about—either supported or changed. From the point at which your thesis solidifies, you are no longer looking for evidence that disproves it (although you should take into account any that emerges); from that point on you are building your case as an honest lawyer would, bringing out supporting evidence and refuting what appears to undermine your case but actually does not.

ORGANIZATIONAL STRATEGIES

The way to make your case journalistically is not to shout louder but to use narrative, description, and quotation to impress upon the readers the rightness of your case. The readers are like jurors but with one major difference: They are free to walk out of the jury box at any time. Your task is to make your case in a way that keeps them interested. One way to do that in a major story is to employ one of the common organizational strategies—circular, spatial, parallel, and linear—that experienced journalists use, sometimes consciously, sometimes without thinking.

A *circular* story begins and ends in the same location or situation; the reader is shown various sites while swinging around the circle. Here is how Roy Maynard's previously cited story on prisons began:

> A brass cross is the focal point of the chapel in the Wynne Unit of the Texas Department of Corrections system. That cross, inmates explain, will likely be removed. "It offends some of the Muslims," explains Eugene, a 35-year-old convict, doing time in this maximum-security facility for a violent crime. "So they're talking about taking it out. Ain't that something? It's about the only thing in here doing any good."

The story then proceeds through various interviews and anecdotes that show how those from various perspectives and backgrounds have come to similar views.

> Eugene, the 35-year-old inmate, has been locked up for 11 years now; he's spent many hours thinking about what can change a criminal's heart. "People talk a lot about education," he says. "Let me tell you, there's a whole lot of educated people in prison. Education doesn't do it. Buildings don't do it. You've got to change a man's heart. Then you'll see some rehabilitation."
>
> Chuck Colson served time in prison two decades ago, in the wake of the Nixon administration's Watergate scandal. He, too, emphasizes changing hearts. . . .

The article ends where it began, with Eugene pointing to the cross and saying:

"Another thing I know is that if I had not been sent here, I'd be in the ground by now. Here is where God talked to me."

He looked over at the threatened cross, and added, "They took God out of schools. Hope they don't do that here."

A *spatial* story, instead of bringing readers circularly to the place where they began, tries to give them a closer look at a subject by moving them from outside to inside, or room by room through a house, or house by house down a street. Here is an example of how to start:

The *Village Voice*, New York's traditional counterculture newspaper, is housed in a crumbling tenement on Broadway at the northern edge of Greenwich Village. Almost every square foot of the building's exterior wall is plastered with handbills for hip-sounding bands or talks at nearby clubs and meeting places: "Lunachicks," "Suicidal Tendencies," "Haunted Toilet," "Hide the Baby," and "Yogo Gupta: Trimmer Body, Calmer Mind, Self-Realization."

A huge trash pile along one side of the building smells of urine and sparkles with empty bottles of Wild Irish Rose and other cheap hits. On the inside, a dark staircase leading to the second-floor editorial department is brightened only by a taped-up flyer offering comfort to "Lesbian Survivors of Abusive Relationships."

Then, the reader is brought inside:

The editorial department is well lit, however. Fluorescent bulbs bring out the detail of scratched linoleum floors, a broken table sitting in the hallway, and a current *Village Voice* that has slid off the table. The lead article in that issue complains of those who have "found common cause with the Jerry Falwells and Pat Robertsons of the world. On the package of issues surrounding abortion, they have allied themselves with society's most repressive and misogynistic forces." Down the hallway lies an open area with dozens of desks; around one of them seven or eight 25-year-olds in tight jeans grimly receive a harangue about the "blow-dried fascism of the Reaganitemare" from a 45-year-old editor in Dockers.

Next comes the introduction of the main character:

Then, from a dim hallway on the other side of the open area, comes shuffling a bent-over, 65-year-old in gray slacks. The Red Sea of young people silently parts before him, and the middle-aged man

offers a sullen look; but no one says hello to gray bearded Nat
Hentoff. The silence is striking, for Hentoff was one of the creators
of the *Village Voice* and its environment. For 33 of the 36 years of the
Voice's existence, Hentoff's articles and columns have attacked anyone attempting to put limits on freedom of expression of any kind,
whether political or pornographic. . . . But in one area—abortion—
Hentoff is a deviate, and for that he has achieved what he calls a "difficult, sometimes pariah status."

From that point on the article takes readers deeper into Hentoff's
views and background. In a sense, a spatial story is like beginning with
a wide-angle lens and then moving in; it can also work the other way,
by starting with a telephoto lens and providing a close-up, then moving out.

For comparing rhetoric and reality, a *parallel* story, which uses the
cutting back-and-forth approach familiar from movies, often works better than the circular or spatial variety. For example, a story in 1994 headlined, "Congress Coddles Social Work Lobby as Children Languish in
Abusive Homes," began with a discussion of legislation.

Before its annual summer recess, the House of Representatives
passed the "Children's Initiative" bill 256 to 163, a margin too small
to override a presidential veto. The legislation combines three separate bills: the "Family Preservation Act," the "Mickey Leland
Childhood Hunger Relief Act," and a deficit reduction measure. It provides $3.5 billion for family preservation, $3.5 billion for food distribution, and $1.2 billion for deficit reduction.

Last week Senate Democrats came roaring back to Washington
promising to pass comparable legislation to "show compassion"
and prove that the Bush administration's concern for families is all
slogan without substance. In stately Senate offices and private dining rooms, liberal senators pledged their commitment to "family
preservation" that would leave no child without a haven amidst
heartlessness.

Then came the reality, italicized in the article to make clear the
alternation.

*Several miles away from the Capitol, in one of the District of
Columbia's rough neighborhoods, conversation is different. There,
citizens talk of four children found locked up by their mother in two*

filthy, roach-infested rooms. The four children—ranging in age from nine to three—had been imprisoned for as long as four years. None was able to speak more than simple sentences. . . .

Back to the legislators:

On Capitol Hill, where lawmakers say the word and create a federal bureaucracy out of nothing, the child welfare program has a simple solution—more money. Whenever a child is killed emotionally or even physically by an abusive parent, the story is the same—the system is overloaded and underfunded. While Congress is trying to give more money to child welfarists in order to "preserve families," critics charge that the child welfare system is so deeply flawed that bigger bucks will not help. . . .

And to the streets:

Quintessa Murreld of New York City died in foster care last year at the age of three. Her uncle, who was also her foster father, pleaded guilty of manslaughter. Quintessa had been placed in foster care because her mother, a crack addict, neglected her. After six months in that foster home, she was not placed for adoption, but was moved into foster care with her aunt and uncle, who made it clear that they had no intention of adopting the child. . . .

The alternating portraits directed readers' attention to the legislators' distance from reality.

A *linear* story (sometimes euphemistically called the "string of pearls") is the most straightforward of the common organizational varieties. It starts with a lively lead, then begins adding details and characters, and stops when enough scenes have piled up to make the point. If the scenes are good enough, the artlessness of the structure does not particularly matter. For example, here is a good opening to a story about the yearning of some Americans for Canadian-style health care:

"Was this the face that launched a thousand ships, / and burnt the topless towers of Ilium? / Sweet Helen, make me immortal with a kiss."
In Faustian legend and lore—especially as told by 16th century English dramatist Christopher Marlowe in his play, *The Tragical History of Dr. Faustus,* Faust made his pact with the devil: his soul

the price for magical powers. After 24 years, Faust was dragged down to Hell.

Where Marlowe meets modern politics is in the awe with which some American politicians regarded Canada's health care system for nearly a quarter of a century.

Canada, it can be argued, is the face that launched a thousand congressional bills and burnt the towers and high-rise office buildings of the American health care system.

But in exchange for a promised magical cure to a free-market health care system's ills, Canada sold its soul to a quasi-socialist system, and exactly 24 years later is finding that the deal struck was no bargain at all.

Then come various expert appraisals, followed by the reporter's analysis:

"In truth, most Canadians sleep well at night knowing that if they get the flu, they can see a provider of primary care," Canadian-born Sally Pipes notes. Ms. Pipes, president of San Francisco's Pacific Research Institute for Public Policy, warns that from across the border, Canada's system shimmers and shines—but up close, it falls short.

Individuals with exotic illnesses, in need of specialized care, quickly enter into Canada's queue zone. They take their place in line and wait and wait, often suffering great pain and prolonged worry, hoping to be treated by a specialist before they are incapacitated."

Next is the reporter's direct summary of the various analyses:

That's not the only problem with the system—the issue of waiting lists is now being overshadowed by the issue of deficit-driven cuts in levels of service. And while President Clinton has begun to distance himself verbally from the Canadian system, major components remain a part of his still-evolving plan. Clinton is brushing aside conservative criticism about costs by promising spending caps. He contends he has rejected the notion of a single-payer system, but his plan embraces centrally controlled budgets and policies. The Canadian model is alive, well, and wedged firmly between the lines of Clinton's musings about "managed competition."

Just when the article threatens to become a policy-wonk piece, the reporter provides "a face," someone to personalize the story, and also provides more description of the environment.

> "I know it's being talked about a lot in the States, but I don't really think Americans would like this system much," said Tom Muecke. His accent is the only indication that this backup quarterback for the Canadian Football League's Edmonton Eskimos grew up in the town of Angleton, Texas, under the Friday night lights of the Lone Star state's football tradition. He played college ball and earned a business degree at Baylor University before signing with the CFL. . . . The clear Edmonton afternoon is a little brisk— Muecke grew up where heat and humidity drove men mad enough to build a domed stadium with fake grass—but other than that, Edmonton could easily be mistaken for a Texas oil town. Developers built out, not up, so the city has that wide-open feeling akin to Dallas. Country music and cowboy boots are common, worn with suits and Wrangler jeans alike. . . .

> As he spoke with *World* last week, Muecke tossed around a football—only his hands were paying attention to it—and he reflected on the Canadian system he'd seen since 1986, when he began to play in the CFL: "It feels great to people, because when they go to the doctor, they know they won't have to pay anything—no money will leave their pockets. But they know they make it up in taxes."

Concluding paragraphs provided other specific indictments of the Canadian system and led to the end.

> Tom Muecke smiled when asked about his future plans, which include attending optometry school in Houston when he's finished with football. Would he like to open a practice in Edmonton? "I don't think so," he said. "The government controls all of that here, and I don't think I'd enjoy that. I'll practice in America, where—hopefully—I won't have to worry about that."

Other types of structures are also usable; you need to find the right structure for your particular material and theme. Circular structures often contribute to a sense that lots of people are talking about problems but few people are finding solutions. Alternating structure works well when you are contrasting biblical and ungodly approaches.

Locational structure provides a sense of looking deeper into an issue, situation, or personality.

If you are having a hard time figuring out how to tell your story, ask yourself questions such as: What interested me about this story? What is it really about? What do I want to teach the reader? If you did not have a firm focus when you started your reporting and interviewing, you certainly need one at this point. You may be able to find your focus by listing crucial conclusions and seeing what you know after doing your research that you did not know before.

The key to successful organizing of a major story is a firm grasp of your theme. You need to be able to summarize your main theme in a sentence that has a noun and a verb; in other words, subject plus action. You will then be ready to see if you have sharpened your angle enough to be able to write a tight article rather than a dithering report.

Whether you are certain or uncertain as to your theme and main points, your next step is to organize your material; if you are uncertain, you may end up reorganizing many times, but it is essential to start on the sorting process anyway. (As you organize, you often will realize that the story you thought was about "x" is actually about "y," with "x " as a subtheme.)

One way to organize as you prepare to write a story is to divide your material into main sections and subsections, either on a computer or using index cards. If you use cards, you may wish to list important points on individual cards, try out the various arrangements, and then develop a plan that can and should be rough. Elaborate outlines tend to be wastes of time as you get into the flow of your writing. As you organize, you want to develop a list of your major points in the order that you think they should go; your outline should be a spine, not a corpse, and it should be brief enough so that you can do quick spinal taps as you think about your material.

Then, as you fish through your notes and folders and try to organize within sections, remember to mix up the three types of evidences and arguments that you are about to provide: narration, description, and quotation. For example, here is the continuation of the story on the culture war in San Francisco, beginning with a long but yeasty quotation.

"San Francisco isn't Sodom," said the pastor, who looks years younger than his 47 years. "But it's vying for second place. . . . What has happened in San Francisco is a grim look into the future of what lies ahead not only for other cities, but for the U.S. health care system, schools, the media, and the church itself. . . . A *coup d'etat* of decadence has occurred in San Francisco. There literally is a new rainbow flag that periodically flies above city hall announcing the new nation—'Queer Nation.' . . . Straight society is now out of power and without influence, living on the fringes of society."

Then came a narrative showing homosexual power in San Francisco:

On June 12, 1990, the school board met to vote on the program; the meeting began with homosexuals hissing the recital of the Pledge of Allegiance.

Catcalls greeted a Christian psychologist's criticism of Project 10. Jean Harris, a lesbian official with a bullhorn, tried to reason with the 200-plus crowd in the room: "I know it's ugly and hateful. Let him get it over with."

Outside, according to Mrs. McIlhenny, an assortment of homosexual activists including gay men dressed as nuns (Sisters of Perpetual Indulgence) and drag queens waited.

The bully tactics didn't surprise Donna McIlhenny; it was the board's reaction to two tearful mothers after the unanimous vote for Project 10 that shocked her.

"Two bewildered mothers cried out to the board, 'You've just given our children over to those people outside,'" Mrs. McIlhenny recalled. "[Superintendent Ramon] Cortines just turned around and walked away."

Then description, conveyed in an active way:

The Castro district is a community of first names and hallowed anonymity. Denny and Michael accepted without question my first name and my honest contention that it was my first time to San Francisco. We walked upstream against the crowds, the gays and lesbians in groups of twos and threes. Rainbow flags adorned every business and bar, and physical affection was displayed with a sense of bravado. There were "straight" tourists—identifiable by their chiseled expressions of disoriented tolerance—but for the most part it was men with men, women with women.

After further description came a second round, beginning with a quotation.

> "It's hell," Michael said. He then cited the oft-repeated round-about logic gays use to justify their lifestyle: "Why would anybody choose to live like this?"
>
> A similar question is put to McIlhenny: Why would any Christian choose to live and minister in San Francisco? "I didn't," he admitted. "I've tried to leave. We've had calls to other churches, even, but things just never worked out."

Then narration (broken up by a quotation):

> McIlhenny had plans to pastor a church he helped start a safe 115 miles away from firebombs and the Castro district—but on the day he was going to announce to the presbytery his intentions of transferring, he instead had to inform them that the presbytery, the church, and McIlhenny himself had been sued. McIlhenny had fired a church organist who was a homosexual.
>
> "Instead of transferring from the church, I had to tell them [members of the presbytery] that we've all got to get lawyers," he explained. "We were here for the duration."

Then more quotation:

> John Whitehead recalls the case—he spent two months preparing the brief alone—and says he realized then the significance of it.
>
> "We won the case [based] on the free exercise clause," Whitehead said. "There was talk of an appeal, but that's all it was. They [gays] knew that if it lost in San Francisco, it wouldn't win anywhere else. There was a lot of clamoring in other cities, a lot of city councils considering similar measures. But when we won, the clamoring stopped for a while. They had been watching the case closely."

But the victory was only temporary. . . .

Then historical narrative, which is not left to stand alone but is connected with the story of the article's leading subject.

> If Stonewall was the gay movement's moment, Harvey Milk was its martyr. He won election to the San Francisco Board of Supervisors in 1977, touting himself as the nation's first openly homosexual politician. He pushed for measures such as legalizing

marijuana, but in 1978 his career was cut short. Another supervisor and political foe, Dan White, shot and killed Milk and then-mayor, George Moscone.

"I was in school at the time—I was taking a master's degree at San Francisco State, just down the street from us," McIlhenny explained. "That day I went into the student quad and everyone was standing around watching the television. We knew that would turn the whole movement around—that a martyr was created."

After showing a familiarity with the particular San Francisco scene, the author could then back off slightly and use a wider angle.

In fact, "portray gays as victims" is one of the four points for achieving the gay agenda, as outlined by homosexual writers Marshall Kirk and Erastes Pill in a homosexual magazine. The others include giving protectors a just cause—if not support for homosexual acts, at least the defensible concept of anti-discrimination; and vilification of those opposed to homosexuality—"The public should be shown images of ranting homophobes whose secondary traits disgust middle America. . . ."

But a little exposition of this sort goes a long way; the particular gift we can give to readers is more description.

We passed through six or eight bars in the span of two hours; Michael and Denny explained that most patrons "make the rounds," considering all of Castro a single party.

With our hands in our coats in the damp, chilling San Francisco night, we passed below the balcony of a lesbian club. Women shouted good-natured abuse at friends and strangers, worn-out gay and lesbian slogans, and sheer nonsense from the balcony, but Denny and Michael took no notice; it was just part of the Castro.

The bars were beginning to announce last call. Although the after-hours places—the espresso bars, the 24-hour restaurants—would remain open and active, a sense of desperation was evident. Men began leaving with other men; those who remained gripped their drinks tightly or left for a quick look into other bars.

Michael seemed determined to make it to yet another bar before closing time. I was a little surprised; because neither he nor Denny had made any sexual advances toward me or other men so far that night, it appeared they were involved in an exclusive relationship, at least for now. I asked Michael why he seemed determined to press on to another bar.

And a closing quotation:

"It's just part of the evening, part of the nightly search," he said. He didn't respond when asked, "What is it you're searching for?"

That type of movement keeps any particular section from hanging heavy. As you organize your material, make sure that you are interspersing the various ways of *showing*—and try to use them all, so that you can keep *telling* to a minimum.

Pacing is vital—and you can control it by pausing for description after you introduce major characters. For example, after a rapid-fire lead about a desperate, unemployed logger, it is time for a pastoral that allows readers to catch their breaths.

The late spring landscape of Washington's Olympic Peninsula probably favors the delicate brush strokes of a watercolor over the firmer brush strokes of an oil. The creator's soft touch enhances rather than diminishes the brilliant colors.

Even in their waning weeks, the western rhododendron stipple the seemingly boundless green with fuchsias, lavenders, oranges, and pinks. . . .

The snow-covered peaks of the Olympic Mountains can be seen from the peninsula's surrounding waters and occasionally through clearings in the forest. But beneath the canopy of pine, alder, cedar, hemlock, and the vital Douglas fir ("Doug fir" to the logger), the scene is less than magnificent.

There is a new and unwelcome silence in the shadowy forest. A once thriving and productive species known as the American timberman has been driven out of his critical habitat—unprotected by the hovering wings of the Endangered Species Act.

Other ways to control pacing include alternation: After readers read through statistics or difficult exposition, reward them with anecdote, colorful detail, or humor. Scatter gold coins throughout the story; readers who find several will keep on reading for more. The key: Show— do not just tell.

Remember throughout that your publication can be a travel guide, taking readers to areas or situations that may be foreign to them, as in the San Francisco story or in this article from the other side of the country.

> Walking down Brooklyn's Fourth Avenue, Leroy Shepherd isn't talking about the New York mayor's race coming next month. Instead, he's explaining how to distinguish a crack addict.
>
> "They walk along the sidewalks, and you'll see them looking into the gutters for old crack vials, in hopes of finding one with a little crack left at the bottom," says the 28-year-old paralegal. "Sometimes they find enough; maybe that day your car won't get broken into."

Whenever possible, try to provide part of the answer, the "who cares?" question by *broadening* the scope and appeal of your story: Show its relevance to a national audience. For the most part your reporting will come from one specific locale, but if you hope to show readers that the problem of culture wars between Christians and their opponents is spreading, you should bring in many examples and have vignettes about each.

For example, the story about Christians vs. lesbians was set in Ovett, Mississippi, but the author explained that it was a microcosm of:

> what happens when quiet, Christian-based communities encounter the challenge of those calling for unbiblical sexual and religious reformation.
>
> Recent examples of similar instances around the nation include:
>
> —Salem, Mass., where about 3,000 of the town's 38,000 people are active witches and feminist goddess worshipers; they are now the dominant cultural influence in the town.
>
> —Fairfield, Iowa, where three of the City Council's seven members are followers of Transcendental Meditation guru Maharishi Mahesh Yogi. Of the town's 10,000 residents, 2,500 have come to the farming community to study TM; in the 1970s, the guru's followers bought a bankrupt college and turned it into Maharishi International University, a Mecca for TM practitioners.
>
> —Antelope, Ore., where sex guru Bhagwan Shree Rajineesh moved his sect in the early '80s, literally smothering the tiny indigenous population of 40.

Whenever possible, put information of this sort high up in your organization plan. Announcements that suggest that cultural trends in one area will be "coming soon to a theater near you" make readers care. They help you avoid the readers' reactions signified in these two acronymns: MEGO (Mine Eyes Glaze Over) and TEK (This Everybody Knows).

Editors and reporters should discuss organizational questions early on. A good editor would rather coach early in the process than fix later on; both methods improve stories, but coaching can improve journalists as well. A reporter should not be offended if an editor reads the draft and then comes back with questions like, What's your theme? What are the most interesting things you saw? What's your evidence for this? What did it look like? What does the reader need to know? How can you clarify this?

The editor's key role at this point is in what is called structural editing, an analysis of how the story moves from start to finish. Editors may demand reorganization: The editor's job is to explain why, and the reporter's task is to be of good cheer through what is at times a painful process. As a reporter, you will tend to feel that everything you have written is important, but a story in which everything is equal most often has the excitement of a posed class or team photograph. A good editor is anti-egalitarian, emphasizing certain elements and downgrading the importance of others.

A stickler for emphasis will place the most important words at the beginning or the end of the sentence, the most important sentences at the beginning or the end of paragraphs, the most important paragraphs at the beginning or the end of stories. He will add emphasis also by arranging ideas within a sentence from least to most important, by varying sentence length, by repeating key words or phrases, and by parallel structure. He will always insist on logical order, and so should each writer: Do not dither as you write, but order elements by chronology, by space (right to left, east to west, and so forth), or by order of climax.

SHORTER STORIES

A shorter story is to a cover story like a quarter-mile run is to a mile run. Milers have to pace themselves; world class quarter-milers sprint the entire way. Shorter articles need description, narrative, and quotation just as longer pieces do, but there is no room in the former for extended descriptive passages, long anecdotes, or extensive personalization; anecdotes have to illuminate issues rather than display faces. Here is an example of an anecdote that quickly gets to the theme of a story about Mexican political changes:

> Mexicans for years have told a little inside joke. They grin and say that citizens of the United States have nothing on them when they brag that they can know the results of a presidential election within a few hours after the polls close. "In Mexico," residents boast, "we know who the next president is before the polls close."
>
> For 65 years that has been so. The nominee of the Institutional Revolutionary Party (known by its Spanish acronym PRI) has been assured the presidency. . . . Something is different this time.

One key to a successful short article is to find the telling joke, the telling anecdote—and to do that you have to know your subject well enough to know what is important and what is trivial. In a quarter-mile sprint you particularly need to highlight the revealing exchanges.

> The day last April that FBI agents assaulted the Branch Davidian compound and it burned to the ground, taking more than 80 lives, Attorney General Janet Reno took every available media opportunity to explain why she had ordered the attack. During her appearance on NBC, Tom Brokaw asked the obvious question of whether she had talked with the president about the tragic turn of events that day in Waco. Ms. Reno responded that she had not [, but] Webster Hubbell had. The exchange was revealing. Hubbell was in important respects the real attorney general.

There are practical differences as well between organizing for shorter and longer stories. If you write a long story you probably will have extensive notes on many interviews, photocopies of background material, and much else beside. You may need to organize your research by placing all of your materials in folders and then by making divisions within the folders. One folder is sufficient for a shorter article: You need one good, straightforward story to tell, and you need to go right at it.

THE THAW PROCESS

Some of my students have found it helpful to work through what I call the THAW process of unfreezing stories—Thinking, Hunting, Analyzing, Writing. The first task is to *think* through a story's theme, go out on a reportorial *hunt* for specific detail, *analyze* what has been gathered, and finally—only after a lot of thinking, hunting, and analyzing— sit down to *write*. If a writer is frozen at the computer, most of the time he or she should not keep sitting there, but go out on a new hunt.

Each of those four phases has several elements: If you were in my class and wanted to remember those elements, I would ask you to picture a Great Dane taking photographs, and then see the following headline describing the event: Fans' Dane Uses Lens. The first word, FANS'—Face, Attitude, News hook, Surprise—summarizes four questions I would ask you about your story idea. First, what is your *face*—your way of personalizing a story? Second, what *attitude* toward your material will you be able to express? (For a Christian, that will relate to the class of rapids in which the story should be placed.) Third, do you have a *news hook*—a way of relating your story to a current event? Fourth, will there be any *surprise* for the readers in what you write? (The classic journalistic phrase for something that will surprise readers is, "man bites dog.")

Next, to describe the ways in which to hunt for elements of a story, picture a Great DANE: Description, Attribution, Narrative, Exposition. That means setting the scene through *description*; interviewing the characters to garner quotations, so that ideas do not float in nothingness but are *attributable* to particular individuals; showing the action in a *narrative*, story-telling fashion; and explaining when necessary through straight *exposition*. As you go out reporting, think about the elements you will need: If you have lots of quotations and adequate descriptive material, be sure to get action adventure material; if you have lots of narrative, be sure to get some quotations; and so on.

The third word, Fan's Dane USES Lens, provides a way of analyzing what you have (and informing your editor) once you have finished your hunting: Will your story lead to Uproar, Sensation, Education, or Snooze? Any of the first three is satisfactory, although a publication's goal is always to make a mark. If your story's potential seems limited to a sleeping-pill function, tell your editor before you spend any more time on it. He may find a way to revitalize it, or he may propose killing it; either way, you will be saving time.

The final word in the formula for thawing a frozen writer is LENS: Lead, End, Nut graf, and Substance. More about these in Chapter Eight.

CHAPTER SIX

The Streets Declare the Sinfulness of Man

L et us go back in history again to see how Christian reporters in America won the opportunity to place God above government. The victory was a long time coming: After the monarchical restoration of 1660 in England, British officials across the Atlantic imitated the lords of London by also placing restrictions on press freedoms. Royal governors appeared to believe that the Reformers' idea of "read for yourself" simply caused too much trouble. In 1671, Governor William Berkeley of Virginia stated that he was glad to have the colony without colleges or printing presses, "for *learning* has brought disobedience, and heresy, and sects into the world, and *printing* has divulged them, and libels against the best government.'"

Virginia was typical in its stifling of any who dared to criticize the government. Philip Ludwell was heavily fined in 1678 for calling Governor Herbert Jeffreys a lawbreaker. When printing finally was allowed, it was carefully regulated: Printer John Buckner received a reprimand in 1682 merely for printing the colony's laws without official permission; Buckner was forced to post a bond of one hundred pounds that would be forfeited were he ever to print anything again. Every few years—1685, 1690, 1693, 1699, 1702, and 1704—proclamations condemned the "over lycentiousnesse of the People in their discourses."

In Maryland, attempts at independence also received severe punishment: In 1666, one critic of government received thirty-nine lashes across his back. Protests concerning such treatment occasionally appeared: In 1689, a Maryland group that called itself the Protestant Association complained that the government had punished "Words and Actions" it disapproved of by "Whipping, Branding, Boreing through the Tongue, Fine, Imprisonment, Banishment, or Death."

During this period, walking the tightrope of reformation without revolution was akin to walking the plank. For example, in 1698, Philip Clark, although a member of the Maryland assembly, was sentenced to six months in jail for criticizing Governor Francis Nicholson. According to the governor's Council, Clark's criticism was incitement to rebellion not because he actually suggested such an activity, but because his critique would reduce the esteem in which the governor was held—and that was seen as the first step toward rebellion.

Only in New England, the center of Reformation thought in the New World, were publication and education emphasized; the Puritans set up a printing press and college in Cambridge, Massachusetts, in 1636, just six years after their arrival in a wilderness where mere survival was not assured. John Harvard's gift of books for a new college was important, but Harvard's founders had to overcome political as well as material obstacles: They were challenging royal authority. In England, the universities at Oxford and Cambridge were arms of the government, which had a monopoly on the granting of college diplomas; Harvard, though, awarded its first diplomas in 1642, without royal authorization. The timing, it turned out, was good: A king besieged and eventually beheaded was in no position to assert his authority.

In the 1660s, however, monarchical restoration in England placed new pressures on New England. Well-connected courtiers in London contested the Massachusetts Bay charter that Charles I had given to Puritan leaders in 1629; the courtiers claiming that they had received previous royal grants to the same land. The Massachusetts legislature, desperate to avoid a royal crackdown, forced evangelist and writer John Eliot in 1661 to retract "such expressions as doe too manifestly scandalize" the government of England. Eliot's book *The Christian Commonwealth*, which advocated election of rulers, was ordered "totally suppressed."

Nevertheless, the Puritans did encourage the reporting of bad news that tended to be swept under the rug in most other places. They were lenient in this way because bad news was seen as a message from God. Boston printer Marmaduke Johnson in 1668 published *God's Terrible Voice in the City of London, Wherein You Have the Narration of the Late Dreadful Judgment of Pleague and Fire*. In 1674, when Benjamin Goad was hanged in Boston for committing bestiality, Samuel Danforth wrote of crime and punishment and offered a why.

> God's end in inflicting remarkable judgments upon some, is for caution and warning to all others. . . . Behold now the execution of vengeance upon this lewd and wicked youth, whom God hath hanged up before the Sun, and made a sign and example, and instruction and admonishment, to all New England.

"News sermons," first presented in church and frequently published, became an established form of New England communication. Twice on Sunday and often once during the week, ministers spoke for at least an hour. Sermons on royal births and deaths, military defeats or victories, election results and government decisions, and crimes (preferably with punishments) were common.

Printers moved naturally from the publication of Bible commentaries, to the publication of theological treatises and sermons, to the publication of news sermons and pamphlets on current events. Most publications in New England in the seventeenth century were event-oriented. Puritan theology not only allowed but emphasized the reporting of bad news, for the coming of well-deserved calamities was a sign that God still reigned. The best-known Massachusetts minister of the late-seventeenth century, Increase Mather, also became its leading journalist. Mather argued in 1674 that God was not pleased with the sins of pride and envy that were common in New England, and that "a day of trouble is at hand."

Mather's forecasts of general disaster hit home in June 1675 when a tribe of Wampanoag Indians burned and looted homes in the town of Swansea and killed nine residents. Indian attacks escalated in August 1675 as Wampanoags led by Chief Metacom ("King Philip") were joined by the Narragansetts and Nipmucks in an attack on towns in western Massachusetts and other outlying areas. A ballad contextualized the news: "O New-England, I understand / with thee God is offended: / And therefore He doth humble thee, / till thou thy ways hast mended."

In the summer of 1676, Philip's forces were within ten miles of Boston, but so many had been killed in battle that a final push was beyond their grasp; when Philip was captured and executed, the war was over. The tribes were left devastated, but one in every sixteen colonists of fighting age was also dead, many women and children had been killed or carried into captivity, and twelve towns were destroyed.

For the Puritans, the war was an exceptionally clear example of judgment upon sinful people, and many ministers and/or writers spoke or wrote about it. Chief among them was Increase Mather, whose *Brief History of the War with the Indians of New-England* was filled with information about who, what, when, and where.

> March 17. This day the Indians fell upon Warwick, and burnt it down to the ground, all but one house. May 11. A company of Indians assaulted the Town of Plimouth, burnt eleven Houses and five Barns therein.

Mather then contextualized the news by seeing God's hand not only in the beginning of the war but in its prolongation; reporting on the aftermath of one battle, he wrote, "Had the English immediately pursued the Victory begun, in all likelyhood there had been an end of our troubles: but God saw that neither yet were we fit for deliverance."

Like other Puritan journalists, Mather was careful to juxtapose evidence of God's anger with dramatic news of God's mercy. When one house was about to be set on fire by hundreds of Indians who surrounded it, it appeared that:

> Men and Women, and Children must have perished, either by unmerciful flames, or more unmerciful hands of wicked Men whose tender Mercies are cruelties, so that all hope that they should be saved was then taken in: but behold in this Jount of Difficulty and Extremity *the Lord is seen*. For in the very nick of opportunity God sent that worthy Major Willard, who with forty and eight men set upon the Indians and caused them to turn their backs. . . . however we may be diminished and brought low through Oppression, Affliction, and Sorrow, yet our God will have compassion on us, and this his People shall not utterly perish.

Mather's reportage was a prototype of the cavalry rescues beloved in Western movies, but the emphasis here was on God's grace, not man's heroism. He reported that when New Englanders recognized their reliance on that grace and renewed their covenant with God, the war ended. He emphasized the importance of accurate reporting—"a brief, plain, and true story"—in understanding the why of the war: God's punishment because of sins such as "contention" and "pride." But he also argued that too much guilt, like too much pride, could "run into extreams." Instead of pouring it on, Mather offered hope: God's "design, in bringing the Calamity upon us, is not to destroy us, but to humble us, and reform us, and to do us good in the latter end."

In applying the Bible to current issues, the Puritans sometimes mistook class-five rapids for class twos—but they did begin a tradition of hard-hitting news analysis. The next step for American journalism came in 1681 when a general meeting of the Massachusetts ministers urged careful coverage of:

> Illustrious Providences, including Divine Judgements, Tempests, Floods, Earth-quakes, Thunders as are unusual, Strange Apparitions, or what ever else shall happen that is Prodigious, Witchcrafts, Diabolical Possessions, Remarkable Judgements upon noted Sinners: eminent Deliverances, and Answers of Prayer.

Here was a definition of news not unlike today's in its emphasis on atypical, man-bites-dog events: "unusual" thunders, "strange" apparitions, and other "prodigious" or "remarkable" happenings—except that the why was different, since for the Puritans all unusual occurrences showed a glimpse of God's usually invisible hand.

The ministers' resolution also provided a method for the recording of events that anticipated the relation of freelancers and editors in later years. First, each minister was to be a correspondent, with the responsibility to "diligently enquire into, and Record such Illustrious Providences as have happened, or from time to time shall happen, in the places whereunto they do belong." Second, to avoid the supplanting of fact by fiction, it would be important to rely on eyewitnesses and make sure "that the Witnesses of such notable Occurrents be likewise set down in Writing." Third, it would be important to find a main writer-editor who "hath Leisure and Ability for the management of Such an undertaking."

That person turned out to be Mather himself—and he proved himself to be right for the job. Mather read widely and well, citing in appropriate places in his writings the work of Johannes Kepler, Tycho Brahe, Robert Boyle, and other leading scientists of the day. Mather himself wrote reports about comets, magnetism, lightning, thunder, and other natural phenomena, and would not report about an event unless a reliable source made a written, signed statement; after noting one extraordinary occurrence, he remarked, "I would not have mentioned this relation, had I not received it from serious, faithfull, and Judicious hands. . . ."

Mather and others thought accuracy important because events were their report card signed by God, and they wanted to know where they stood, for better or for worse. Mather wrote about not only political events but storms, earthquakes, and fires: all such events, he wrote, were "ordered by the Providence of God. . . . When a fire is kindled among a people, it is the Lord that hath kindled it." Puritans also set the stage for an honoring of the journalists themselves. The idea that God was acting in the world made journalism significant, for Increase Mather wrote that "it is proper for the Ministers of God to ingage themselves recording the providentiall Dispensations of God." Increase's son Cotton even wrote that "To *regard* the illustrious displays of that Providence wherewith our Lord Christ governs the world, is a work, than which there is none more needful or useful for a Christian."

When one Christian in 1690 took the next step by trying to put out a regular newspaper, he encountered trouble. Benjamin Harris knew persecution: Jailed in 1679 and sentenced to a harsh prison regime for publishing in London an independent newspaper, *Domestick Intelligence*, Harris said simply, "I hope God will give me Patience to go through it." After Harris did go through it he continued to print pamphlets that exposed wrongdoing. Aided by Cotton Mather, Harris, on September 25, 1690, published the first newspaper in America, *Publick Occurrences Both Foreign and Domestick*.

Belief in Providence was evident throughout the four-page newspaper. Harris's expressed purpose for publishing it was in line with his previous writing: "That Memorable Occurrents of Divine Providence may not be neglected or forgotten, as they too often are." Harris's combination of reporting and teaching showed as he reported "a day of Thanksgiving to God" for a good harvest and noted, concerning a tragedy averted, that God "assisted the Endeavours of the People to put out the Fire." When a man committed suicide after his wife died, Harris explained that "The Devil took advantage of the Melancholy which he thereupon fell into."

When Harris emphasized God's sovereignty over international relations as well, controversy followed. Harris's report of mistreatment of prisoners by Mohawk Indians, and his criticism of royal officials for making an alliance with those Indians in order to defeat French forces in Canada, was based on his belief in Providence.

> If Almighty God will have Canada to be subdu'd without the assistance of those miserable Savages, in whom we have too much confided, we shall be glad, that there will be no Sacrifice offered up to the Devil, upon this occasion; God alone will have all the glory.

Furthermore, Harris took seriously reports of adultery in the French court. British officials, hoping at that time for peace with France, were refraining from comments that could arouse popular concern about trusting those of low morals; since sexual restraint was not a common court occurrence in Restoration England either, they probably thought such news was non-news. Harris, however, went ahead and reported that Louis XIV "is in much trouble (and fear) not only with us but also with his Son, who has revolted against him lately, and has great reason if reports be true, that the Father used to lie with the Sons Wife."

Puritans who liked to emphasize God's sovereignty over all human activities were pleased with *Publick Occurrences*; Cotton Mather called it "a very noble, useful and laudable design." The royal governor and his council were not amused, however: Four days after publication, the newspaper was suppressed, and Harris was told that any further issues would give him new prison nightmares. Harris gave in. He stayed in Massachusetts for a time and was given some public printing jobs because of his good behavior but returned to England in 1695.

Other newspapers emerged over the next four decades, but for the most part, they were unwilling to criticize government officials. Newspapers did provide a service in helping readers to know "how to order their prayers and praises to the Great God." Local news continued to be reported in reverential context, as in this coverage of a storm.

> The Water flowed over our Wharffs and into our streets to a very surprising height. They say the Tide rose 20 Inches higher than ever was known before. . . . The loss and damage sustained is very great. . . . Let us fear the GOD of heaven, who made the sea and the dry land, who commandeth & raiseth the stormy wind, which lifteth up the waves; who ruleth the raging of the sea, and when the waves thereof arise, He stilleth them.

"Remarkable judgments" such as earthquakes also caused excitement. In October 1727, a "horrid rumbling" and "weighty shaking" was felt throughout New England. "The motion of the Earth was very great, like the waves of the sea" one report noted, using good specific detail: "The strongest Houses shook prodigiously and the tops of some Chimnees were thrown down." Aftershocks over the next nine days, "mightily kept up the Terror of it in the People, and drove them to all possible needs of Reformation."

The first newspaper outside New England, the *American Weekly Mercury*, commented from afar on God's sovereignty in politics. Editor Andrew Bradford wrote that Massachusetts royal officials were "remarkable for Hypocrisy: And it is the general Opinion, that some of their Rulers are rais'd up and continued as a Scourge in the Hands of the Almighty for the Sins of the People." But criticizing officials close at hand was more dangerous, and until the 1730s no editor after Benjamin Harris took the risk.

The editor who did was John Peter Zenger, a New Yorker who believed so strongly the ideas taught in the Dutch Reformed church at which he played the organ each Sabbath—God's sovereignty, the Bible above all—that he was willing to take on William Cosby, the royal governor. Cosby clearly thought that he was above the law. When a farmer's cart slowed down Cosby's coach, the governor had his coachman beat the farmer with a horsewhip until he nearly killed him. When Cosby desired some land owned by Indians, he stole their deed and burned it; when he granted new lands to those who applied legally, he demanded and received bribes often amounting to one-third of the estates.

Cosby made enemies who were willing to fund Zenger's newspaper and provide anonymous articles for it, but it was Zenger whose name was on the newspaper, and it was Zenger who would go to jail. He first sent a message in the *Journal's* second issue by publishing a piece that differentiated an absolute monarchy from one based on biblical principles of fixed law and limitations on power. In an absolute monarchy, the article argued, the "Will of the Prince" was over all, and "a Liberty of the Press to complain of Grievances" was impossible. In a limited monarchy, however,

> laws are known, fixed, and established. They are the streight Rule and sure Guide to direct the King, the Ministers, and other his Subjects: And therefore an Offense against the Laws is such an Offense against the Constitution as ought to receive a proper adequate Punishment.

Law (applying biblical principles) was above the king, not under him, just as the Bible itself was over all human royalty. An essay in the *Journal* pointedly asked, "If we reverence men for their power alone, why do we not reverence the Devil, who has so much more power than men?" The article concluded that respect was due "only to virtuous qualities and useful actions," and that it was therefore "as ridiculous and superstitious to adore great mischievous men as it is to worship a false god or Satan in the stead of God." Subjects had the right to evaluate their king; obedience was not guaranteed.

The *Journal* prominently featured "Cato's Letters," written in England by John Trenchard and Thomas Gordon. They argued that governmental authority must be limited, and that such limitation was possible only if individuals were free to speak the truth to those in power. Everyone was to be restrained by biblical principles of conduct: "Power without control appertains to God alone, and no man ought to be trusted with what no man is equal to."

By publishing such material, Zenger was spreading ideas long current in New England; as minister Ebenezer Pemberton had argued in 1710,

> kings and royal governors must govern themselves by unalterable Principles and fixed Rules, and not by unaccountable humours, or arbitrary will. They take care that Righteous Laws be Enacted, none but such, and all such, as are necessary for the Safety of the Religion

& Liberties of a People . . . [Rulers] that are not skilful, thoughtful, vigilant and active to promote the Publick Safety and Happiness are not Gods but dead Idols.

New York's royal governor, not wanting to admit that the state's domain was limited, brought a charge of "seditious libel" against Zenger and threw him into jail. Journalists at that time had little defense against such accusations; if they proved that their statements were true they might be even worse off. (Under English law truth made the libel worse by making it more likely that the statements would decrease public support for the king and his officials; a common legal expression was "the greater the truth, the greater the libel.") Jurors were only to determine whether the accused actually had printed the objectionable publication; if they agreed that he had, judges decided whether the statements in question were critical and deserved punishment.

At Zenger's trial in 1735, however, defense attorney Andrew Hamilton placed Zenger in the line of Martin Luther, John Foxe, John Stubbes, Marchamont Nedham, Increase Mather, and others. Zenger was one more victim of what Hamilton called "the Flame of Prosecutions upon Informations, set on Foot by the Government, to deprive a People of the Right of Remonstrating (and complaining too), of the arbitrary Attempts of Men in Power." Hamilton's biblical references were frequent. He argued:

> If a libel is understood in the large and unlimited sense urged by Mr. Attorney, there is scarce a writing I know that may not be called a libel, or scarce any person safe from being called to account as a libeller: for Moses, meek as he was, libelled Cain; and who is it that has not libelled the devil?

The spread of Reformation principles concerning literacy, independent journalism, and the rights of citizens to read for themselves, allowed Hamilton to turn to the jurors and ask them to support the truth teller, regardless of what royal officials desired. Zenger, Hamilton said, was merely following the lead of the Bible, which attacked corrupt leaders as "blind watchmen" and "greedy dogs that can never have enough"(Isa. 56:10–11). Zenger's defense, essentially, was that if God's authors produced such a critique, so could he.

Judges in red robes and white wigs were ready to convict Zenger for his criticism of the royal governor, but the jury included "common People" among whom Zenger's newspaper had "gain'd some credit." A packed courtroom sympathetic to Zenger kept the judges from silencing Hamilton when he turned directly to the jurors and suggested that they declare Zenger innocent even though he admitted to printing the material in question and was thus under the power of the judges. Hamilton argued that Zenger deserved such support because he had been "exposing and opposing arbitrary power by speaking and writing Truth," and the jurors agreed. They delivered a verdict of "not guilty"; royal officials decided not to provoke a riot; Zenger went free.

The verdict meant little legally: A runaway jury had disobeyed English law and had gotten away with it. But the verdict reverberated through the colonies and through England itself, encouraging Christian editors and discouraging officials from trying printers for seditious libel; no case of that sort was brought anywhere in America after 1735. The year after the Zenger case, *Virginia Gazette* editor William Parks exposed corruption, including the stealing of sheep by a member of Virginia's House of Burgesses. Threatened with prosecution, Parks used the Zenger defense of truth-telling: When he produced court records showing that the accusation was accurate, the case against him was dropped.

By midcentury most newspapers were independent of governmental control and free to provide, as *Maryland Gazette* editor Jonas Green promised his readers, not just "a Weekly Account of the most remarkable Occurrences, foreign and domestic," but also an examination of "whatever may conduce to the Promotion of Virtue and Learning, the Suppression of Vice and Immorality, and the Instruction as well as Entertainment of our Readers." Newspapers ran lively debates on many subjects, including politics.

The idea that fundamental law came from God, not from the state or from any persons, opened the door to the questioning of many political traditions, including even monarchical control. Journalist Elisha Williams argued in 1744 that:

the Powers that be in Great Britain are the Government therein according to its own Constitution: If then the higher Powers for the Administration rule not according to that Constitution, or if any King thereof shall rule so, as to change the Government from legal to arbitrary . . . no Subjection [is] due to it.

Articles repeatedly pointed out that liberty without virtue could not last. Young Samuel Adams wrote in 1748, "Neither the wisest constitution nor the wisest laws will secure the liberty and happiness of a people whose manners are universally corrupt. He therefore is the truest friend to the liberty of his country who tries most to promote its virtue." Adams concluded that:

> if we would most truly enjoy this gift of Heaven, let us become a virtuous people: then shall we both deserve and enjoy it. While, on the other hand, if we are universally vicious and debauched in our manners, though the form of our Constitution carries the face of the most exalted freedom, we shall in reality be the most abject slaves.

By the 1750s, colonial newspapers were free to bring charges of graft against those supplying American troops during the French and Indian War; for example, the *New York Gazette* and *Weekly Post-Boy* reported that many of the guns purchased were out-of-date and practically useless, and that the soldiers' beef was more effective than powder because its odor would drive away the enemy. That such charges, when accurate, could be made without legal repercussion, showed how firmly independent journalism had established itself in America. The colonists thus found themselves surprised when, after the war, England began to crack down.

Samuel Adams led the protests in Massachusetts. If transported to our present age of television journalism, Adams would be a washout: He had a sunken chest, a sallow complexion, and "wishy-washy gray eyes." Adams's lips twitched and trembled, for he suffered from palsy. His clothes were drab and sometimes sloppy. In addition, Adams was a financial misfit who lived in an old, shabby house, writing much but earning little. John Adams put the best complexion on the surface prospects of his cousin when he wrote that "in common appearance he was a plain, simple, decent citizen, of middling stature, dress, and manners."

Looking beyond appearances, however, Samuel Adams possessed advantages. His strong Christian and classical education made ancient times as real to him as his own; references to the political ups and downs of ancient Israel, Greece, and Rome came easily to his pen. He had the ability to write under almost any conditions. Adams typically composed his columns after evening prayers; his wife Elizabeth would go to bed but would sometimes wake in the middle of the night and hear only the sound of her husband's quill pen scratching on and on. But when Adams had to, he could write forceful prose amidst a town meeting.

Adams was also in the right place, at what in God's providence became the right time. He lived in America's largest port city, and the second largest city in all of the colonies, after Philadelphia. The twenty thousand residents of Boston in 1770 may not seem like many now, but at that time they were enough to support a half-dozen weekly newspapers, including, during the decade before revolutionary warfare broke out, the *Boston Gazette*. The *Gazette* was published every Monday afternoon, and a crowd often awaited its issues hot off the press. Adams had a regular column but never signed his own name to it. Instead, he used a pen name—such as "A Puritan"—that connected him with biblical journalism's honorable lineage.

Furthermore, Adams was modest. He had no problem with being in the background; he argued that "political literature [was] to be as selfless as politics itself, designed to promote its cause, not its author." Adams's self-effacement has made life harder for some historians: John Adams wrote that his cousin's personality would "never be accurately known to posterity, as it was never sufficiently known to its own age." (A minister wrote on October 3, 1803, the day after Adams's death, that there had been "an impenetrable secrecy" about him.) But Adams's willingness to have others take the credit worked wonders during his time. He chaired town meetings and led the applause for those who needed bucking up; for example, he pulled John Hancock onto the patriot side and promoted Hancock's career.

Most important was Adams's strong belief in the God of the Bible. The Great Awakening had made a permanent theological impression on him. That impression is evident in Adams' writings and actions, in his prayers each morning, and in his family Bible-reading each evening. He frequently emphasized the importance of "Endeavors to promote the spiritual kingdom of Jesus Christ"; in good or bad times he wrote of the need "to submit to the Dispensations of Heaven, 'Whose Ways are ever gracious, ever just.'" During the struggle of the 1760s and 1770s Adams regularly set aside days of fasting and prayer to "seek the Lord." When Adams in 1777 wrote to a friend about the high points of one celebration, he stressed the sermon delivered that day; the friend wrote back, "An epicure would have said something about the clams, but you turn me to the prophet Isaiah."

Adams, in short, worked within the tradition of Foxe and Mather; John Adams called him the Calvin of his day, and "a Calvinist" to the core. William Tudor in 1823 called Adams "a strict Calvinist . . . no individual of his day had so much the feelings of the ancient puritans." For Tudor, that meant Adams had "too much sternness and pious bigotry." Yet, Adams did not merely rely on established procedures; he is a model for today's directed reporters in four ways.

First, observing that "mankind are governed more by their feelings than by reason," Adams emphasized appeals to the whole person, not just to a disembodied intellect. Emotions were to be taken seriously, for the "fears and jealousies of the people are not always groundless: And when they become general, it is not to be presum'd that they are; for the people in general seldom complain, without some good reason." Adams argued that ordinary citizens could "distinguish between *realities* and *sounds*; and by a proper use of that reason which Heaven has given them, they can judge, as well as their betters, when there is danger of *slavery*."

Second, Adams emphasized investigative reporting more vigorously than any American journalist before him had: He did so because "Publick Liberty will not long survive the Loss of publick Virtue." Adams argued that it was vital to track activities of those who are:

> watching every Opportunity to turn the good or ill Fortune of their Country, and they care not which to their own private Advantage. Such Men there always have been & always will be, till human Nature itself shall be substantially meliorated.

He went on to praise exposure of leaders who "having gained the Confidence of their Country, are sacrilegiously employing their Talents to the Ruin of its Affairs, for their own private Emolument." At the same time, however, Adams emphasized restraint in such exposure: Only those "capable of doing great Mischief" should be held up "to the publick Eye." Adams realized extremely well the dangers of investigative journalism to the journalist; he noted that the writer who exposes does so "at the Risque of his own Reputation; for it is a thousand to one but those whose Craft he puts at Hazard, will give him the odious Epithets of suspicious dissatisfiable peevish quarrelsome & c."

Third, Adams defined more thoroughly than his predecessors the limits of protest. His strong sense of lawfulness is indicated by his reactions to two incidents: the Stamp Act demonstrations of August 1765 and the related attacks on private homes such as that of Thomas Hutchinson, the royal governor. Adams favored the former action because legislative methods and petitions already had failed; the House of Commons would not listen, so the demonstration "was the only Method whereby they could make known their Objections to Measures." He opposed the assault on the Hutchinson home, calling it an action of "a truly *mobbish* Nature." When Adams and his colleagues planned the Boston Tea Party, they made it clear that nothing except tea was to be destroyed; when the patriots dressed as "Indians" accidentally broke a padlock, they later replaced it.

So far was Adams from revolution in the way the term is currently understood that he wrote, in the *Boston Gazette* in 1768, that "the security of right and property, is the great end of government. Surely, then, such measures as tend to render right and property precarious, tend to destroy both property and government; for these must stand and fall together." Adams opposed dictatorship, whether popular or monarchical.

> The Utopian schemes of levelling, and a community of goods, are as visionary and impracticable, as those which vest all property in the Crown, are arbitrary, despotic, and in our government unconstitutional. Now what property can the colonists be conceived to have, if their money may be granted away by others, without their consent?

Fourth, Adams argued that writers should pay careful attention to the connection between attacks on political rights and attempts to restrict religious rights. In a *Boston Gazette* column that he signed, "A Puritan," Adams described how he was pleased with attention paid to politics but:

surpriz'd to find, that so little attention is given to the danger we are in, of the utter loss of those *religious Rights*, the enjoyment of which our good forefathers had more especially in their intention, when they explored and settled this new world.

He saw acquiescence in political slavery as preparation for submission to religious slavery.

I could not help fancying that the Stamp-Act itself was contrived with a design only to inure the people to the habit of contemplating themselves as the slaves of men; and the transition from thence to a subjection to Satan, is mighty easy.

Other writers came to similar conclusions. A columnist in the *Pennsylvania Evening Post* declared that "resisting the *just* and *lawful* power of government" was rebellion but resisting "*unjust* and *usurped* power" was not. The *Virginia Gazette* saw British authorities moving to apply "the Rod of Despotism" to "every Colony that moves in Defense of Liberty." In Connecticut, the *Norwich Packet* argued that liberty was like an inheritance, "a sacred deposit which it would be treason against Heaven to betray."

The patriotic journalists sometimes used nonpolitical stories to make their points. The *Boston Evening Post* reported a hanging: "Saturday last was executed Harry Halbert, pursuant to his sentence, for the murder of the son of Jacob Wollman. He will never pay any of the taxes unjustly laid on these once happy lands." Rather than raging against the British system generally, they pointed to specific violations by the "salary-men" who were "hourly multiplying on us." In New Hampshire, the Executive Council was supposed to provide the governor with a broad array of colonists' views; the colony's correspondent complained in the *Boston Evening Post* that relatives of Governor John Wentworth filled all but one Council seat.

Journalists saw such exposure of corruption as part of their calling. Adams wrote in the *Boston Gazette*, "There is nothing so *fretting* and *vexatious*, nothing so justly TERRIBLE to tyrants, and their tools and abettors, as a FREE PRESS." Isaiah Thomas, editor of the *Massachusetts Spy*, wrote that, without a free press, there would be "padlocks on our lips, fetters on our legs, and only our hands left at liberty to slave for our worse than Egyptian task masters."

Adams was at his best when he took Bible-based theories and heightened them journalistically. In his printed response to the adoption of the Declaration of Independence, he wrote that "the hand of Heaven appears to have led us on to be, perhaps, humble instruments and means in the great providential dispensation which is completing." He stated plainly his sense of the Declaration of Independence.

> We have explored the temple of royalty, and found that the idol we have bowed down to has eyes which see not, ears that hear not our prayers, and a heart like the nether millstone. We have this day restored the Sovereign to whom alone men ought to be obedient.

Adams followed those statements with his key rhetorical question: "Were the talents and virtues which Heaven has bestowed on men given merely to make them more obedient drudges, to be sacrificed to the follies and ambition of a few . . . ?" He responded, "What an affront to the King of the universe to maintain that the happiness of a monster sunk in debauchery . . . is more precious in his sight than that of millions of his suppliant creatures who do justice, love mercy, and walk humbly with their God!"

Adams crescendoed with the editorial fervency that moved a generation.

> The hand of Heaven appears to have led us on to be, perhaps, humble instruments and means in the great providential dispensation which is completing. We have fled from the political Sodom; let us not look back, lest we perish and become a monument of infamy and derision to the world!

Adams, "the last Puritan," was able to lead a revolution because the Reformed emphasis allowed him to pay attention to the streets that declared man's sinfulness without losing sight of the heavens that showed God's glory. As you report and edit, under circumstances much more favorable than those that Zenger and Adams initially faced, remember Adams's understanding that we are "humble instruments." And ask: Have Christians in journalism become a monument of derision? If so, are we looking back toward Sodom, or are we looking to God?

CHAPTER SEVEN

Investigating and Profiling

C hristian exposers of corruption like Marchamont Nedham and Samuel Adams began their work with reflection on the biblical truth that all have sinned and fallen short of the glory of God. Wherever there is extensive power and influence, corruption is likely to follow unless leaders of organizations fear God. Even when the leaders do fear God, a fall may follow, but the likelihood is less.

INVESTIGATION

Bible-based investigative reporting dates back to Luke, and more recently (four centuries ago) to John Foxe. But when investigation results in the exposure of corrupt individuals, a question is often raised about the relationship between reporting scandal and a famous passage in Matthew 18:

> If your brother sins against you, go and show him his fault, just between the two of you. If he listens to you, you will have won your brother over. But if he will not listen, take one or two others along, so that every matter may be established by the testimony of two or three witnesses. If he refuses to listen to them, tell it to the church; and if he refuses to listen even to the church, treat him as you would a pagan or a tax collector. (vv. 15–17 NIV)

Christian journalists should keep three aspects of that passage in mind. First, the injunction refers to "your brother"; non-Christians should also be confronted with the facts against them and given an opportunity to comment, but this particular procedure is for use among Christians. Second, the passage refers to private offenses ("sins against you") rather than instances of community-affecting corruption such as stealing from the temple treasury. Third, the passage deals with the initial way in which a person is helped to confront sin; normally, by the time a reporter learns of a public-affecting, sinful activity deserving of exposure, the steps listed in Matthew 18 already will have occurred—at least in part.*

The overwhelming majority of exposure situations that reporters face do not involve Christian brothers in private situations concerning issues with which they have never before been confronted. Typically, the offender already will have been challenged by an associate or associates, and will have decided to continue on his downward path. The reporter should attempt to find out if that initial confrontation has occurred, and if not, why not. The logic of Matthew 18 suggests that great care must be taken in reporting public as well as private offenses, but it does not argue for nondisclosure.

But what about those situations in which a Christian brother engaged in personal rather than public offenses has acknowledged his sin following confrontation and shows signs of repentance and reconciliation? Here is where it is helpful to remember the title of the first American newspaper, *Publick Occurrences Both Foreign and Domestick*. A news publication should emphasize public occurrences, not private affairs, unless those affairs have public ramifications. A minister's adultery, for example, can have an effect on a congregation different than that produced by the waywardness of a regular congregant member. For people in public positions who are supposed to model virtue and elicit trust, every offense has public ramifications.

When dealing with specific cases, particular nuances need to be

---

*The breakdown of biblical patterns of discipline within many churches during the past several decades means that the confrontation by two or three often is not followed by taking the offense before the church, and that is all the more reason for a Christian publication to become involved.

taken into account, but the ethic of reporting need never be situational, for the principle that Christian journalists should expose wrongdoing is clear. A crusading minister-journalist of the 1830s, John McDowall, laid out the biblical rationale in his time; Appendix B contains excerpts from his analysis.

Investigation often is difficult because many people in sensitive situations and aware of potential repercussions do not want to talk on the record. Your task in a stressful situation is not to sweet-talk the source but to be forcefully honest with him about hardships as well as the benefits to be gained by truth-telling.

The good news about investigation is that often, sooner or later, someone who has been part of a cover-up decides to talk. Sometimes God has been at work on the person; sometimes he simply sickens of the deception. When a source during an investigation does talk, verification is vital. Those with strange tales should be asked to repeat them several times, to different people as you listen and see if the details change. Documentation is important: Ask sources to get verification of their stories on paper from files to which they have access.

Always ask for specific detail. Half a century ago, when Whittaker Chambers was trying to show that he had been the courier for Alger Hiss's disclosure of diplomatic secrets to the Soviet Union, he mentioned that Hiss had been excited about seeing a prothonotary warbler during a bird-watching expedition. Hiss had denied knowing Chambers, but his deception began to unravel when he was questioned about his hobbies and mentioned how he had been entranced by the sight of a prothonotary warbler.

Ask sources to describe a specific place at which an incident occurred, and the weather at a specific time. When you verify detail by detail, sometimes the whole is as great as the sum of the parts. Here, for example, is part of a story based on the testimony of thirteen witnesses who offered solid specific detail:

> Although Larson urges the hurting to call his radio program for comfort, screeners are instructed to make sure the callers want to talk about the day's subject. Former employee Tammy Brown, who answered the ministry's crisis-referral line and screened calls for "Talk-Back," said she has hung up on weeping callers whose problem wasn't on the day's agenda.

"A desperate listener can find hope and help by dialing 1-800-821-TALK," Larson wrote in *Satanism: The Seduction of America's Youth*. But this toll-free number is answered only two hours each day during "Talk-Back", and even then a desperate caller must get past screeners.

The ministry offers two other lines. The Communicator Club line, a toll-free line reserved for donors, is open ten hours per day, five days a week. The Compassion Connection's Hope Line, the line for helping the hurting, is open only four hours per day, five days a week, and it is a toll call.

Compassion Connection only refers callers to other agencies, although many former employees say Larson listeners believe it offers counseling and crisis intervention. Some listeners who can't afford the long-distance cost call the toll-free donor line.

"We weren't allowed to talk to them, because it was an 800 line. We would be reprimanded if we were caught counseling. It cost the ministry money," says Charlene Erickson, who worked in BLM's donor services until last August, when she says she resigned.

"We had to give them the toll number to Compassion Connection. They weren't allowed to call that collect, either. They weren't allowed to get any free help from the ministry. They always had to pay for the phone call."

On more than one occasion, supervisors who thought an operator was spending too much time on the phone instructed the operator to hang up even on distraught callers, say Ms. Erickson and other former operators.

"I hated that part of the job, hanging up on someone who was suicidal," Ms. Erickson said.

Unnamed sources can best be used when they are supporting information given by named sources, and when readers are given an explanation as to why the name of the source should not be revealed.

At least once, an operator transferred the call to the referral line without getting caught. "I went over the boundaries and gave it to a person in the Compassion Connection," said the woman, who wishes to remain anonymous for fear of retribution.

She once refused a direct order to hang up on a caller, which she believes contributed to her dismissal a few weeks later.

Reporters are sometimes reluctant to investigate organizations that claim to be charitable, but you need to remember the biblical lament,

"They rob widows." Given man's sinfulness, it is not surprising to find financial corruption occurring all over—in big governmental or business structures—and within charities as well.

Charitable and religious organizations actually may be the easiest to steal from, since the assumption that no one would take candy from a sick baby sometimes leaves resources inadequately fenced; the New Era scandal of 1995 provided one more cautionary tale. And yet, since the financial records from these organizations are often public information, the results of covetousness can become visible.

> On "Talk-Back," Larson frequently bemoans the ministry's financial condition. But in the years 1989–91, the ministry paid Larson salaries totaling $607,806, according to Internal Revenue Service records. In 1991, the ministry provided an expense account of $76,300, which is more than Billy Graham's salary. Larson's expense account was $35,750 in 1990, according to the records, which by law are open to public inspection.
>
> Other records show that those totals do not include royalties from his 21 books and consulting fees paid to Larson by the Canadian arm of Bob Larson Ministries.

Divorce records show family tragedy but provide insight.

> Bob and Kathryn J. Larson exchanged marriage vows in Hamilton, Ontario, on Jan. 24, 1968. Eighteen years later, in the same year Larson condemned divorce in his *Book of Family Issues*, the Larsons began receiving counseling for their troubled marriage. Four years later, Larson asked his wife of 22 years to move out of their home and initiated their divorce.
>
> The 1990 tax records show the ministry paid Larson $178,167 and allowed him an expense account of $76,300. Larson certified to the court under oath that his income in 1990 was $403,310.
>
> When they divorced, the Larsons owned five pieces of real estate, including two in the Rocky Mountains, worth $539,200.
>
> Between them, the Larsons owned more than $4,000 worth of porcelain, $13,000 worth of ivory, $8,000 in crystal and china, nearly $8,000 worth of carvings, $6,575 in jewelry, $3,000 in paintings, more than $4,000 in rugs and $8,000 worth of taxidermy.
>
> The value of their marital assets at the time of the divorce was $1.4 million.

Public records—you may obtain previously closed ones through federal and state freedom-of-information statutes—often can show the amount of the take. Then, it is useful to detail how such wealth was won.

> Larson expects screeners to prime callers for a dramatic encounter. "Bob would put them on hold and we would have to manipulate them, push them over the edge, so they could go back on the air with "Talk-Back" and be saved by Bob Larson," Mrs. Brown says. "We had to push until they said, 'OK, I need God.' We're not to do that, the Holy Spirit is. I felt like I was being used to make Bob more money."

"They rob widows," the Bible laments, and organizations in recent times have done the same; others have misused funds designed for orphans. *World* reported charges by:

> Thomas Naylor, an economics professor at Middlebury College, [who] blew the whistle on the Christian Children's Fund and was then ousted from the Richmond-based CCF's board of directors . . . he asked, "Is it humanly possible to stuff $112 million in five layers of management aimed at 400,000 kids in 40 countries, and have a clue as to whether it's working or even what's happening to the money?"

Naylor went on to point to specific incidents of mismanaged and misappropriated funds.

> In Brazil, a project director gave his fiancee $31,000 in bonuses; in Oklahoma, funds meant for Cherokee Indian children were used to run a video rental business.

The article did not stop there, but moved on to the deeper question of whether the Christian Children's Fund, even if the money was going to hungry children, is Christian at all.

> CCF spokesperson Cheri Dahl explained that "there are no stipulated spiritual activities required for participation in our programs . . . the Christian in our name simply refers to the Christian philosophy of helping thy neighbor."
> That's not enough, says Ronald Nash, professor of philosophy and theology at Reformed Theological Seminary in Orlando. There has

to be an emphasis on the gospel as well as on giving . . ."those children should keep receiving the aid even if they reject the gospel—but you don't stop offering the gospel."

Sometimes investigations do not require undercover searches, deep-throat interviews, or any other behind-the-scenes work; sometimes the information is out in the open but requires someone to conscientiously scoop out bits of data and analyze their significance.

For example, one *World* story took a complaint frequently heard at pro-life meetings—that many ministers shied away from taking a stand on abortion—and concluded, in a cover story headlined "Silence of the Shepherds," that large numbers of evangelical pastors have "offered their flocks little or no leadership as abortion practices have grown more lenient and the death toll has risen." Investigative work needs to be thorough to warrant a broad charge of that sort, and reporters need to spell out, with even pedantic detail, the way in which they gathered evidence.

Three sets of evidence bear this out.

In a study by *World* of the preaching of 20 noted Christian leaders, only six men provided a full sermon preached on abortion, and only three more could provide even an excerpt.

World phoned each pastor's assistant to notify them of an incoming fax requesting a sermon—printed or on tape—addressing abortion; or, as a second option, an excerpt on abortion from a sermon. An electronic confirmation verified that each fax was successfully transmitted. *World* followed up with phone calls to each pastor or his assistant, continuing to seek a response.

The second set of evidence concerning silence in the pulpit is a new study by Molly Stone of Last Days Ministries in Tyler, Texas. For her master's thesis at Regent University, Ms. Stone polled 104 pastors from evangelical, charismatic, mainline, and fundamentalist churches in the South Hampton Roads area of Virginia. She found that while 76 percent agreed that life begins at conception, and 69 percent believed the church should take a clear stand on the issue, only 39 percent ever devoted an entire sermon to abortion.

The percentage who preached a sermon on abortion was higher among those classified as evangelical in the study pool—58 percent—but Ms. Stone's basic conclusion remains the same: "The average clergyman does not actively encourage his church to be involved in pro-life activity," she wrote. Ninety percent of the clergy had at least mentioned abortion some time in a sermon, but less than half ever announced a pro-life event from the pulpit or church bulletin.

"Even actions that clergy say are highly acceptable are typically not performed," notes Ms. Stone. For instance, 70 percent of the pastors said crisis-pregnancy centers were their pro-life activity of choice, yet the exact same number said they did not actually support a crisis-pregnancy center.

Only a third ever encouraged walking in a march for life or ever showed a pro-life film. Only one-sixth had endorsed pickets or prayer at abortion clinics. Rescues had been encouraged by 7 percent.

The third body of evidence *World* drew from in identifying a silence·in America's pulpits was the unanimous opinion of ten pro-life leaders interviewed for this article.

The response of Life Issues Institute Director John Willke, medical doctor and former president of the National Right to Life Committee, is typical. The silence of pastors is documentable and "deadly," says Dr. Willke. "You see it in every denomination."

It is the silence of the shepherds.

In such a broad investigative story, opinions of informed sources are not a substitute for documentary evidence, but they can be excellent supporting material. Writer Joe Maxwell bulwarked the claim of "a gaping hole of silence from the Protestant pulpit" on abortion by quoting experts.

"One of the greatest travesties of the church is its silence on abortion," theologian R.C. Sproul of Ligonier Ministries told *World*, "particularly the evangelical church."

Said O.S. Hawkins, pastor of First Baptist Church (Dallas, Texas), in a recent sermon: "The main reason convenience abortions on demand are the law of the land is not because of the militant minority of the women liberationists and liberal politicians. . . . Perhaps the thing that is most amazing is the silence of the grand old flagship churches in the hearts of cities across America. Where are all the voices from all the First Baptist Churches of our land? Where are the voices from the First Presbyterian Churches and the First Methodist Churches?"

It is important to show, when some people defend themselves by saying that a particular failure or omission was inevitable, that others similarly situated acted wisely. For example, when over one hundred

Christian organizations lost millions of dollars to the Foundation for New Era Philanthropy, which was engaged in a pyramid scheme, *World* reported that Westminster Theological Seminary (Pennsylvania) fell for the scam but "Westminster's sister campus in California 'was wary' of the proposal and declined an invitation to give money."

Similarly, the "Silence of the Shepherds" story included specific detail about a Christian leader who had realized that silence is wrong.

> Preaching outright on abortion wasn't an easy decision for Charles Swindoll, recalls his friend James Dobson in a foreword to Mr. Swindoll's book, *Sanctity of Life*. "I was sitting in my office at Focus on the Family . . . when the telephone rang," recounts Dr. Dobson. "A minute or two later, my secretary came in to inform me that Dr. Chuck Swindoll was on the line." He was calling to say he had decided to speak out "with intensity" against abortion, a decision that had Dr. Dobson "fighting back the tears."
>
> "Making a strong public statement against abortion was an evolving decision in Chuck's mind," he continues. "It is not a position at which [Swindoll] arrived with ease." Mr. Swindoll worried about dragging his church into politics. "But on this issue of abortion," Dr. Dobson notes, "we are confronted with one of the most terrible evils of all times. . . . How can we as Christians continue to sit in our services and ignore this unprecedented crime against humanity?"
>
> Finally, Mr. Swindoll told himself, "Remaining silent . . . is no longer an option."
>
> So in January 1990, around the time of the 17th anniversary of *Roe v. Wade*, a convinced Charles Swindoll stepped into his pulpit at First Evangelical Free Church in Fullerton, Calif., and did something he had never done before: He preached to his congregation against abortion.

Whether an investigation requires undercover work or reading not only the covers but the insides of many reports, the hard-and-fast rule is: Be very careful, and verify everything numerous times. Inflammatory words should be avoided; when writing up the results of an investigation, remember the motto, Sensational Fact, Understated Prose.

PROFILES

Profiles are in one respect at the opposite end of investigative stories—profiles tend to be friendly, investigations adversarial—but they require considerable digging as well.

The first step in writing a profile is to do background research. You should run down newspaper and magazine stories about the subject; the computerized service Lexis/Nexis, or resources available over the Internet, are helpful. You may also ask the interviewee to send biographical data. It is convenient and respectful to have basic information before the interview: this includes the spelling of the subject's name (be careful), his place of residence, age, and marital status; the number and ages of his children; his educational and work background.

You will also want to talk with your subject's friends and enemies, often including colleagues, competitors, neighbors, and relatives. If you can find some generally obscure piece of information with which to confront the subject, you will be able to show him that you mean business.

As far as the interviewing process itself, you should use information in the chapter on reporting and interviewing, but keep in mind that the subject of a general interview is not the interviewee; in profiles, the subject of the interview is the interviewee, and he or she is more than words.

Since profiles are great ways to express ideas and make points, some committed reporters have the tendency to make them a set of sound bites. That is a mistake: The goal of a profile is to bring a person to life through descriptive detail and narrative, along with contextualized use of quotation.

You will need to spend time in person with the subject of your profile: Remote-control profiles based on news clips or telephone interviews are almost always inferior to those that give a sense of the whole person. Profiling with discernment requires not only perceptiveness but the kind of close, in-person observation that leads to three-dimensional portraits, with the subjects almost seeming to walk off the page.

Good profiles require investment not only of interview time but also of time searching for anecdotes and impressions from all who know the subject. As discussed in the chapter on interviewing, you always need to press for revealing stories. That is particularly true for biblically directed profiles, for they should get into the deeper questions. Ask about beliefs; give your subjects opportunities to declare their faith in Christ, if they have it.

Along those lines, keep in mind the acronym PROOF: Purpose, Road, Obstacles, Overcoming, Future. That means: Ask a subject about his *purpose* in life; ask how he started down the *road* to fulfilling that purpose; ask about the *obstacles* he encountered, his ways of *overcoming* those obstacles, and his expectations of *future* obstacles.

Ask questions in a down-to-earth style: What do you really hope to do? What do you have to do to fulfill that hope? What problems have you faced, how did you handle them? What is your next step? In general, start with specific questions: not, Do you enjoy being in the major leagues? but, Why did you suspect that the pitcher would throw you a fast ball in that situation? And ask short questions: Get the subject's voice on tape, not yours.

Remember that you want to see as well as hear. You will certainly want to describe physically the subject of your profile. Since at least one photo generally accompanies a profile, facial features are the least important aspect for you to describe; more significant is how the person moves or sits (stolidly or shifting). Watch body language and facial expressions when you ask hard questions. (One interviewee who had "grown" from his evangelical background easily danced around abstract theological questions, but poured out buckets of sweat in reaction to the straightforward, "What do you think of Christ?")

To show a person in action, you may want to spend a few hours with him as he goes about his business, but you can also obtain anecdotes from the subject and from others. One way to push subjects to provide anecdotes (and in a way that reveals worldviews) is to use "superlative" questions: What was the happiest day of your life? What is the angriest you have ever been? Which experience was the most exciting? the most dangerous? If a particular approach yields an anecdotal pearl, fish some more: What was the second most exciting experience?

Here is a basic checklist of what you generally should know by the time you complete the interview:

- Physical Characteristics:
    Description of home or workplace, outside and inside.
    Subject's overall appearance, clothing style, hair style.
    Subject's mannerisms.
- Basic Background:
    Birthdate, birthplace
    Schooling
    Military service?

- Religious Experience:

   If a Christian, when he became one, how has he developed since then, how he puts faith into practice; denominational and church affiliation.

   If not a Christian, what he believes, why he believe it, does he think that what he believes is objectively real or is it something that makes him feel good.

- Family:

   Spouse—when married, spouse's activities.

   Children—ages, names, activities.

   Parents—what he learned from them, what he did not.

- Personal:

   Hobbies, recreations, pets.

   Favorite books, movies, presidents, hymns.

   Volunteer work, other community service.

   Memberships in organizations.

As the start of the checklist indicates, it is vital to see the subject in his surroundings—generally, his place of work or home. You will want to convey a sense of the person by relating your perceptions of him to your description of the environment.

Ron Lewis' church is not easy to find—unless you know your way around Hardin County, Kentucky, like he does. More people are finding out about Lewis, and the kind of people he represents, since a May special election put him in Congress. The 47-year-old Lewis, a conservative Republican Christian, is the kind of person that Democratic Party leaders say Americans should fear. People in Kentucky's 2nd Congressional District see it differently. And they've seen Lewis up close.

White Mills Baptist Church sits on a hill away from Highway 84, tucked between the White Mills Christian Church and a campground. You know you've gone too far when you take a sudden turn and you're on a one-lane iron bridge across a river. Though the church's exterior looks like it might have appeared a century earlier, the steps are covered with new indoor-outdoor carpet. Central air conditioning is evident inside the glassed foyer. Like Lewis, there's subtle sophistication here—a savvy about technology that works. An advanced electronic soundboard blinks just inside the rear doors.

Observe, observe—see what the subject likes in clothes, home furnishings, office momentos. Often you will not be able to get into an office beforehand, so rejoice if your subject is interrupted for a minute or two: This is an opportunity for you. A person's office shows important things about him or the way he wants to present himself to the world.

> A look at Henry Hyde's inner office suggests more ambivalence than first meets the eye. His two Illinois-obligatory busts of Abraham Lincoln are outnumbered by three statuettes of Don Quixote, whose impossible dreams were not of, by, and for the people. Standard photos of Hyde handshakes with smiling Presidents are overshadowed by a large portrait of a weary George Washington at Valley Forge: "His force of character kept 11,000 men together during a terrible winter," Hyde says.

What is not in an office can be as important as what is.

> Don Wildmon does not have embroidered Bible verses hanging around his office. In fact, his small office, which has the faint aroma of cigar smoke, has absolutely nothing hanging on the walls. His desk serves as a cluttered file cabinet, yet he knows where everything is.

After tying together setting and person, the next step in profiling is to look closely at the person. Do not be shy about making obvious physical characterizations: big or little, beard or clean-shaven, suit or shirtsleeves, wingtips or boots, shoes scuffed or polished, manicured fingernails or nose ring:

> Wildmon is an unlikely national celebrity. He is not a charismatic leader, per se. He does not turn heads when you walk with him into a restaurant. He does not wear Armani suits and his shirts do not have stitched monograms, let alone cuff links. He does not wear Christian lapel pins or try to impress you with his importance. He does not try to turn up the charm when he talks to the press.

Be sure to include gestures and mannerisms: Does he speak quickly or slowly, does he move his hands as he talks, does he pause before answering questions, does he reach for hamhocks with both hands? Record not only what he says but what he eats, what he drinks, whether he smokes, whether he smiles just with his mouth or with his eyes also. How do people respond to him? Watch, smell, take notes.

> On Sunday after church, before he has to hurry back to Washington, Lewis and his wife, Kayi, pull into a small drive-in down the road from the church. Before Lewis can make it across the parking lot a man jumps from a parked car to shake his hand. Wide-eyed, he tells Lewis he has followed the campaign and hopes the congressman can "turn things around." They talk for a moment, and as they part, the man says, "We're with you all the way." Lewis first met his wife across drive-in lanes in Ashland, Ky. Today, she orders the food for them. This drive-in is famous for steakburgers and thick onion rings—topped with local chatter. The lot is full of open car doors and people less intent on eating than on seeing each other.

In questioning the subject, ask about crucible experiences: tragedies, births of children, military experience. Ask about beliefs: about God, about man, about life and death. Then connect the dots. How does a person's worldview affect his actions on the job, as well as his habits: Does he like gangsta rap or Rotisserie baseball? Show what your subject thinks about his work, past and present. Here is an example:

> Jack Kevorkian despises the banal. More than 30 years ago, he found his style cramped in an oil painting night class with little old ladies whose artistic tastes ran from clowns to kittens. Planning to quit the course, he decided to assault sensibilities and exit remembered.
>
> "[I painted] a skull, with the top of the skull leaning back a little, the jaw twisted to one side, like it's kind of laughing out of the side of its face. . . . Then, there were some bones coming underneath, and a broken femur under the thing. . . . Tacked up on the wall behind, where you can barely see it, I have this pasty yellow-green skin, peeled off the head and hanging there. . . . I called it 'Very Still Life.'" They loved it.
>
> Paintings followed: "Fever," "Nausea," and "Coma." But when 64-year-old Jack Kevorkian quits his earthly course, he will not be remembered for his offbeat paintings or his own exit but for assisting others in theirs.

If possible, you should schedule about ninety minutes for an interview, because you have many questions to ask. Some of them will relate specifically to the subject's reason for being newsworthy, but others are more generic: Who or what has had the most impact on your life? What is the most important thing you have learned during the past year? What was your most frustrating experience? What would you change about yourself if you could? What do people say about you behind your back? If you could invite any person or persons for dinner, whom would you invite? What do you like most about your job? What do you dislike the most? What are your best and worst habits?

Do not be afraid to ask bland, prepared questions such as some of those above, or others including: What do you expect to be doing ten years from now? If you could make that decision over again, what would you decide? Was there a turning point in your life? Are you satisfied with your present job or way of life? People who take pride in their craft are generally willing to explain how they accomplish a particularly difficult task. Ask a couple of how-to questions; the answers may be instructive, and they give you a safety net.

Also ask about parents and children: What did your parents teach you? What do you hope to teach your children? You want to provide readers with a sense of the person as a member of a family, not a disembodied voice or a Lone Ranger—unless he is one. And be sure to ask about the person's attitudes toward God; come back to the question several times in different ways if the subject dodges.

As in other directed-reporting assignments, you will have a tentative theme as you go into the story. After you gain chunks of information from your interview, and supplement that material with information gained from others, you need to arrive at a definitive theme: Who is this person you have interviewed, as best you can determine? When you feel that you have a fix on that, go through your notes and see what specific details are salient.

As with other articles, profiles can have a variety of structures. One workable variety proceeds locationally: from outside a person's office or dwelling, to inside, then to the person. Another starts with an anecdotal lead that suggests the essence of the subject, then includes a paragraph presenting the theme and explaining why the profile is significant, and then moves chronologically to summarize the subject's past, present, and future.

A third type of structure begins with a catchy lead but then delib-

erately alternates achievements and warts; such a story often con-
cludes with an anecdote that tries to reconcile the contradictions.
Other profiles may follow the lead with a chronological account of a
person's day; such articles may lack drama but tend to evoke a sense
of realism.

Often, it is useful to see the subject in action, responding to questions from others and working at his craft. This is particularly true
when profiling teachers, coaches, and others whose job it is to interact
with other people.

> Some people can gaze at a spreadsheet and glimpse the problems
> of a corporation; others can look at a magazine article and see how
> it should be restructured; hitting coach Mike Easler, standing at the
> batting cage, can watch a swing and instantly know the correction that
> is needed. "Keep that right shoulder down," he reminded third base-
> man Scott Cooper. "Timothy, you must think right-center," he
> instructed Tim Naehring. "Control with your hands, power will
> come," he told Mo Vaughn.
>
> "I've been in baseball for 25 years and I can see the physical auto-
> matically," Easler, who is also a licensed Baptist minister, noted.
> "What I really work on is reading the personality." Easler said he
> counsels non-Christians and Christians differently: for Christians, he
> shows them Scripture about Providence and God's care, and for non-
> Christians, he brings out material from Proverbs about hard work.

The student's view of impact is relevant:

> This spring Mo Vaughn talked about what Easler's teaching had
> meant to him: "He knows how to prepare you not only about bat-
> ting but about life. . . . I don't go to a church and stuff like that, but
> I know there's Someone you've got to answer to. You've got to look
> truthfully at yourself and not worry about failure, as long as you're
> prepared."
>
> In spring training, Vaughn still had not grasped the truth about
> God's grace: Vaughn said that his belief is, "You have to be good, and
> good things will happen to you." But Easler is at work: "Mo is think-
> ing, but he hasn't accepted Christ as Lord and Savior. I'm not going
> to try to force it on him, but I'm going to let him know, 'That's going
> to be your big battle in life, that's what will make you complete.'
> We're talking, and this year, before spring training is out, I *will* pre-
> sent the gospel to him, point-blank."

Whatever the structure, it is vital to avoid falling into a series of sound bites. The best way to do that is to couch quotations in brief descriptive material.

> Hyde is relaxed as he rocks softly in his office chair, but there is an edge to his voice as he talks about colleagues who roll over under media pressure: "People want to do what's right, but unfortunately they would rather be *perceived* as doing right than as actually doing what's right. I think they are torn, and perception wins out, because the adoration of the secular press is heady."

Physically descriptive material can be related to current concerns.

> Hyde is concerned about future leadership for the pro-life cause. He was once square-jawed and lean, but years on the rubber-chicken and chocolate-mousse circuit have softened the lines. He senses a similar aging taking place in the prolife movement. The future of abortion, he argues, is tied to development of a new generation of prolife leaders.

Biographical detail can be placed in the context of current reputation.

> Now Hyde walks the floor of Congress with burly grace, but almost a half-century ago, during the last half of a 1943 NCAA playoff game, Hyde at 6'3" and 180 pounds ran the floor of a basketball court well enough to hold DePaul great George Mikan to one point. Hyde has similarly outplayed top-rated liberal politicians year after year so that even Cokie Roberts of Left-leaning National Public Radio grudgingly admits, "Hyde is one of the smartest men that ever walked."

When you profile someone who is not a Christian but has broken from liberal secular orthodoxy, your goal is to get at the why.

> Hentoff read widely and was surprised in 1984 to find that every article about an infanticide case much in the news that year, that of Baby Jane Doe, had an Orwellian spin to it. . . .
> . . . When some of his teammates on the Left then asked him why he was making a "big deal" about a "late abortion," Hentoff realized that the slippery slope spoken of by pro-lifers was angled more sharply than he had supposed. When Hentoff began to label killing

of children born or unborn as just that—killing—he again got strong pressure to back off.

Contextualize biographical anecdotes in a discussion of why the subject did not give in to conventional pressure.

Pushing at the headstrong Hentoff has never worked, however. He regularly tells interviewers of the time he was 12 years old and sat on the porch of his parents' house on Yom Kippur, the holiest last day of the Jewish year. On that porch, in full view of the Orthodox Jews walking past the house to the synagogue a block away, he ate a huge salami sandwich very slowly. Many of the passers-by shook their heads in disgust. One shook his fist. Another spat and Hentoff, in his autobiography, *Boston Boy*, recorded the overall experience as "quite enjoyable."

Do not hesitate to push theologically, and then come to an evaluation:

Hentoff has a glib answer when pressed on religion by his theistic prolife allies: "I've always wished I could make the leap of faith and believe, but I can't." And yet, Hentoff does not seem to have any desire to try; despite his voluminous reading, he admits to having never read any evangelical theology. When pressed harder, he simply snaps, "I'm an atheist. I'm really not interested. . . ." Clearly, Hentoff has a sense of right and wrong, and admirable courage in standing by his core values and beliefs: "You shouldn't lie. You shouldn't kill developing human beings." But when asked why others should listen to him, he is unable to ground right and wrong beyond his own rationality: "I have developed for myself a moral sense." And if others have developed other moral senses? "They're wrong," he says with a twinkle. And why? "They are." In the end, this self-described member of "The Proud and Ancient Order of Stiff-necked Jewish Atheists" sees himself as a god unto himself—and the urgent need for God's grace becomes more evident than ever.

A good ending to a profile often places the subject once again in his environment, to suggest either the isolation of the interviewee or the community in which he revels.

Hentoff drinks from a *Village Voice* coffee cup and decorates his office door with a sign that reads, "Card-Carrying Member ACLU."

His windowless office (about 7 by 8 feet) is so crammed with books, folders, and jazz albums that when Hentoff sits in the chair behind his paper-strewn desk he almost seems to be sinking beneath a sandbag barricade. He does not join the young *Village Voice* staffers scurrying to the conference room to preview a new MTV commercial for the newspaper. Nor does he head off to "a 401(k) Pension Plan presentation" for all permanent staff. Soon Hentoff will take the elevator down to the first floor and walk away from the building that is both home and isolation cell. He will walk through a neighborhood that is in many ways a consequence of the ideas he has expressed, past signs advertising "Urban Scarecrows," "Hell in a Handbasket," and "Biohazard: Infection Approaching." But in the meantime, Hentoff sits in his bunkered office, alone.

The profile of Hentoff ended in sadness; the profile of Congressman Lewis ended on an upbeat note.

Lewis' time before had been split between people in the pews and people across the bookstore counter; his time is split differently now, but those same groups are his concern. At a recent congressional meeting a woman approached him and remarked that a few weeks earlier he had been "just like us." The difference, Lewis says, is that now he has taken a step down. Now he is their servant.

Is the Hentoff ending too sour, or the Lewis ending too sweet? It is hard to say from afar; that is why the profilist has such a responsibility to be discerning enough to do justice to his subject. Just as reporters need to avoid thinking the worst of those they are investigating until the proof rolls in, so reporters who cover attractive individuals, need to avoid adoration. We should adore God but suspect man, and that means we should distrust profiles that contain no criticism. Trust, but verify, by asking for opinions about the subject by those who know him: How is he different from his reputation? What are his shortcomings?

When profiling Christians, we need to concentrate not so much on testimony about the time of conversion but on what has happened to the person since: How has the subject walked the talk? All have sinned and fall short of the glory of God, and those who are redeemed remain sinners; the question to ask is whether that sin is decreasing as the years go by and whether the enjoyment of God's grace is increasing.

A profile in *World* of the Cooneys, who as mentioned in chapter two have adopted many children, brought out this aspect well. First came scene-setting.

> Bel Air is a town set just off the interstate that passes from Maryland to Delaware, and it's not too fancy. Along the highway are malls recently erupted from raw earth, and behind these are aging subdivisions. At the foot of a cul-de-sac is a circle of modest ranch-style homes; the one in the middle, the one with the big gray van with pro-life and adoption bumper stickers, looks like it could belong to any suburban family.

Then, the distinctiveness:

> This is not an ordinary family, but a Rainbow Family. Terri and Jim Cooney founded Rainbow Families five years ago, to bring together people who, like them, had adopted kids across racial lines. . . . The Cooneys began their family the usual way 27 years ago with a son, Andrew; he is now a Methodist pastor. When no further pregnancies ensued they adopted a daughter, Christine, who lives near enough to come help her mom with the laundry.
>
> "Then Nathan came to us as a foster child in 1982," Terri says. "He is African-American and Mexican; his dad took flight when he heard Nathan was on the way." Nathan, almost 13, is serious and quiet, but is prevailed upon to show some of his artwork.
>
> Then came Leanna, 9, and Joshua, 7. Joshua, who has been in and out of the room during this conversation, looks heavy-lidded, lethargic, and big. "At his one-year checkup Joshua was very normal, and at his two-year checkup he was very abnormal," Terri says. An initial diagnosis of autism has been amended to "severe manic depression with thought disorder. He became very manic and violent, would hallucinate, would cry for no reason. With medication he's coming around."

Amidst the gravity come touches of humor.

> At this moment Joshua comes up the stairs with his pants around his ankles, and Terri exclaims, "Yay! You left your pants on!" then confides, "Usually he strips." Isaac is laid on the couch while Terri goes to redress the situation.
>
> Terri takes her shoes off as she resumes her narrative. "When Joshua was diagnosed we had already adopted the next one, Sarah, who's now 6. Up to that point we felt that we were not to handle special-needs children, but once we got through the grief with Joshua we

found we could handle this kid and find joy. We knew from that point on that we would request special-needs kids." But it was not a ministry they could undertake alone. "Through prayer we came to understand that God was not sending this child only to us, but to the whole body of Christ."

Joshua comes up the stairs wearing matching purple T-shirt and underpants, but the underpants are on his head. "Well, it was nice of you to match!" Terri says. "Joshua, look at Mommy's face. Go to your room and find some pants."

At this point Jim comes home with the other kids, who have been to an Easter party at the mental health nursery where 4-year-old Janee attends. ("She has bipolar disorder," Terri says. "So does Leanna, but we didn't realize that until after Joshua was diagnosed.") Janee shakes a plastic Easter egg and rattles the pennies inside.

More background about the children constantly pours out, not in textbook manner but in the context of a flowing narrative.

> Terri settles on the floor as a tide of children flows around her. Leanna wants to go to the park alone, but her parents explain that it is too dangerous. She suddenly bursts into sobs, then just as suddenly stops. Two-year-old Stephen comes in wearing yellow star-shaped sunglasses, and Terri exclaims, "Look at you! You are downtown!"
>
> Stephen, she says, was born at 28 weeks and weighed only two pounds; doctors said he would probably never walk. It appears they were right: He runs everywhere, and has broken the blades off two ceiling fans by hanging from them. "He's very, very hyper. We asked God to touch him, and now we wish maybe he'd done a little bit less." As we watch, Stephen steps up on the hinge of the storm door and, reaching up with a book, flips the hook latch open. He is immensely pleased with himself.
>
> Sarah is small enough to look like Janee's twin. The two little girls come in with babydoll strollers that they propose to ride in, though Terri suggests this will not work. Joshua reappears with his shirt on his head and his pants down. "Sweetie, I love you, and it's a good thing," Terri says to him, and to me: "Lithium causes very loose bowels."

We will discuss in a later chapter how authors may involve themselves in stories; here, writer Frederica Mathewes-Green gracefully did it in a way that moves readers to understand even more the immense task that the Cooneys have taken on.

While Terri tends to Joshua, I change baby Isaac's diaper. He wiggles and grins, and the white dot of a cataract shows in each pupil. When Terri returns I am not ready to give up holding him.

Finally, with readers given a vivid sense of the who-what-when-where-how of the Cooney home, discussion of the why comes naturally.

"Our story challenges everybody's reasons for not adopting," Terri says. "Age, income, space . . . we had all of those problems. But if everyone in the body of Christ would adopt just one! There are thousands of kids out there who need homes, but they're older, black, or special-needs. If we could just embrace one we could take care of the kids. Why save them from abortion if you're not going too save them for the kingdom?"

Because you want to have a tidy, quiet, comfortable life. Terri and Jim got a glimpse of that life; their two older kids saved for four years to surprise them with a 25th anniversary party and a week in Hawaii. "We stayed in the best hotels, ate the best food, and listened to retired people talk all about their travels. At the end of that time we realized that we had chosen the better portion. That was when we came home and applied to adopt Stephen."

Leads, Nut Grafs, Bodies, Ends, Headlines

LEADS

Once your journalistic research is done and you have a strong sense of how you want to organize the material, it is time to think of a lead. Sometimes, you will have thought of the lead as you are gathering material, and the organization will flow from it. But remember that in journalism, the perfect is often the enemy of the good: Look for a good beginning, not the perfect lead.

Generally, it is better to rough out the article and then come back to wrestling with the lead. I have provided a chapter on organization before discussing leads because many writers either get hung up at the lead or construct a pretty lead that does not connect well with the bulk of the article. Remember that most leads do not have to be grabbers: They can ease readers into stories.

Feature leads, like other parts of articles, vary in length according to the size of the overall article, but their purpose remains the same: They are to give the reader a sense of what the article is about, establish a mood, and entice the reader to march on. Feature leads are *not* supposed to summarize the news. Feature and standard newspaper leads are opposites: The latter variety is designed to save the reader from reading the entire story, but the former is to push him or her into doing that.

There are many different kinds of leads: I have listed eight here, four of which are generally superior, four of which need to be handled with care.

Superior Leads

First on the superior list is the *anecdotal lead*: It is often the best because it gives readers a character with whom to identify and action to grasp. In directed reporting, an anecdotal lead is a specific ministory that begins teaching the reader about the nature of the overall problem. Here is an example:

> Jim Gold was bankrupt, burdened with depression, and, through it all, born again. He was also wide awake, notwithstanding the handwritten note left on his windshield:
>
> "Wake up fool! Forests aren't just for chopping down. Many of us prefer to have them for owls and recreation, rather than have fatso fools like you chop them down, never to be replaced. Look over your shoulder. Earth First is watching you!"
>
> The threatening note was long on sentiment and short on scholarship. But it wasn't just a product of an eco-terrorist's bad-hair day. It was, in fact, a seedy but faithful reflection of federal policy.
>
> It was not what Gold needed after perching for 5 1/2 frustrating hours on the boom of his swing yarder in front of the Washington capitol in Olympia. He would rather have been harvesting timber in the vast forests of the Olympic Peninsula where he had operated an independent logging business for 16 fulfilling years. Now the U.S. Fish and Wildlife Service, armed with the Endangered Species Act, had locked up federal timberlands. And, in Gold's words, the state had then "caved in to the federal government," locking up most state timber as well.
>
> "You've Gone Too Far" read the placard mounted beside him on the rusty boom. It was a last whimper from a vanquished culture, catching only the ear of a state trooper who ordered Gold to move his machine away from the unmoved and unmoving legislature.
>
> There was nothing left to do but abandon the yarder for the bank to sell for scrap. He returned to his home north of Hoquiam, drained in pocket and in heart.

Anecdotal leads are good for arousing immediate interest by

involving the reader in the story. Often, anecdotes with people in them humanize what could be dry, or personalize what could be merely sensational. The anecdotal lead has to be true to the rest of the story: It should be colorful but directed, accurately representing the article and pointing the reader to it. An anecdote that is colorful but does not begin directing the reader to a deeper understanding of the problem can be used further down, but should not be the lead. The anecdote should be factual, an actual scene, not a composite or a product of the imagination.

Second on the superior list is the *descriptive lead*: It presents a scene without including characters or action. A descriptive lead works particularly well when the physical setting or the emotional mood is key, as in this example.

> A large black crow is furiously flapping against the blustery south wind sweeping over the desert of northern New Mexico. Silhouetted by rolling mounds of cracked orange sand that roll upwards into a perfect blue sky, the crow is neither moving forwards nor backwards. It is only maintaining, bounced up and down by wind sheers whipping under and over it.
>
> Such is the case today with those trapped in pockets of rural poverty in America. The neglected segment of Americans that are the rural poor finds that it is a battle to maintain while faced with a barrage of forces bouncing it up and down like a cork. The rate of rural poverty in America (16.1 percent) is higher than the much more publicized rate of urban poverty (13.7 percent).
>
> Why doesn't the crow ascend to higher, more helpful winds? Its instinctual nature should tell it to do so. Yet it seems frozen in space, destined to remain in the currents it now rides. In thirty minutes, would it still be there?
>
> Likewise, social and cultural forces such as government dependency and ill-equipped churches seem to be keeping many rural poor people stuck in thin air.

Descriptive leads are photographs rather than videotapes, but they can focus wonderfully.

Third on the superior list is the *situation lead*: It presents a problem and raises a sense of conflict or suspense about how a person will escape. Here is an example:

It's just after 11 p.m., and Houston police officer Al Leonard has his gun drawn as the elderly black man approaches the patrol car. The 9mm pistol is out of sight, pointing through the car door. Leonard rolls down his window and casually greets the man.

"What can I do for you?"

The man shakes his head in disgust. "Some kids," he says. "They was throwing bricks. Up over there on the corner. Broke my windshield. Musta been 10 or 12 of them."

Leonard nods. "When did it happen?"

"Few minutes ago. . . ."

What will Al Leonard do? The lead pushes us to read on; it is a purposefully incomplete anecdote. A situation lead should end with a sense of imminent trouble, or at least a circumstance demanding resolution.

Fourth on the superior list is the *multivignette lead*: It communicates a sense that many people are undergoing a particular problem. You can show several actual examples—do not make them up—and thus communicate the reality.

> *Although she wanted more children, Janet White felt that a tubal ligation—severing the fallopian tubes—was "the thing to do." Never questioning the "pressure from society for small families," she felt she had pushed the limit with three. But since then, her desire for more children has intensified—after her ability to have them was gone.*
>
> *Jennifer Barfield's marriage, on the other hand, was in shambles. She didn't want her husband around the two children they already had. Her husband didn't seem to care, so she took the bus to a doctor's office and had the option of more children surgically removed from her life. It became a decision she and her second husband later regretted.*
>
> *John Barja underwent sterilization surgery because doctors warned that pregnancy might endanger his wife's health. It nagged at him for 11 years.*
>
> Now, in the early '90s, a number of men and women, because of various circumstances, are changing their minds. A small but slowly growing movement is taking a closer look at the rights and wrongs of reproductive sterilization. . . .

Handle-with-Care Leads

Along with the superior or classic feature leads, four others are useful, but should be used sparingly. The *summary-lead* is the first type of sparingly used opener. This mainstay of news reporting is rare in a feature story, but useful when leading into a first-person account or some other story that will appear to have minor news value unless its significance is explained. Summaries of this kind should be printed in italics, with the main story in standard type; for example:

> *President Clinton's proposal to allow openly homosexual men and lesbians to serve in the military is in obvious trouble on Capitol Hill. During Senate hearings on the proposal, influential lawmakers have pushed a compromise "don't-ask-don't tell" policy, which would prohibit recruiting officers from inquiring about the sexual practices of potential enlistees while effectively keeping homosexual soldiers in the closet—for now. Hours of expert testimony have dealt with the negative impact of open homosexuality on combat effectiveness, unit cohesion, and esprit de corps in the armed services. . . .*
>
> *What the senators—and by extension, the public—saw illustrated was the prospect that the way of life that has preserved their freedom could be destroyed. Is it a way of life worth preserving?* World *sent Norm Bomer, editor of the God's World current-events newspapers, to Nellis Air Force Base in Nevada, where the top guns of the top guns train, to observe military life firsthand. Here is his report.*
>
> The heads-up flight data display monitor blocked my view directly ahead. I couldn't see the pilot, Col. Bentley Rayburn, until he leaned slightly to the side and peered around at me. His eyes twinkled from under his gray helmet. I knew his oxygen mask covered a joyous grin.
>
> I grinned back with a thumbs up that belied unconvincingly my gripping nausea. I had adjusted the power air vents between my knees to hit me full in the face. I wasn't sure Col. Rayburn could distinguish my skin from my olive drab flight suit. . . ."

The story goes on to show, through action, the esprit de corps of the flyers, and suggests that it can readily be threatened by congressmen who do not ask about it and do not care to listen when officers tell them.

The *quotation lead* is the second type of sparingly used opener. It often does not work because the quotation needs to be explained, and explanation slows down the story. But if a person is quoted while in action or in an evocative situation, a quotation lead can work, as in the following example.

> Brian, a young scriptwriter, sinks deeper into his chair but speaks into his jacket collar loud enough to be heard. "A friend who was working on the set with River Phoenix last summer said that he was shooting heroin between his toes every day. What did I do with that? All I did was take it and gossip it. I didn't intercede for him. I never prayed for River Phoenix."
>
> There is a long moment of quiet in the fellowship hall at Sherman Oaks Presbyterian Church, where a normally chatty group of Hollywood writers, directors, and producers called Associates in Media has gathered for its monthly meeting.
>
> The next day the coroner's office for Los Angeles County will confirm that Phoenix, who collapsed Oct. 31 outside a Hollywood night club, died of a massive drug overdose.

The *book-excerpt lead* is the third type of sparingly used opener. It should only be used to present a gripping story directly tied to the theme of the article that brings in foreshadowing, foreboding, or some other form of drama, tension, or suspense. For example, a story about psychobabble began:

> A man claims, "I am God." He is breathing hard and writhing. Richard Ganz hesitates, then responds by reading the New Testament: "False Christs and false prophets will arise."
>
> The man suddenly calms down and asks what Ganz is reading from. Ganz gives him the New Testament. Four weeks later the man calmly walks into Ganz's office and announces, "I want to become a Christian."
>
> Richard Ganz was a clinical psychologist working at a state hospital. The man who claimed to be God had not spoken a word for several years. Nor did he speak again until he told Ganz that he wanted to convert. After that, however, he could not stop speaking of the healing power of Jesus Christ. He was able to leave the state hospital soon afterward, a changed man.
>
> Shortly after he left, Ganz left too. Ganz was also a changed man. Before the incident he had been a secular psychologist who happened to be a Christian. But when confronted with an apparent incurable who suddenly wanted to know about the gospel, Ganz became a Christian counselor. His boss gave him a chance to apologize for using the Bible and pledge to sin no more, but he refused.

That account of Richard Ganz's heresy and resulting excommunication from secular psychology is described in "Confessions of a Psychological Heretic," the first chapter of his forthcoming book *Psychobabble: The Failure of Modern Psychology—and the Biblical Alternative*. Ganz's work is the latest sally in a battle taking place within evangelicaldom over the value of clinical psychotherapy within Christianity.

And the controversy is growing.

The *essay lead* is the fourth type of sparingly used opener. It lends itself to pontificating. For example, this lead came in a draft and had to be excised.

> To most outsiders, Russia is a country with little hope. . . .
>
> Still others think that Russia is stumbling toward stability. . . .
>
> Both perspectives, however, are right. Russia is a country in economic and political despair, yet there are glimmers of hope that remain. . . .

This lead was actually throat clearing, a false lead before the story's real beginning in a fourth paragraph that showed the "kiosks and tables all through the city that sell anything from live chickens to furniture. . . ."

Quantitatively and qualitatively, lead writers have great variety to choose from. The length of a lead often is tied to the length of the article—short for short, long for long. A good rule of thumb is that the lead should not be more than 10 percent of the story, but there is much leeway. The crucial point to keep in mind is that the lead should draw attention to the theme of the story, not to itself.

Lead construction is not either/or. It is not necessary to adopt one or another of the types of lead listed above; forms can be combined, as long as the lead does not dither but comes to a point. The following opener, for example, is both descriptive and anecdotal.

> Inside a small Bedouin goods shop in Jerusalem's Old City, the smell of strong Arab coffee cuts through the foreign aromas that have combined into a confusing but unforgettable blend. Outside the shop, a commotion . . . reaches a peak. Shouts and screams in Arabic are heard, and a moment later an Arab youth is carried away atop the shoulders of eight or 10 of his friends. His shirt is off and blood from knife-wounds flows freely. . . .

NUT GRAFS

What comes directly after the lead goes by many names—point statement, theme-paragraph thesis, justifier—but I like the pungent journalistic expression, nut graf.

The nut graf is the essence, the underlying idea of a story.
Generally following an anecdotal or descriptive lead, the nut graf
gives the basic news value and describes the significance of what the
reader has just been shown. The nut graf is expository writing: After
a lead that shows, the nut graf tells. The nut graf is vital because it
explains that the story is not about an isolated incident, but that many
people are affected.

Lack of a nut graf confuses readers and opens the door to dithering.
Lack of one also wastes a good author's tool: Once the nut graf is in
place, sentences and paragraphs throughout the body can be measured
against it and discarded if they do not help to make the point or provide
reflection upon it.

The nut graf should be one paragraph, sometimes one sentence. Here
are various examples:

> This scenario is far-fetched, but proposed legislation in Congress
> that would establish a nation wide computer-tracking system for inoc-
> ulations is getting a closer look.

■

> And that's not the only problem. The president is counting on
> national anxiety over a "health care crisis" to generate support for his
> plan. But the public is unsure that there's really a crisis at all.

■

> The shy, reclusive ninth-grade dropout from Texas has evolved
> into a despotic cult leader, able to command hundreds of followers
> and hold off 400 federal agents for days outside his dusty Mount
> Carmel compound.

■

> NBC has handed a sword to those who believe that many jour-
> nalists deserve skewering.

This abortionist shortage represents the soft underbelly of the multi-million dollar industry that has grown up around the concept of choice and personal sovereignty.

■

Prisons are in the news this month because a Republican-sponsored amendment to President Clinton's crime bill (up for debate in both the House and the Senate) sets aside $3 billion for new jails. But Christian leaders are divided over whether more prisons are necessary.

You should remember that readers want news, but they want it in an interesting, lively way. They want color but need connection. You can kill two birds with one nut graf—draw the reader forward by hinting at what is coming.

Here is an example of how to go from lead to nut. First, you powerfully present the situation.

They kicked open his door in the middle of the night during a power outage last month, blinded him with flashlights while others in the house were being beaten and interrogated. Six others who accompanied Dennis Balcombe on that trip to mainland China last month were arrested as well. Three are still missing, at first rumored to be executed, but now said to be held without being allowed visitors.

Then comes the nut graf:

Dennis Balcombe sees little of the progress China is claiming in its human rights record, progress the Clinton administration says must be made before China's Most Favored Nation trade status is extended in June. China, Balcombe says after his four-day ordeal, is repeating the atrocities of Mao.

An investigative report often presents the subject in action. First comes the lead.

Satanists and the demon-possessed show up frequently in Bob Larson's ministry, and they love to dial 1-800-821-TALK for apocalyptic showdowns with the energetic radio talk-show host. For two hours every day, via satellite from Denver, almost 200 radio stations across the country hear Larson's slugfest with the supernatural, "Talk-Back" with Bob Larson.

"What do you want? Mr. Milquetoast?" he says in a promotional tape. "Hey, flip the dial. This is me, this is real, this is 'Talk-Back.'"

Then the nut graf:

But 13 past Larson associates interviewed for this story—nine speaking openly, four confidentially—challenge Larson's public image.

The follies of secular liberalism often lead to a three-part lead-nut opening. First comes the news, with an emphasis on how big media spun it.

Nine women members of Congress marched last week in an attempt to swing the vote on demoting Adm. Frank Kelso upon his retirement—just as some women marched during the Anita Hill–Clarence Thomas hearings. The press covered last week's march with the same ear for righteous indignation given to Miss Hill and her supporters among the nation's feminist leaders.

Second, spotlight the contradiction.

But so far, no one has marched for Paula Jones. In fact, most people haven't heard of the 27-year-old woman who states that she was sexually harassed by then-governor Bill Clinton in 1991. Nor have the press or feminist leaders taken up her cause—one based on more evidence than was Miss Hill's.

Third, provide the explanatory nut (and sometimes a good quotation works well here).

"It's politics, pure and simple," says Tim Graham, associate editor of *Media Watch*. "There's such a dramatic difference between this and the response to the charges made by Anita Hill. With Anita Hill, there was no need to check her background, to check her witnesses, to check her facts. *The Washington Post* ran the Anita Hill allegations the day after the story broke. But now, it says it's taking months to investigate Paula Jones's allegations."

The nut graf is a highly directed part of *World* reporting style. By itself, it can be obnoxious; but when it follows specific detail and leads into a strong body, readers need and value it.

RUNNING THE RACE: THE BODY OF THE STORY

Many stories that start well become mushy in the middle: There is no sequence of ideas and sensations, no pattern of cause and effect, no narrative, no pearls—just puddles. Here is where it is important to turn constantly to the nut graf, and to remember that your goal is to convey information in support of that point. Ask yourself every step of the way as you write: What is my point?

Writers who are trained in writing for newspapers or writing for children sometimes fear long sentences, on the theory that they slow down readers. Actually, a well-organized longer sentence takes no longer to read than a series of short sentences, because periods are like stop signs. The real issue is complexity of material. The more complicated the idea, the shorter the sentences and paragraphs should be, in order to slow down the reader. But a narrative sentence can be long if it is good.

Keep thinking of readers, and then help them by relating the unknown to the known (for example, faraway place X is like nearby place Y). Do not overuse confusing statistics or technical information: A little goes a long way. Translate jargon into regular English, and give a face to a fact by explaining macro matters in human terms: Let the small represent the large.

Keeping readers in mind is especially important when dealing with big numbers. Instead of merely noting that the national debt is about $5 trillion, you should point out that there are about 100 million taxpayers; thus the average taxpayer's portion of the national debt is about $50,000. Instead of merely mentioning that New York spent $2 billion in ten years on 25,000 homeless persons, you should do the division problem for the skimming reader and note that the per person per year expenditure was $8000.

Logical transitions also contribute to the cause of moving readers from one chunk of information to the next. Write tightly, but do not neglect transitional words such as *and, but, nevertheless, still, meanwhile*. Do not bury good information in the middle of a paragraph. Key points of emphasis are the beginnings and ends of sentences, paragraphs, and stories. Your best stuff should be in the most emphatic locations.

Some editors use readability formulas. Rudolph Flesch in the 1940s had a famous one: He called seventeen to nineteen words per sentence ideal, and desired 150 syllables per one hundred words. Robert Gunning's "fog index" in the 1960s had writers adding the average number of words per sentence and the percentage of words having three or more syllables, then multiplying by 0.4 to determine the number of years of school the reader would need in order to understand.

Practical literacy has decreased during the past three decades, so it is even more important to pay attention to reading capacities. Still, commonsense checking may work better than formulas. For example, reader-friendly prose places the subject before the verb, uses the active voice rather than the passive, and uses the past tense. Some novice writers think that present tense is better because it supposedly makes the action more immediate, but it also can make reporting sound like a breathless romance novel.

The most important thing to remember throughout the body of the article is the inclusion of specific detail. Beginning writers often fall in love with their material and try to compress anecdotes and description so they can force everything in. Sometimes even experienced reporters with a lot to say cut out descriptive and narrative material so they can include all their points. But good stories require showing, not telling, and showing takes space: Selection, not compression, is the key.

You may also find it possible to use quotations more concisely. Try not to quote more than a sentence at a time (unless the goal is to throw a spotlight on the sentences themselves, as in this book). When quotations just state facts, put them in your own words, unless it is important that a particular person is acknowledging a particular fact. Quote colorful words: "The sacks are juiced" is better than, "The bases are loaded."

In general, end quotations with "he said," unless you want to call attention to his particular way of saying. *Noted* implies that you agree with what the speaker is saying, *argued* that you disagree. *Maintained* means he is sticking to his story, *insisted* means that he is under fire. When in doubt, stick to *said*—it moves the story along, without calling attention to words of attribution.

Try to use, subtly, some literary devices, such as alliteration (words in a sentence beginning with the same initial letter), assonance (same internal sound), and onomatopoeia, which features the sounds of a word or words suggesting the meaning: Bees buzz.

Another way to summarize material quickly is to quote public-policy jargon but, instead of going on about it, merely place the question under the biblical lens.

> He defines behavioral poverty as a "cluster of social pathologies including dependency and eroding work ethic, lack of educational aspiration and achievement, inability to control one's children, increased single parenthood and illegitimacy, criminal activity, and drug and alcohol abuse."
> In a word, sin.

Journalists sometimes fall into some of the mistakes listed above, but if you are a typical writer you will be particularly susceptible to the sin of coveting so-called inspiration and not working unless you have it. Remember, though, that although good writers work in a variety of ways, they all work hard. Some prefer morning, some afternoon; some write by hand, some type at computers; some need silence, some do well with children running through the room. The common denominator in success is perseverance: keeping at it, staying with it. Like a baseball player, you might get a hit the first time up and then strike out four times. Similarly, you might strike out in the first inning and hit a game-winning home run in the ninth.

When you do get stuck, ask yourself if you have done enough reporting. If the answer is yes and you still are stuck, you might try to describe to a friend what you saw or found out; type your good quotations, write lead-ins and follow-ups to them, and then eliminate some of the quotations; imagine yourself telling the story to a child—and then, and then. When the writing is going very poorly, you might try typing a page or two quickly without worrying about the sense of it; then print out the page(s), circle what is important, and rearrange the circled materials into an outline.

Other writing tips include: Be sure to identify in some way the people you quote or cite; vary sentence structure and length; and—as T. S. Eliot said when a young writer asked for advice—when it is cold, wear long underwear. For a good, brief compilation of basic stylistic pointers, you might pick up the classic and readily available little book by Will Strunk and E. B. White entitled *The Elements of Style*.

ENDS

Endings give readers a sense of closure and a sense that the writer knows what he is doing. You need to ask yourself what you want the reader to remember; often, last is most in memory. You should compare the lead and the ending: They should make the same point. (Sometimes, they can be more effective if switched.)

Of the several different types of endings, summary endings (like summary leads) are functional but weak. Four popular kinds of endings are the metaphorical, the next step, the nail-it-shut, and the circular. With all four kinds, do not hesitate to appeal to the emotions as well as to the intellect.

A *metaphorical* ending works well when you want to evoke a response either by making a biblical reference or placing the problem you have reported on in some other cultural context. For example, a story on the highly publicized tug-of-war concerning an adopted child ended, "No one is proposing that the child be cut in half physically; most people are hoping that Jessica will not be sliced and diced emotionally."

The *next-step* ending tells readers what happened after the time span emphasized in the article. Here is the end of a story about a woman who did abortions in China but escaped having one herself.

> As for Chi An and her family, they live in the southwestern United States. Now that Mahwae is in kindergarten, Chi An is studying for her nursing credentials. She hopes one day to work in a maternity ward, helping to deliver babies, not destroy them.

The *nail-it-shut* quotation has one of the persons quoted strongly elucidating the story's central theme.

> "At his funeral, they were saying what a tragedy it was—that Gary was a Christian and had even been a missionary. I didn't know anything about that part of his life. I knew he was a good officer, a good person. But I told God right then that people I ride with aren't going to hear [for the first time] at my funeral that I was a Christian. I knew I had to do better at letting people know what I am. Because like I said, without God I couldn't make it."

We have already discussed circular structure in stories; *circular* endings that bring back for a final look a central character of the article can increase reader identification.

> A full set of logging equipment for a site operation is called a side. It includes a yarder (a diesel-powered dragline and tower), a shovel, and a cat. In 1988, Jim Gold owned three complete logging sides, employed 14 men, and had a net worth of $700,000. It's all gone. . . .
> "When you've lost everything, threats don't matter," he says. "We've got no fight left."

In all these types, look to make a Christocentric point if you can do so without preaching at readers or seeming smarmy. An article about illegal Chinese immigrants in jail ended powerfully.

> One detainee's wife wrote to him and warned him not to return, unless his new God was a powerful one.
> "As to your pursuit of Christianity, as mentioned in your letter, I will leave it up to you to decide whether you want to believe it or not," she wrote. "It is very dangerous to come home now. The village officials are still working on your case, which is why I am still in hiding. You know very well the consequences. If deported, your fate wouldn't be better than the one who took his life. I can only hope you can be saved by the Jesus that you mentioned in your letter. I hope you can count on the power of Jesus to avert the unthinkable."

Now as in the past, only that power can yank humanity out of sin and individual men and women from the clutches of those still totally captive to it.

HEADLINES

The job of traditional newspaper headlines, like leads, is to tell the essence of the story. Magazine headlines, however, are designed to draw the reader into the story. Since magazine headlines can more readily evoke and provoke than their newspaper counterparts, there is room for occasional wit.

Some of my favorite headlines, of the many excellent ones written by *World* managing editor Nickolas Eicher, are "No Advance, No Retreat," to discuss Newt Gingrich's decision to turn down a book advance but stick with his writing plans; "PC on the Pecos," concerning a review of a new, ideologically up-to-date Disney movie, *Tall Tale*; "God Save the Monarch," over a story concerning butterflies; "cybershark@-aol.com," for a story about computer pornography, pedophiles, and children; "Political Science," for an article about how the federal government's subsidies for scientific projects do better at propping up particular interests than promoting breakthroughs; and "Foundation of Lies," concerning the Foundation for New Era Philanthropy's pyramid scheme.

There are some technical details to be mastered, but the bottom line on these top lines should be: Have fun.

CHAPTER NINE

Theocentrism or Egocentrism?

S tyle has changed over the years, but a kiss is still a kiss, an idea is still an idea, and it's thoughts that continue to count, as time goes by. The conservative uprising of the mid-1990s is showing the power of ideas; the patriots of the American Revolution clearly saw their triumph as a victory of ideas, disseminated through newspapers. The editor of the *New York Journal* noted in a letter to Samuel Adams, "It was by means of News papers that we receiv'd & spread the Notice of the tyrannical Designs formed against America, and kindled a Spirit that has been sufficient to repel them."

British officials such as Ambrose Serles had a different perspective: He complained that, "Among other Engines which have raised the present Commotion, next to the indecent Harranges of the Prechers, none has a more extensive or stronger influence than the Newspapers of the respective Colonies." British leaders were appalled that Samuel Adams's central idea of corruption in leadership had defeated their official story of faith in King.

Had the British better known their own country's history, the shock would have been less. Adams was another in the great cloud of witnesses that included John Foxe, Marchamont Nedham, and many who had been executed for Christ. By the time of the American Revolution, 250 years had passed since Martin Luther first showed the power of exposing corruption through the publication of specific detail. During that time, the uses of biblical sensationalism, investigation, and accurate exposure had become apparent, and principles of reforming but nonrevolutionary journalism had been established.

Those concepts formed the baseline for journalism in the new republic. Deism, which denied God's continuing sovereignty over that which He had created, was on the march during the last quarter of the eighteenth century, yet reports of crime retained their Christian edge. Coverage of a New Hampshire execution emphasized the evil that had been done, but concluded "O may that God / Who gave his only Son, / Give you his grace, in Heaven a place, / For Jesus' sake—Amen."

Newspapers, rather than embracing deism, often portrayed it as containing the seeds of its own destruction. In 1782, six days after a man had killed his wife and four children and then himself, the *Connecticut Courant* reported the news and then contextualized that:

> The perpetrator had rejected all Revelation as imposition, and (as he expresses himself) renouncing all the popular Religions of the world, intended to die a proper Deist. Having discarded all ideas of moral good and evil, he considered himself, and all the human race, as mere machines; and that he had a right to dispose of his own and the lives of his family.

The *Courant* related how the man gave opiates to his family and then went around slaughtering the sleepers with knife and ax—but the damage initially occurred when the man "adopted this new theoretic system which he now put in practice." Ideas had consequences.

Columnists of the period argued that the nature of man would lead to attempts at dictatorship, unless careful restraint was maintained. Robert Yates wrote, "It is a truth confirmed by the unerring experience of ages that every man, and every body of men, invested with power, are ever disposed to increase it." John Adams, after noting that the Constitution stipulated the election of key leaders, asked:

> How are their characters and conduct to be known to their constituents but by the press? If the press is stopped and the people kept

in Ignorance we had much better have the first magistrate and Senators hereditary.

In Alexandria, Virginia, the *Gazette* also thought the press had an essential role in limiting governmental power, for:

> here too public men and measures are scrutinized. Should any man or body of men dare to form a system against our interests, by this means it will be unfolded to the great body of the people, and the alarm instantly spread through every part of the continent. In this way only, can we know how far our public servants perform the duties of their respective stations.

The rise of French revolutionary ideas in the 1790s led to attempts to crack down on press freedom, but newspapers survived. The number of newspapers in the United States shot up from 37 in 1775 to 359 in 1810 to 1,265 in 1834—and, as one contemporary observer noted, "Of all the issues of the press three-fourths are theological, ethical, and devotional." The *New York Christian Advocate* was the largest circulation weekly in the country, with twenty-five thousand subscribers in 1828 and thirty thousand in 1830. Ninety of these newspapers were dailies.

Hundreds of unsung editors went about their business of reporting both sinfulness and special providences. One typical editor, Nathaniel Willis, born in 1780, was impressed by French revolutionary ideals. Willis from 1802 to 1807 edited a vitriolic radical newspaper and was happy to "spend Sabbaths in roving about the fields and in reading newspapers." One Sunday, however, he went to hear what he thought would be a political speech by a minister, and was surprised to hear instead a discussion of biblical basics. Willis, "much interested," eventually came to believe "that the Bible is the Word of God— that Christ is the only Saviour, and that it is by grace we are saved, through faith."

Applying that understanding to his occupation, Willis decided that good journalism required biblical analysis of issues; he began putting out a newspaper, the *Boston Recorder*, that emphasized individual responsibility rather than grand societal solutions. *Recorder* columns argued that civil government has strictly limited jurisdiction, and should be turned to only for defense or punishment of crime. Family, church, and charity groups were to take leadership in dealing with social problems.

Other newspapers also emphasized the moral questions involved in both personal and governmental actions. The *Lexington Western Monitor*, a Kentucky newspaper, was typical in its summary of one major role of the press: "To strengthen the hands of virtue and to rebuke vice." *The New York American* viewed "the Press as the great instrument of Liberty," as long as there was a "FREE and INDEPENDENT PRESS, FREE from all controls but that of religion and morality, INDEPENDENT of any influence but the good of our country and mankind."

These newspapers also covered international news in line with their theological concerns. For example, many publications complained that the British East India Company—agent for the British government in India—was restricting the activities of missionaries for fear that Christian development would "prove fatal to the British government in India." The *Columbian Phoenix* complained that British leaders thought "the Religion of the Most High God must not be suffered to interfere with the arrangements of the British government." Sensational stories about India's "Juggernaut festival"—in which people prepared for sacrifice to local gods were "crushed to death by the wheels" of a moving tower while onlookers shouted with joy—led into reports that British agents were collecting a "Juggernaut tax."

Great Britain's peaceful coexistence with human sacrifice, wife burning, and infanticide was attacked by *Niles' Weekly Register*, which reported that two American missionaries were evicted from India because "the revenues of Juggernaut must not be unhinged." A Rhode Island newspaper argued that the British government would "sponsor the worship of Beelzebub if the state could make money off of it." The *New Hampshire Patriot* complained that "British leaders take a premium from the poor ignorant Asiatic idolater to indulge him in falling down and worshipping the moulten image, Juggernaut. By this piece of religious fraud, they raise a handsome revenue to the British government."

Many publications were hindered, though, by a tendency to emphasize essays rather than hard-hitting reporting and exposure of corruption. George Wisner, editor of the *New York Sun* during the 1830s, was a Christian who understood that it is neither accurate nor stimulating to pretend that all is well in the world. You can learn much from his emphasis on what we might call the ACES of journalism: Accuracy, Clarity, Specificity, and Exposure. Like Increase Mather, he wrote of how news stories:

> must generally tell of wars and fighting, of deeds of death, and blood of wounds and heresies, of broken heads, broken hearts, and broken bones, of accidents by fire or flood, a field of possessions ravaged, property purloined, wrongs inflicted. . . . The abundance of news is generally an evidence of astounding misery, and even the disinterested deeds of benevolence and philanthropy which we occasionally hear of owe their existence to the wants or sorrows or sufferings of some of our fellow beings.

Wisner's practice followed his principles: He ran moral tales concerning the consequences of seduction, adultery, and abandonment. Believing that specificity was important both to win readers and to make his product morally useful, he listed names of all criminal offenders and defended:

> such posting as an inhibitor of others inclined to vice: Much complaint has been made from a certain quarter, and emanating from a particular class of individuals, against the publication of the names of persons who have been arrested by the watch, [but . . .] such publications have a tendency to deter from disorders and crimes, and to diminish the number of criminals.

A typical story shows Wisner not afraid to shame offenders.

> Patrick Ludwick was sent up by his wife, who testified that she had supported him for several years in idleness and drunkenness. Abandoning all hopes of reformation in her husband, she brought him a suit of clothes a fortnight since and told him to go about his business, for she would not live with him any longer. Last night he came home in a state of intoxication, broke into his wife's bedroom, pulled her out of bed, and pulled her hair, and stamped on her. She called a watchman and sent him up. Pat exerted all his powers of eloquence in endeavoring to excite his wife's sympathy, but to no purpose. As any sensible woman ought to do who is

cursed with a drunken husband, she refused to have anything to do
with him hereafter.

Following the Reformed view that the heavens display the glory of
God and the streets show the sinfulness of man, Wisner told stories to
make his points, and also displayed a sense of humor. For example,
Wisner opposed dueling but once accepted a challenge from a seller of
quack medicines whom he had criticized. Given his choice of weapons,
Wisner said that they would have to be syringes filled with the doctor's
own medicine, at five paces. The duel was called off.

The most articulate journalistic writer on politics and morality during the 1830s was William Leggett of the *New York Evening Post*.
Leggett's major political principle was support for "equal rights," by
which he meant that law should not discriminate among citizens, bene-
fiting some at the expense of others. (With this position Leggett was following the emphasis of chapter 23 of Exodus, which commands us to
show partiality neither to rich nor to poor in their disputes.)

Leggett believed it unfair for government to be "offering encour-
agements and granting privileges" to those with political clout. He set
about to expose any governmental redistribution of income, whether
through taxes, tariffs, or government aid to individuals, businesses, or
labor groups. He foresaw problems whenever "government assumes the
functions which belong alone to an overruling Providence, and affects to
become the universal dispenser of good and evil."

Leggett especially did not want government to become: "the greater
regulator of the profits of every species of industry," and in that way to
"reduce men from a dependence on their own exertions, to a dependence
on the caprices of their Government." He complained that some already
were beginning to insist:

> that because our government has been instituted for the benefit of the
> people, it must therefore have the power to do whatever may seem to
> conduce to the public good. Under the sanction of such a principle, a
> government can do any thing on pretense of acting for the public
> good.

Leggett in his columns reported the attempts of "designing politicians, interested speculators, or crack-brained enthusiasts" to use gov-

ernment for their own public-interest purposes. Leggett thought his work of exposure vital because if Washington's expansive tendencies were not stopped early, Americans would "become the victims of a new species of despotism." Once a system of governmental favoritism was established, Leggett pointed out, changing it would be difficult.

> One of the greatest supports of an erroneous system of legislation, is the very evil it produces. When it is proposed to remedy the mischief by adopting a new system, every abuse which has been the result of the old one becomes an obstacle to reformations. Every political change, however salutary, must be injurious to the interests of some, and it will be found that those who profit by abuses are always more clamourous for their continuance than those who are only opposing them from motives of justice or patriotism, are for their abandonment.

Yet, if change did not occur, citizens would be left enslaved.

> A government administered on such a system of policy may be called a Government of Equal Rights, but it is in its nature and essence a disguised despotism. It is the capricious dispenser of good and evil, without any restraint, except its own sovereign will. It holds in its hand the distribution of the goods of this world, and is consequently the uncontrolled master of the people.

In God's mysterious providence, both Wisner and Leggett died young during the 1830s. By 1840 new voices were arising, in response to theological trends. Increasingly, liberal ministers began to proclaim that man was not inherently sinful, and that if man's environment were changed, man himself could become perfect. A host of panaceas, ranging from diet change (meat was out, graham flour was in) to the abolition of private property, became popular as ways of changing mankind.

Many of the proposals for change involved an opposition to property rights, which journalists—aware of the importance of privately owned printing presses to editorial independence—had strongly favored over the years. Unitarian leader William Ellery Channing clearly named one of the assumed villains: "Avarice was the chief obstacle to human progress. . . . The only way to eliminate it was to establish a community of property."

Channing later moderated his communistic ideas concerning property, but he typified the liberal New Englander's approach to the problem of evil. Evil was created by the way society was organized, not by anything innately evil in man. Change society and evil could be eliminated.

Such ideas were part of Unitarianism's reaction against the Reformed worldview's emphasis on man's fallenness and God's holy sovereignty. Harvard College, which early in the nineteenth century became the Unitarian Vatican, published the influential *Monthly Anthology* and *Boston Review* and gained supporters such as William Emerson, minister at the First Unitarian Church and father of Ralph Waldo Emerson. Some Christian newspapers fought back, but others contented themselves with singing, "A Mighty Fortress Is Our God," all the while forgetting that a fortress was an offensive as well as a defensive weapon: From it soldiers could make sorties.

Another of the radical attacks on private property was led by Albert Brisbane, who had journeyed to Europe in 1828, at age eighteen, and had eventually become a disciple of Charles Fourier. Fourier, famous in Marxist history as a "utopian socialist," argued that man's natural goodness could be restored if society was reorganized into small units called phalanxes, each with 1,620 members. Each phalanx member would be paid from the common product and would live in a common dwelling called a phalanstery, with a common dining hall featuring seven meals a day. Bodies would also be in common, since "free love" would be encouraged. The communes would emphasize agriculture, but each member would be free to work when and where he wanted.

For Fourier and Brisbane, this economic vision came from pantheistic theology and was designed, in Brisbane's words, to create "a humanity worthy of that Cosmic Soul of which I instinctively felt it to be a part." But Brisbane, desiring success and believing that material change would lead to spiritual transformation, learned to downplay his theology before the public. Searching for journalists who could popularize his ideas, he latched onto a talented but somewhat loony editor named Horace Greeley.

The collaboration of Brisbane and Greeley changed American journalism. Greeley in 1841 was a thirty-year-old New York Unitarian and frustrated office seeker just starting up a new penny newspaper, the *New York Tribune*. Greeley was enthralled by the "ennobling tendencies" of Transcendentalism and enamored with the movement's leaders: "Its apostles are mainly among the noblest spirits living." He called himself a mere popularizer of Emerson's transcendentalist teachings, and at the same time a Universalist who believed in salvation for every man and salvation of society by man's efforts. Greeley also wanted people to revere him as a great thinker; as fellow editor E. L. Godkin noted, Greeley castigated office seekers, but he was "as time-serving and ambitious and scheming an old fellow as any of them."

Naturally, Greeley was attracted to Brisbane's proposal of salvation through commune. With a new convert's enthusiasm Greeley published a magazine edited by Brisbane and entitled *The Future, Devoted to the Cause of Association and a Reorganization of Society*. He then gave Brisbane a front-page column on the *Tribune* that provided an opportunity to "spread ideas broadcast over the whole country, gaining a great number of adherents." As one Greeley biographer noted, "The *Tribune* threw itself wholeheartedly behind Brisbane, and soon found itself building up news interest, discussion, and circulation at an extraordinary rate as it helped him popularize his cause."

Greeley was the first American editor to become a national celebrity. He threw himself personally into the commune movement, as he attended Fourierist conventions and became president of the American Union of Associationists—*association* becoming the American term for commune. Greeley received ample stroking; in 1844, for example, when he went to a New York City banquet honoring Fourier's birthday, Greeley was toasted by Brisbane as the man who had "done for us what we never could have done. He has created the cause on this continent. He has done the work of a century. Well, then, I will give a toast: One Continent, One Man!"

Greeley's political activities helped him attract many young, idealistic writers, some of whom—Margaret Fuller, George Ripley, and Charles Dana particularly—had great literary skill. The *Tribune* became *the* place to work; as editor E. L. Godkin would note, "To get admission to the columns of the *Tribune* almost gave the young writer a patent of literary nobility." One *Tribune* reporter recalled that the furnishings were poor, but:

> ill-furnished and ill-kept as the *Tribune* office was in those days, it harbored a moral and intellectual spirit that I met nowhere else dur-

ing my thirty-five years of journalistic experience. Every member of
the force, from reporter to editor, regarded it as a great privilege to be
on the Tribune and to write for its columns. . . ."

Greeley himself had great journalistic instincts. He demanded from
his reporters "vigor, terseness, clearness, and simplicity." He emphasized
comprehensive news coverage, and described how an editor should make
sure that nothing "of interest to a dozen families occurs, without having
the fact daily, though briefly, chronicled." He noted that if an editor can
"secure a wide-awake, judicious correspondent in each village and township" and have him send "whatever of moment occurs in his vicinity," the
subscription list would be fruitful and multiply.

Greeley also insisted on good typography. One anecdote shows
how even Greeley's fiercest competitors respected the *Tribune's* superiority in this regard. It seems that Greeley once fired a printer who mis-
read Greeley's notoriously messy handwriting and thought the editor
was calling not for an early morning milk train to bring the fruits of
farm labors to New York City, but a "swill train." When the editorial
was published and an angry delegation of Westchester County farmers
assaulted Greeley, he in rage scribbled a note to the composing-room
foreman ordering that the printer be fired. The foreman knew Greeley's
writing and could read the message, but to the average reader only the
signature was clear. The fired compositor asked to hold onto Greeley's
note as a souvenir. He then took it to other newspapers and answered
questions about previous employment and reliability by flashing the
note. The name of Greeley on it—all else being illegible—was
accepted as all the recommendation needed.

All of these factors allowed Greeley the freedom to make his newspaper a proponent of social revolution without unduly alienating otherwise delighted subscribers. Since the 1840s was a decade of utopian
hopes that in some ways paralleled the 1960s, some readers also were
excited by commune coverage. In 1846, however, Greeley was challenged
to a series of newspaper debates by his former assistant editor on the
Tribune, Henry Raymond, who five years later would found the *New York
Times* as a Christian newspaper. Greeley later wrote that he had never
seen "a cleverer, readier, more generally efficient journalist" than
Raymond. The philosophical differences between the two were sharp: In

1854, journalist James Parton would muse, "Horace Greeley and Henry J. Raymond, the one naturally liberal, the other naturally conservative—the one a Universalist, the other a Presbyterian."

Two newspapers—*The New York Courier and Enquirer*, where Raymond was assistant editor, and the *Tribune*—agreed to publish twenty-four articles of the debate, twelve from each side. The first six statements from each side emphasized economic points. Raymond then stated his fundamental position: Only the "personal reform of individual men," through Christianity, can lead to social progress. Raymond argued that reformers should seek "personal, moral transformation. When that is accomplished, all needed Social Reform will either have been effected or rendered inevitable."

Greeley, in his seventh statement, had two replies to Raymond. First, Greeley argued that personal change among the best and the brightest would lead to societal transformation that in turn would lead to change among the masses.

> Give but one hundred of the right men and women as the nucleus of a true Social Organism, and hundreds of inferior or indifferent qualities might be rapidly molded into conformity with them.

Greeley could write this because he saw man as a product of his environment: "I believe there are few of the young and plastic who might not be rendered agreeable and useful members of an Association under the genial influences of Affection, Opportunity, Instruction, and Hope." Greeley's emphasis on plasticity—the doctrine that there is no human nature, and that man can be molded into almost anything—prefigured twentieth-century Marxism's attempts at human engineering.

Second, Greeley's arguments pointed toward future ideologies by putting forward what a half-century later became known as the "Social Gospel": He tried to show that Raymond's demand for Christ first was absurd, because "Association is the palpable dictate of Christianity—the body whereof True Religion is the soul." In arguing that Associationism was Christianity-in-practice, a material emphasis that necessarily went along with the spiritual, Greeley described slum living conditions and asked:

Can any one doubt what Christianity must dictate with regard to such hovels as these? Can any fail to see that to fill them with Bibles and Tracts, while Bread is scanty, wholesome Air a rarity, and Decency impossible, must be unavailing? 'Christianity,' say you! Alas! many a poor Christian mother within a mile of us is now covering her little ones with rags in the absence of fuel. . . .

Greeley's statement jarred Raymond to lay out his full position on January 20, 1847. He first noted partial agreement with Greeley as to the need for action: "The existence of misery, and the necessity of relieving it, are not in controversy, for we have never doubted either. It is only upon the *remedy to be applied*, that the *Tribune* and ourselves are at variance." But Raymond argued that Greeley was unnecessarily revolutionary when he insisted that:

to benefit a part, the whole must be changed; that to furnish some with good dwellings, all must abandon their houses and dwell together under a common roof; that the whole fabric of existing institutions, with all its habits of action and of thought, must be swept away. . . .

Raymond, rather than linking philanthropy with upheaval, praised "individuals in each ward, poor, pious, humble men and women, who never dreamed of setting themselves up as professional philanthropists," but daily visited the sick and helped the poor. He also argued that:

Members of any one of our City Churches do more every year for the practical relief of poverty and suffering, than any Phalanx [the Associationist name for communes] that ever existed. There are in our midst hundreds of female 'sewing societies,' each of which clothes more nakedness, and feeds more hunger, than any 'Association' that was ever formed.

Raymond then portrayed Greeley's ideas as abstract and ineffective.

Hundreds of thousands of dollars have been expended by the Associationists, in propagating their theories of benevolence, and in making benevolent experiments, yet where is the practical good they have accomplished? . . . The *Tribune* sneers at practical Christianity. . . . Does the taunt come with good grace from a system which theorizes over starvation, but does not feed it; which scorns to give bread and clothing to the hungry and naked, except it can first have the privilege of reconstructing Society?

Finally, the two debaters were focusing on the basics. Raymond had called Greeley superficial for not getting the root, spiritual causes of material poverty, and now Greeley struck back with his assessment that capitalism, not spiritual decay, was the culprit: "Association proposes a way . . . of reaching the causes of the calamities, and absolutely abolishing Pauperism, Ignorance, and the resulting Vices."

Journalists, Greeley went on, should not merely praise those who mitigated "woes and degradations," but should fight for revolutionary change: " 'Relieving Social Evils' is very well; we think eradicating and preventing them still better, and equally feasible if those who have power will adopt the right means, and give them a fair trial."

Increasingly the debates hinged on the view of man that divided the two editors. When Greeley argued that all man's problems "have their root in that isolation of efforts and antagonism of interests on which our present Social Order is based," Raymond replied by emphasizing individual corruption rather than social oppression as the root of most social ills. Greeley believed that "the Passions, feelings, free impulses of Man point out to him the path in which he should walk"; Raymond argued that evil feeds on man's natural inclination, and that sinful tendencies needed channeling into paths of work and family.

The last three debates showed even more clearly the conflict of two faiths. Greeley's Associationist belief was that human desires are:

> good in themselves. Evil flows only from their repression or subversion. Give them full scope, free play, a perfect and complete development, and universal happiness must be the result . . . create a new form of Society in which this shall be possible . . . then you will have a perfect Society; then will you have the Kingdom of Heaven . . .

Raymond in response argued that:

> this principle is in the most direct and unmistakable hostility to the uniform inculcations of the Gospel. No injunction of the New Testament is more express, or more constant, than that of self-denial; of subjecting the passions, the impulses of the heart to the law of conscience.

Greeley would not assent to Raymond's assertion that Association-ism was anti-Christian; rather, he made social universalism a Christian necessity.

> The duty of every Christian, every Philanthropist, every one who admits the essential Brotherhood of the Human Family, to labor earnestly and devotedly for a Social Order, which shall secure to every human being within its sphere the full and true develop-ment of the nature wherewith God has endowed him, Physical, Intellectual, and Moral.

Raymond, however, refused to concede that the "social order" was the focus of evil: He pointed to the sinfulness of the heart and insisted that the remedy "must reach that cause, or it must prove inefficient. The heart must be changed."

Thus, the line was clearly drawn. Greeley believed that "the heart of man is not depraved, and that social distinctions of master and servant, rich and poor, landlord and landless," cause social problems. Raymond concluded by arguing that

> the principles of all true REFORM come down from Heaven. . . . The CHRISTIAN RELIGION, in its spiritual, life-giving, heart-redeeming principles is the only power that can reform Society: and it can accomplish this work only by first reforming the indi-viduals of whom Society is composed. Without GOD, and the plan of redemption which he has revealed, the World is also without HOPE.

As the debates ended, interest in them was so high that *Harpers* quickly published all twenty-four of the articles in a pamphlet of eighty-three closely printed, double-columned pages, which sold out. What Raymond and Greeley were really arguing about was what the "central idea" for Americans, and American journalists, should be.

The battle was not one of change vs. the status quo. Raymond agreed with Greeley that social problems were great—"Far from denying their existence, we insist that they are deeper and more fundamental in their origin." But Raymond saw himself as arguing for "a more thorough and radical remedy than the *Tribune* supposes"—namely, the change of heart that acceptance of Christianity brings.

Biblical direction was common in the Christian journalism that dominated the early nineteenth-century press. Directed reporters showed the universality of sin and the need for repentance. But the Bible did not remain dominant in American journalism. Instead of seeing sinful man and a society reflecting that sinfulness, Horace Greeley and his followers believed that man, naturally good, was enslaved by oppressive social systems. Greeley, in the debates, developed the rationale for journalists to become advocates of secular liberalism.

CHAPTER TEN

Biblically Directed Reviewing

Previous chapters on the journalistic craft have emphasized reporting: Covering a story, to many writers, is at the opposite end of the universe from writing a review, which is seen as an opportunity to express personal opinion. In directed journalism, however, the distance between reporting and reviewing is not great: Both forms emphasize specific detail, not abstract theorizing, and both should present a biblical perspective, not individual bias. Since both demand thorough reporting, the writer on arts and media ideally should spend time not just in the theater or at the computer, but in an office where a persevering Christian producer is waiting to see whether his television show will be renewed.

It's a mid-November day in Southern California, and Dave Johnson is working in the San Fernando Valley town of Chatsworth. . . . Chatsworth is barely 15 miles from the NBC studios in Burbank, but it seems worlds away from Hollywood. . . . Production on *Against the Grain* has shut down. The scaled-back crew is mostly waiting: Eight episodes have been shot, six have been televised, and a call from NBC renewing the show or canceling it is long overdue.

The phone rings, but it is . . . a fan from Texas, the show's fictitious location. Don Ohlmeyer, NBC's president in Burbank, is who Johnson wants to hear on the other end, and he wears the sleep-deprived look of a campaign manager on election eve. He has done his share of watching the polls these past few weeks. . . . He's gotten support from Concerned Women for America, Family Research Council, and Focus on the Family. To anyone who will listen, he asks for an endorsement and a letter to NBC executives.

Similarly, writing about music should include reporting about its audience and effects; as one *World* article noted,

> "gangsta" rap, the brutally verbal and musically simplistic category into which much of the controversial music falls, seems to be no longer 'hip' in the hip-hop, or black community. [Nevertheless], the gradually declining but still formidable sales of hard-edged rap albums and singles suggest a faithful core audience [that] congregates toward the younger end of the 12-to-24-year-old demographics.

Most of the time, reviewers cannot be on the set, of course, but they still should think of their work as a form of directed reporting, rather than either dithering summary or sheer editorializing. Reviews, like news features, should have characterization and description, leads and endings; since readers rely on reviews not only for understanding but for action, writers need to avoid both stylistic and substantive wishy-washiness.

Ideally, review pages accompany news developments. *World*, for example, commissioned a review of a new book by Stephen Breyer as he was parading past the Judiciary Committee on his way to the Supreme Court. The review's lead pointed out both positives and negatives.

> In a slim volume devoted to regulatory law our newly nominated associate justice of the Supreme Court reveals both his admirable grasp of data and his inability to see its basic implications.

The review summarized major parts of Breyer's analysis.

> Breyer points out that the cost of attempts to improve safety and health through regulation reach a point at which safer environments simply become too expensive. Further, when very small risks are in view, backing away from them often means backing unknowingly into greater risks.
>
> Much of our federal and state regulatory apparatus is harnessed to a misbegotten attempt to remove all risks whatsoever and has become counterproductive and too expensive. Breyer includes tables

showing estimates of the cost of regulations per human life saved. The EPA's ban on asbestos in 1989, for example, bears an estimated cost of over $110 million per premature death averted.

The review then proceeded to a worldview analysis.

> The author fails to see the larger lesson—that civil government has no divine appointment by God to micromanage everything, that God has set up other institutions of governance, and holds none accountable for minuscule risks inherent in the fabric of a fallen world—events that were called "acts of God" before the death of God and the birth of EPA, OSHA, FAA, and their siblings.
>
> Breyer's answer, alas, is yet another layer of regulation. He proposes a kind of super-regulatory agency that would regulate the regulators, insulated from political control, operating on supposedly scientific and logical principles. This elite oligarchy would be professionally [in]bred to its role by years of circulation through the judiciary, universities, bureaus and the like.

The review did not get off track onto trivia, but provided a conclusion that emphasized the threat represented by Breyer's thinking.

> Breyer enthuses that this "small powerful group" would have success which would lead to even more power. Their interests could range as near to home as the transportation of cancer patients to clinics and as far as the deforestation of Madagascar. Breyer . . . forgets that our federal union was structured out of mistrust for concentrations of power in the hands of fallen mankind. It is precisely through the regulatory fourth branch of government that our Constitution has been most handily outflanked. The man seeks efficiency over freedom. Our Constitution may be headed back through the shredder.

Reviews in Christian publications should be theologically distinctive. Secular publications can dissect the technical aspects of a director's technique, but the special function of Christian publications is to point out to readers the worldviews embedded in various artistic products as well as the skill of the artists.

In doing so, reviews should distinguish among different genres. Light action-adventure films such as *True Lies* that content themselves with providing thrills should be evaluated differently from films such as

Forrest Gump that aspire to send religious chills up and down our spines. Readers need to know about serious films such as *Tender Mercies* that present the truth about original sin and God's grace, and they also should be referred to films designed for fun. Christian reviewers should not endorse products that preach man's natural goodness.

When you decide to write a review, you should not suddenly neglect reporting and become an essayist; journalistic fundamentalism still applies. For example, finding a lead that will interest skimming readers challenges reviewers as it does feature writers. Anecdotal leads can work well when the plot of whatever you are reviewing is lively.

> In October of 1980 an intruder brutally murdered a nursing student in Oak Park, Ill. The police told neighbors to provide anything that might be of help, no matter how silly it seemed. Steven Linscott, a Bible school student, took their advice and it changed his life forever.

You have to be careful, though, to avoid sounding as if you are copying a publicity agent's release. It is best to pick out a particular scene from a book or movie and describe it: If it seems that you could have written your lead paragraph without having read the book or seen the movie, it is not a good lead.

Generally, judgment trumps suspense in review leads. The judgement can emphasize either the particular work or, when the artist under review is well known, a body of work.

> Several years ago Johnny Cash began telling interviewers that, after two decades of lackluster recordings, he was ready to make a really good album again. With *American Recordings* he's made good on his promise.

The body of the review needs good transitions so that the review builds to a climax. A review, like a feature story, needs to be more than a series of fragments. As in writing a feature story, you need a clear theme before you begin, and you need to think through a structure that carries along the reader.

You should avoid three common mistakes. First, do not talk down to the reader: "*Much Ado About Nothing* is one of William Shakespeare's comedies, the very title implying frivolity." Second, do not show off the abstruse insider knowledge you may have obtained: "His inclusion of that double-fogged scene was a tribute to the little-known German director. . . ." Third, do not state what the reader already knows; thus making mine eyes glaze over: "The relationship of religion and politics is obviously an important one these days."

As you think through what you should be sure to cover in a review, remember that you are the reader's regent: You should have some idea of readers' interests so you can function more effectively as their eyes and ears as well as your own. You are also the reader's teacher. Just as a good senator finds the right mixture of representing constituents' views and goes beyond them to leadership.

To both teach Christians and represent them, you should be anchored in a church community. You should not worship the arts or any artistic products. Your job is not to promote books, movies, or anything else, except God's truth.

All of these complexities show that innocent bystanders who think reviews are easy to write—"You're just giving your opinion"—have it backward. A good reviewer needs the ability to bring out theological implications and the firmness to avoid going gaga over a movie just because it makes some religious allusions; on closer inspection, Hollywood's theological profundity tends to be an illusion.

In 1994, for example, some critics praised the "purity of vision" in the movie *Forrest Gump*, but a column in *World* noted that the vision did not include Christ—and did not need to, according to the film's coproducer, because "the child-like innocence of Forrest Gump is what we all once had" and need to develop anew.

It is not necessary to criticize most movies for showing no awareness of original sin; most are light entertainment, and leave it at that. But since *Forrest Gump* went from film to sociological phenomenon—$200 million in tickets sold, over one million copies of the book in print, "Gumpisms" widely quoted—Christian critics had an opportunity not only to comment on a movie but to teach discernment. The first step was to place the movie in the context of the current culture war.

> Never say that Hollywood does not respond to pressure from Christians protesting promiscuous sex, violence, and obscenity in the movies. This summer's surprise box-office sensation, *Forrest Gump*,

has none of these: Gump is a saint who honors his mother, consistently loves one girl/woman, and never gets angry. . . . Gump's virtues are a byproduct of his IQ of 75: simple thinking leads him to the salvation of simple living. The apostle Paul thought about running the race; Gump just runs.

Then, after summarizing the box-office and critical success of the movie, the reviewer presented his nut graf.

Forrest Gump, in short, has become one of those cult films that tells us much about contemporary culture: in *Time* magazine's summary, Gump is "all-innocent and all-powerful, the ideal guru for the nervous '90s: Forrest God." The enthusiasm this story of a sinless person generates among some Christian critics shows how far discernment and expectations have fallen.

Just as reporters research stories, so reviewers when possible should not rush from theater to computer. In this case, the reviewer read the book that undergirded the movie and offered a comparison.

The success of the movie is particularly revealing because it differs so radically from the novel on which it is based, *Forrest Gump* by Winston Groom. Hollywood always transforms books, and has to, but in the novel (which sold only 10,000 copies when first published in 1986) Gump develops a heavy marijuana habit, neglects his mother (who is forced into the poorhouse and cries herself to sleep every night), and becomes a professional wrestler ("The Dunce"). In the novel he ends up a transient wandering through the south, playing a harmonica and other instruments in city squares while folks throw quarters in a tin cup, and sleeping with a waitress from a striptease joint.

Then came the opportunity to connect the dots:

The book shows a person who sins and needs Christ. It begins with Gump not as a naturally pure child but as one who scorns kids worse off than himself, "retards of all kinds and spasmos." It shows him in adult life not as a rock for flower child Jenny but as a rolling stone: Jenny in the book finally walks out on Gump and marries the assistant sales manager of a roofing company because *she* wants to settle down with a home and family. (In the movie, Jenny dies of a mysterious disease, apparently AIDS; in the book, she starts going to church.)

The movie-makers in essence switched the characters of Gump and Jenny, so that the person of below-normal intelligence desires marriage and other tender mercies that give long-term satisfaction, and the smarter person avoids responsibility. *Forrest Gump* the movie is Hollywood's joke on the religious right: Here's your ideal American, and he's a simpleton.

A two-paragraph ending, with the first paragraph summarizing the message of the review and the second paragraph generalizing to a challenge concerning discernment, can sometimes work well.

Christians who call Forrest Gump a theological film are right—but the movie is a spiritual counterfeit. The apostle Paul knew the limitations of man's wisdom, but he did not substitute for it man's stupidity. He wrote that "Greeks look for wisdom, but we preach Christ crucified . . . for the foolishness of God is wiser than man's wisdom, and the weakness of God is stronger than man's strength." *Forrest Gump* the movie tells us that *man's* weakness is stronger than man's wisdom.

Discerning Christians, by comparing Paul and Gump, can use the movie as a springboard to evangelism. For Christians who embrace *Forrest Gump*, however, the title of a J.B. Phillips book rings true: *Your God Is Too Small*. If we desire movies that display faith in original innocence, our cultural goal will be the humanistic movies of the Production Code era and the television shows of the 1950s. But, since the Bible presents the truth about original sin and God's grace, should we settle for so little?

What are we willing to settle for? In part, that depends on what we expect, and that in turn relates to the pretensions of authors (or *auteurs*) and conventional critics. When critics try to turn theological milk into meat, as occurred when Gump went over the hump and became a blockbuster, it is important to point out overreaching. On the other hand, when milk is depicted as poison, it is time to come to the rescue, as in this coverage of the controversy surrounding one television show.

Gentle Barney has become passé among the grade-school set. The Power Rangers are kick-boxing him into extinction. Today the top-rated children's show is the Mighty Morphin Power Rangers, the Fox Network's saga of five teenagers who transform into karate-chopping superheroes. Children's enthusiasm for the Power Rangers—and for the accompanying merchandise—has turned them into a billion dollar industry.

During the "Freshman orientation" for new Republican legislators, the lawmakers' children were elated to discover that their babysitters were none other than the Power Rangers. While Newt Gingrich praised them as "multi-ethnic role models," the Canadian Broadcast Standards Council banned the program. After three boys, aged six and five, kicked to death a 5-year-old girl, Norway pulled the show from the air. So did Sweden and Denmark. Parents and teachers around the world are noticing how playground rough-housing now includes karate moves and power kicks.

With background set out, it was time to ask key questions, and then suggest some answers.

Are the Power Rangers good role models, as the Speaker of the House says, or are they a violent threat to children and society? Should Christians let their children watch the Power Rangers?

In evaluating children's television, the issue is not merely whether a program contains acts of violence, but what the violence means. Some studies, which attempt to be scientific by formulating quantifiable data, simply count the number of violent acts in a program. Thus, a clown getting hit in the face with a pie counts the same as a woman getting bludgeoned to death. Under this methodology, a Road Runner cartoon comes out looking worse than a slasher movie. But violence in a slapstick comedy, or in a drama where good is in conflict with evil, has a very different meaning and impact than the violence in a program that glorifies evil by giving viewers the vicarious experience of butchering someone.

In the Power Rangers, the forces of good are battling the forces of evil. Wholesome teenagers are joining forces to protect the world from the villains Lord Zedd, Rita Repulsa, and their hordes of monsters. The Power Rangers inhabit a universe of moral clarity, with sharp boundaries between right and wrong and no ambiguity about what is good and what is evil. In our age of moral relativism, Christians should applaud the clear-cut moral universe of the Power Rangers, in which absolutes are real and worth fighting for.

Reviewer Ed Veith, while noting that children who are kicking each other are watching too much TV and need to be taught the difference between fantasy and reality, thus blew away overblown concerns about violence. He then went on to present some real problems with the program.

> Although the show distinguishes between good and evil, its treatment seldom goes beyond the symbolic. The bad guys are ugly; the good guys are "cute." While traditional children's stories used the symbolism of appearance, good and evil were also matters of character. Villains were bad because they did bad things: They stole, bullied, and hurt people. Heroes and heroines were good because they were kind, brave, and just. Though the Power Rangers often give heavy-handed lessons about eating healthy food, going to school, and protecting the environment, they seldom model the deeper inner virtues.

What differentiates a Christian worldview review from the garden variety is the deeper thrust contained in the final three paragraphs.

> The major value communicated by the program is group identity. The five teenagers, of various races and genders, constitute an in-group. They go to school together, hang out together at the local juice bar, and then morph into superheroes. Themes of friendship, belonging, and group solidarity are brought out strongly on the show. Though these qualities can be valuable, the effect on children who are obsessed with popularity, peer pressure, and conformity may not be wholly benign.
>
> This exaltation of the group over the individual is part of the Eastern influence that is looming ever larger in American popular culture. Japan not only animates most of the Saturday morning cartoons, it is supplying the new breed of children's heroes, from Ninja Turtles to the "Superhuman Samurai Syber-Squad"—complete with zen-masters and allusions to Eastern mysticism. The Western tradition is worth passing down.
>
> Traditional American heroes have been rugged individuals, even social outcasts, who often stood up against the group. The Power Rangers are a clique. Christians need to teach their children that in order to stand up against the Lord Zedds of the world they will sometimes have to be Lone Rangers.

That is a good review: turning upside down the usual critique and always probing deeper but with specific detail rather than hysteria. It is not necessary to go looking for theological significance in films: Even thoroughly undistinguished efforts try to ground themselves in something greater by playing off biblical references that resonate even when—and perhaps especially when—viewers have only a dim memory of the stories from whence they come.

Hollywood's look at the salvation of society takes a quirky turn down the dusty trails of the Old West in *The Quick and the Dead.* Starring Sharon Stone as Lady Ellen, this melodrama is replete with sexual and religious references, not the least of which deal with salvation. Lady makes her significant entrance to the remote township of Redemption via the way of all men: the unkempt graveyard. She not only scorns death but brings death: Her goal is to even the score with an old enemy, John Herod (Gene Hackman), by means of an annual shootout contest. Herod is the boss of Redemption, the murderer of children, and an extortionist who persecutes the townsfolk to the point of desperation.

Many of the most interesting westerns offer a biblical counterpoint to frontier savagery, and here the character of Cort (Russell Crowe), a former member of Herod's gang turned minister, is supposed to perform that function. But Cort is confused: He tells Lady of his conversion, then confesses that his good works are penance for sins he believes can never be forgiven. Lady agrees.

Again, in classic form, Cort has sworn off gunfighting but is forced by bad guys into a series of shootouts. Cort comes out ahead. Instead of rejoicing over his survival, however, Lady is cynical and throws mild insults his way. As a subplot, Lady makes points for feminists by blasting a rapist to smithereens, revealing sensitivity about all this nasty gunslinging, and dressing for (sexual) success.

Eventually, Lady and Cort cooperate to overcome Herod, but after Lady delivers the mortal blow she remains as jaded and dead inside as when she arrived. Cort makes Lady no offer of hope. He receives the Marshal's star from Lady's hand, but there is no new creature or new creation in this town; no one has changed as a result of Lady's life or Herod's death. . . . It's really no laughing matter that revenge is labeled as redemption. In short, there is no redemption in Redemption.

Along with distinguishing between biblical wisdom and gussied up attempts to make foolishness seem profound, cultural correspondents need to keep in mind their task of both representing readers and teaching them. Reviewer Pam Johnson, as she blasted to smithereens the pretensions of *The Quick and the Dead*, did not fail to note "explicit, close-up depictions of slimeball gunfighters being shot through various parts of their anatomy."

It is always important to warn readers about violence, sexual suggestiveness, and profanity, but merely totaling up the unseemliness is a task for an accountant, not a writer. While one major reviewer error is not to tell moviegoers about what will repel them, another is to attempt to be holier-than-God by declaring that evidence of man's depravity, which the Scriptures emphasize so emphatically, is off-limits for Christians today. One *World* review avoided both debacles by noting that the film *Rob Roy* was not:

> an easy film for Christians today to watch. Audiences should be prepared for the unblinking eye of director Michael Caton-Jones: Crudities and ruthless evils were common in this period, and the film includes explicit scenes of sexual violence and torture. The difference that sets *Rob Roy* above other films is the point of view . . . within which context man's depravity is explored. Watching *Rob Roy*, the audience rightly cringes at cruelty and weeps with the defenseless.

That review in *World* drew much harsh criticism from readers, and thus raised important questions about the fit of a reviewer's two goals (representing readers but also teaching them). "The warning for Christians was not strong enough," one writer of a letter to the editor stated. "Many like me will not want to subject minds and spirits to that level of evil." Another letter, after objecting to the description of *Rob Roy* as "high artistry" despite its inclusion of violence, provided "notice to cancel our subscription and refund us the rest of our money before you use it to support something else that we don't believe in."

World came right back with reviews of three more violent films. Two of them, *Johnny Mnemonic* and *Die Hard with a Vengeance*, were easy to characterize as not God-glorifying. But the third film, *Braveheart*, required Pam Johnson to use the first person in her review so as to warn potential viewers while not giving a philosophical inch.

> Some Christians will say that *Braveheart's* realistic, graphic scenes of medieval warfare and torture should never have been filmed. I disagree. The context of violence is vital, and no one who

sees *Braveheart*'s historically accurate portrayal of war as hell is likely to join the nearest gang.

Still, Christians who disapprove of all violence in film should not see this movie. If they do, they will miss a stirring depiction of William Wallace, 13th-century Scottish freedom fighter.

A later paragraph provided warning about the film's ending.

One final caveat for potential audiences: History records that Wallace was drawn and quartered, and *Braveheart* faithfully depicts his death—including his final prayers asking God to help him through it. It is all extremely heroic, but it is not comfortable watching the public torture and execution of a good man.

The goal was not only to represent the readers but also to treat the film fairly while standing up for a biblical point—and an important one it is. One irritated letter writer quoted Paul's injunction in Philippians 4:8 to meditate about "whatever is noble, whatever is right, whatever is pure, whatever is lovely, whatever is admirable. . . ." However, Paul writes about explicit evil in the first chapter of Romans and elsewhere: He clearly does not mean us to be unaware of depravity.

Should it be said that inspired biblical authors write about problems but do not describe violence or unlawful sexual practices, passages such as those highlighting Jael's assassination of Sisera (Judges 4 and 5 describe it in five graphic ways); the gang-rape, murder, and subsequent dismemberment of the Levite's concubine (Judges 19); and the adultery of God's people (Ezekiel 23) are vivid. Many other biblical passages make it clear that—to emphasize the point again—the heavens declare the glory of God but the streets display the sinfulness of man.

Should it be said that those passages are inappropriate for us, we need to be reminded of God's promise: "All Scripture is God-breathed and is useful for teaching, rebuking, correcting and training in righteousness, so that the man of God may be thoroughly equipped for every good work" (2 Timothy 3:16–17 NIV). We cannot do better than the inspired authors of the Bible: They show us that even the grotesque, in Bible-based context, is useful for our education and sanctification.

Often we are not equipped for good work until we comprehend the bad and understand from our own experience the need to fight it. You should not praise movies or books that revel in evil and glorify evildoers, but some education concerning man's depravity increases our understanding of the need for Christ's sacrifice. Sadly, the tendency of Christian publications in film reviewing, as in other areas, has been to praise movies with smiling faces and warn against those with red blood. Many reviewers roll over for smarmy products officially designated as "uplifting," but uplift apart from Christ is idolatry.

What has rightly been decried as the "feminization of the church" often had led reviewers to shy away from action-adventure pictures that, when based in biblical morality, portray the development of character under extreme pressure. That is too bad artistically and theologically: Movies are best when they move, and Christianity is not a *nice* religion. Just as priests used hyssop to spray the blood of sacrifices on the people in Moses' time, so Christ had to shed his blood, not just preach, to free us from sin. Christians should not hide from hard realities either in life or on film.

The same issues—how much depravity to show, how it should be contextualized, and how an unwillingness to acknowledge the presence of monsters in the world—can be debated in assessments of children's literature.

At the American Booksellers Association convention last month, the long-term tendency to make children's stories reflect the evening news continued: There were books on divorce, wife and child abuse, and so on. In many of the books it seems as if no one's right and no one's wrong. Things just happen. The father walks out. The kidnapper cometh. The rapist returns. There's no protection against evil, no reason for it, and not even much rhyme in these sad books for sophisticated kids.

In the output of some publishers at the Christian Booksellers Association convention last week, however, the other extreme is evident. One "beginning reader" book about the Exodus has colorful drawings of Egyptians chasing Israelites across the Red Sea. There's tension in the text also: "'Hurry up,' said the people. 'Hurry up!'" But, when we turn the page, the water has rolled back, with no mention of massive Egyptian drowning. A pop-eyed Pharoah stands on the opposite bank but the Egyptian soldiers have simply disappeared for a time, perhaps soon to reappear.

Other books in an early reader series tell the story of hiding the baby Moses, without mentioning the Pharoah's murderous intentions, and the story of Noah, without mentioning why God sent a flood or what happened to those outside the ark. In a book titled *Bing!* David bings Goliath on the head with a pebble; the giant is woozy. Since there is no mention of David cutting off Goliath's head, a child might wonder whether there will be a rematch.

These monster stories lack true monsters and do not make clear their demise. The stories show part of God's love, but they omit his holiness. Some secular psychologists have pointed out the usefulness of semi-gruesome fairy tales: Children know there is danger in the world, and they need to have a feeling of control over it. But Christian understanding, based on real biblical history, goes deeper: There is danger in the world, and sometimes we cannot overcome it in our own power, but Jesus can in his.

The facts of man's sinfulness are crucial for reporter or reviewer to relate, and films such as *Nell* that espouse natural human goodness deserve spirited criticism.

Although sprinkles of Scripture, fundamentalist phraseology ("The Lord led you here"), and spiritual buzzwords ("evildoers," "guardian angel") find their way into the dialogue, the filmmakers do not embrace the biblical fact of the Fall. They do not separate depraved nature from God's original creation, but instead deal with the evident problem by turning to romantic rationalism. By the end of the film, Nell's "natural" morality has brought about the redemption of people corrupted by civilization and caused them to discover human love and higher truth.

At a child's level, Disney's *The Jungle Book* was offering a parallel antigospel with a twist of feminism, pointing:

its bony finger at terrible men who intrude upon the jungle with their greedy civilization. This picture could have been a student production at PC University: All the men in the picture are attributed a greater or lesser degree of guilt for the woes of this world, but every woman is either an innocent or desirable mate. Apparently the female of the species is pollution-free.

While *Nell* is nuanced and *The Jungle Book* is melodramatic, they share an unrealistic view of reality . . . *Nell* and *The Jungle Book* are based on the premise that a child left to the education of Mother Nature will grow up to be a purely good person.

What a good reviewer does, in short, is to take the same things that other people see and place them under a biblical lens to examine both their brilliant facets and their flaws. In that sense, although both a reviewer and a reporter practice biblically directed journalism, the reporter's task is generally to cover what most readers have not yet looked at, and the reviewer's what they have observed but not truly seen.

CHAPTER ELEVEN

First Person Accounts and Sports Stories

One of the most frequently asked questions by new reporters concerns whether, or how much, they can become part of the story. Part of the question is stylistic: Is first person ever allowed? Part is substantive: Should a reporter be a "fly on the wall," listening to conversations but not affecting them in any way?

As we have seen, Samuel Adams was content to keep himself in the background. His reluctance to become part of the story was tactically brilliant: By assuming the role of reporter rather than protagonist he was able all the better to massage the egos of those who demanded attention, such as John Hancock. It was also biblically correct: We are not to grab the best seats at the table or at church.

Throughout much of the twentieth century, American journalists also have tried to remain out of the story, and have demonstrated that standoffishness by going to great lengths to avoid the use of the first person: Writing "This reporter" rather than "I" has been one of the clumsy circumlocutions. Sometimes a modesty like that of Adams made writers more comfortable with such devices, but often their rationale emerged from the secular understanding of objectivity: describing an impersonal universe impersonally.

The rebellion against impersonality that has gone on for a generation now has mightily influenced journalism. With neutrality disappearing in appearance as well as fact, the battle of the future will be between existentialist subjectivity and biblical objectivity. The choice for reporters, although most will not understand it in these terms, will be, "Do I present my version of the story, or God's vision (as close as I, a fallen sinner, can come to it)? Do I practice egocentrism or theocentrism?"

INNOCENTS ABROAD: FIRST PERSON ACCOUNTS

Reviewers, as the last chapter noted, should not only represent readers but also educate them. Reporters can use the first person altruistically and intelligently, rather than in a self-glorifying way, when they show themselves not as superheroes but as innocents abroad (to use Mark Twain's term). Use of the first person is suicidal when reporters put on airs, but used in a self-deprecating way, with the writer becoming a partly naive tourist, it can be a dead-on transformer of dull, faceless stories into ones with plots.

For example, one *World* investigative cover story examined whether members of the Evangelical Council for Financial Accountability who have tax-deductible status were making available to the public some basic tax records, as required by law. The issue is important, since we are to render unto Caesar what is Caesar's—Jesus specifically mandated us to do so in relation to a question about taxes—but it is not one that quickens the pulse or is likely to generate a made-for-TV movie. Writer Joe Maxwell, however, turned what could have been a quagmire for readers into a quest.

> Tree-sparse Gundersen Drive in Carol Stream, Ill., has lost some tax-exempt tenants to upstart Colorado Springs, but numerous evangelical superstructures remain.
> I'm driving my tiny rental car into the National Association of Evangelicals parking lot on what is known locally by some as "Holy Row." This is the first leg of a week-long journey to 10 evangelical organizations based in and around Chicago, Ill., Orlando, Fla., and Washington, D.C.
> I'm on a quest of sorts—searching for financial disclosure.

The article had to include financial details, but a spoonful of specific detail garnered during visits to the various groups made that medicine go down.

> A wooden pelican with a fish in its mouth stands on the table in the NAE receiving room. . . .
>
> The Orlando boulevard to Campus Crusade for Christ's massive headquarters is lined—even in mid-winter—with blossoming pink azaleas. After I speak with two receptionists, an impressive man clad in tie, blue blazer, and pressed shirt asks me into a nearby conference room. . . ."I don't think we publish that [the Form 990], but you are welcome to the [audit] report," he says in a rich, baritone voice that could convince Attila the Hun to accept all four Spiritual Laws.
>
> At Ligonier Ministries in suburban Lake Mary, Fla., a painting of an English fox hunt hangs over a receptionist.

The writer, by putting himself in the story, is also able to convey the nervousness of officials.

> I'm taking notes on a yellow legal pad. He seems to notice. "I can give [the information] to you," he eventually says. . . . "Are you writing a story?"
>
> She is not sure about the tax returns. I pull out a copy of the federal law on disclosing Form 990s. She reads highlighted portions. "To be honest, I'm caught a little bit off guard."
>
> She'll gladly give me an audit (which she does), but adds: "Tax returns? No. . . . Why? To my knowledge we've never released those to somebody coming off the street."
>
> "It's public knowledge," I say politely.
>
> "No, tax returns aren't."
>
> "Do you file a 990?"
>
> "Yes."
>
> "Then it's public knowledge."
>
> "Okay, if you say so. . . . I still don't know just what it is you are doing," she says.
>
> A story on Christian 501(c)3s.
>
> "I can't go by something you hand me. That doesn't mean anything to me."

The first-person usage also allows for self-deprecating humor, with a running gag about lacking a business card.

An older woman sits at a desk, answering phones. "Hello. My name is Joe Maxwell and I would like to see a copy of your most recent annual audit and tax returns."

"Do you have a card?"

Oops. I don't! I've got to get some of those things.

They ask who I am, and to see credentials. I say I'm a journalist with *World*, and apologize for not having a business or press card. I show them a copy of *World* magazine.

Jeff is flipping through it. "We're just a little suspicious," he says.

After calling their finance manager, Carolyn suggests I make a "formal" request in writing. From my briefcase I produce a typed request, which is not, however, on *World* stationery, and Carolyn views it skeptically.

"I guess we're just suspicious," Jeff reiterates.

But there is a serious point to all this, which the writer makes explicit at the conclusion of the story.

In the coming years, Christian organizations can, in fact, expect tough scrutiny from segments of society increasingly hostile to religion—and $5,000 fines could be serious threats. Outsiders—hostile or not—will ask tough questions. Christian groups that use federal tax exemptions should not deny any taxpayer a chance to examine the top salaries.

Yet four of ten groups surveyed by *World* flatly refused a request for lawful disclosure. Beyond that, two more—the NAE and CCC—initially refused disclosure, claiming to be exempt churches, an assertion any non-Christian might reasonably question.

World's survey was not designed to evaluate the work or mission of any of the organizations visited; in fact, they were chosen because of their good reputations. But good groups that do not comply with every detail of the law are handing a sword to those who would seek to destroy Christian nonprofits. The best form of resisting such hostility—overt or disguised—is not by refusing lawful requests, but by so adhering to high moral and legal standards of disclosure that an adversary can do nothing but commend a group's integrity.

Many evangelical organizations live in this tension—being not of this world and yet, by their tax-free status, being very much tied to it. If they accept the benefits of Caesar's policy, then the witness of

ECFA-member organizations must include a cheerful willingness also to live by Caesar's rules. My journey for disclosure complete, it would appear that Jesus' words aren't yet fully realized among many evangelical organizations: In the United States, "Render therefore unto Caesar the things which are Caesar's" also means disclosing some financial information.

Action-adventure stories also can be improved at times by the judicious use of "*I.*" Roy Maynard's *World* story about illegal immigration along the Texas-Mexico border first set the stage.

> The carriage-driver's horse wore blinders, but he was too old and too tired to be spooked by the cars rumbling past him in the streets of Piedras Negras. His back sagged lower than the peso against the dollar, and a jutted-out left hip showed that he'd be crippled by arthritis within a year. The horse's name was Samuel, and the cabby was Ernesto. That's about the extent of useful information he was willing to provide. Yes, he said, this Mexican border town was known for its nightly tide of illegal immigration into the United States. But no, he said, he didn't know anything about it. He knew about the tourists, and would I like to see another market, find a nice restaurant?
>
> The carriage, painted with garish pastels and upholstered with a fabric surely once used as drapery, rattled over the potholes. It rolled past the occasional federale and by the dozens of young men smoking cigarettes on the street corners.
>
> "What about these men?" I asked through an interpreter.
>
> "They are maybe going to go across, yes," Ernesto replied. "Many of them stay in the hotels until it is the night they are to go. . . ."
>
> "What about the river?" I asked.
>
> "No, no, it is not safe. I will not take you there. I will stop working soon anyway. You don't know what you will find. The coyotes, they are dangerous."
>
> He was speaking of the alien smugglers, the men who charge fees of $300 to $500 for a supervised river crossing and the promise of a van ride to San Antonio, Fort Worth, or Dallas. Stay away, Ernesto said, stay away from the coyotes.

After descriptive detail about the border town and its short-term residents waiting to go across, it was time to come back to the river and the coyotes, with the first-person presence of the writer adding drama.

To the left was a decaying railroad bridge with timbers and ties blackened with creosote-soaked preservative. There was no sign of anyone; it seemed that the nightly crossings must have already been made. The Rio Grande was a 30-feet-wide slow eddy at this point, quiet and unhurried. When the cab stopped, I got out to take a closer look. How far to the other side? How deep? How cold?

"Everyone has left," Alphonso said through his friend. "Maybe I can bring you back tomorrow, during the daylight, and you can see people then."

I shook my head and started toward the embankment. The hillside leading down to the river wasn't steep, and the bright moon outlined a rough pathway. I went down slowly, carefully, and reached level ground about 20 yards from the river. I found myself walking on denuded sand, indicating the Rio Grande was down a little.

To my left, between the bridge and me, I heard murmuring. I came around a small hill and I saw them. Men, Hispanic men of various ages and shapes and sizes, all of them quiet and intently following oral instructions. There were about two dozen of them; they were hunkered down, taking off their clothes, down to their briefs, and laying their blue jeans in front of them lengthwise. I was about 25 feet from the group; I wondered if they had seen me.

They had. The only one not taking his clothes off—the coyote, I assumed—put his hand inside his unbuttoned shirt. The half-dressed men turned to him, but he paid no attention. He wore a denim shirt, sandy boots, and a white straw cowboy hat. His mustache was untrimmed and his jeans had holes at the knees. He watched me for a moment, and when I didn't react, the tension seemed to ease. His hand came out of his shirt; it was empty.

"American," I said. "Journalist." The words were similar in Spanish, so I thought that might get the idea across. The coyote seemed to consider this for a moment, and he turned his attention back to the men. I must have seemed to present no threat—I probably wasn't the first American to stumble across a moonlight crossing.

The coyote's instructions to the men continued, and they began to place their belongings—shoes, a watch, a wallet, a crucifix—on their jeans. They rolled the jeans into a tight bundle, which the coyote showed them how to hold: he pressed a pantomimed bundle against his ear with one hand. The men did the same with their bundles. Another few sentences in Spanish, and the men looked to each other for a buddy—someone to link hands with for the crossing.

When the coyote nodded, the men stood and formed a line, two-by-two, then slowly walked into the water. For the first 10 feet, the water was only ankle-deep. Halfway through, it was waist-high. At the deepest part, just a few feet from the American bank, it reached chest-level. And then they were across. None stopped to redress; they simply began to climb the embankment on the other side.

Later the cabby told me there was likely a van parked just past the crest of that hill; the coyote would no doubt have an associate who was waiting to receive the men and begin the long drive to San Antonio or Dallas.

When the men had crested the hill, the coyote looked at me. After a few moments he walked off, through the bridge supports and out of sight.

That first person gave life to what could have been a MEGO (Mine Eyes Glaze Over) article. It provided drama and personal involvement for an issue that would otherwise be abstract. The first person can also be used to describe the mazelike qualities of bureaucracy; since almost all readers have had the experience of being shunted from one place or telephone answerer, Joe Maxwell's attempt to learn who truly runs the federal school lunch program provided a point of contact for readers and humor as well.

"Do you know where to find the National School Lunch Program?"

The middle-aged man in a white short-sleeve button-down and tie removes his cigarette from his lips. "Pardon?" he asks.

"Do you know where to find the school lunch program? It's supposed to be housed in the Department of Agriculture."

Standing on the steps of the south wing of the U.S. Department of Agriculture's gargantuan main building, the man wearing a USDA badge blows smoke up toward a crystal blue sky and replies: "I have no idea. Try inside, maybe."

After providing background about the half-century-old program and its role in current political debates—children will starve if Republicans have their way, it was said—the Quixotic quest could continue.

Two guards inside the south wing of the Agriculture Department building aren't any help; they fumble through their directory looking for a listing for the National School Lunch Program. On the walls behind them are photos of the first, small, national headquarters for the USDA, a second larger one, and then the current mammoth "Agriculture Complex," which runs at least 5 city blocks by 5 city blocks. "I got the Food and Drug Administration," a male guard says. "Try calling them up."

Dialing the number he offers taps into the Department of Health and Human Services. No good.

"Do you have any idea where the school lunch program is?" the other guard, a female, is asked.

"No," comes her terse answer. Frustrated, she suggests trying across the street at the USDA's administrative building.

Another building? How could USDA possibly need another building?

Another guard awaits at that entrance. She has no idea where to find the National School Lunch Program offices. What about Ellen Haas? I ask. One recent newspaper article quoted her as running the program.

The directory, in fact, does list Ellen Haas, and the guard calls her to say she has a visitor. Ms. Haas, it turns out, is Undersecretary of Food, Nutrition, and Consumer Services for the U.S. Department of Agriculture. School lunches must somehow fall under her realm.

Up on the second floor, down the wood-grained halls and past oil portraits of former Agriculture Secretaries, is an impressive set of glass doors opening into a suite of about eight offices and a receptionist.

A man in his thirties and a double-breasted brown suit is walking out the door and asks if he can help.

"Is this where the National School Lunch Program is run?"

"That's in Alexandria," he says.

"Doesn't Ellen Haas run the school lunch program?"

"Oh yeah, she runs it," explains Neal Flieger, Ms. Haas's public relations man. (His real title is: Deputy Administrator, Governmental Affairs and Public Information, U.S. Department of Agriculture, Food and Nutrition Services.)

He explains that Ms. Haas just deals with big policy issues, and that the the real administration is done by nearly 2,000 "bureaucrats" in another building in Alexandria.

"The way the bureaucracy works is that people [like Ms. Haas] at the subcabinet level are responsible for developing policy. But the programs are run out of another building," he says.

Another building? Wow. Is a tour possible?

Mr. Flieger seems a bit irritated at this unannounced visit. "Why do you want to see a bunch of people sitting in cubicles?" he asks.

Nonetheless, he offers to meet at the Alexandria building the next morning.

The innocents-abroad theme—*Wow*, the reporter has himself saying—adds humor, but the point again is serious: Readers are being
shown—not just told by orators—that bureaucracy is siphoning off
some of the funds supposedly going to fight hunger. The uncovering
continues.

> In the middle of an affluent section of Alexandria, Park Center
> Office Building 1's downstairs directory lists several commercial
> offices and vendors on the first floor, including a travel agency, fur-
> niture rental company, and hairstylist. Plants and green tile floors give
> the lobby a luscious look. The remainder of the directory, however, is
> exclusively occupied by one entity: "WELCOME TO THE USDA, FOOD
> AND CONSUMER SERVICES," the sign reads, and then lists three long
> columns of USDA Food and Consumer Services departments, sub-
> departments, on and on and on. . . .
>
> The national Food and Consumer Services office in Alexandria
> has about 600 staffers [that administer] seven regional FCS offices
> nationwide with 1,200 staffers. Together they "provide cash and
> food" to state offices that route it to local schools.
>
> Each school district hires its own school food services director, a
> trained professional who makes out meal plans in May and June for
> the entire upcoming school year and submits them to a state nutrition
> supervisor, hired by the state to insure sound nutrition standards at the
> local school level. These state directors then communicate with fed-
> eral employees. . . .
>
> Mr. Flieger hastens to add: "The vast majority of people who are
> involved in administrating and delivering school meals work for the
> state or local government." There are 60,000 or so individual school
> food service directors. . . .
>
> He goes to a desk and produces a copy of a flow chart full of lines
> and boxes. Under Office of the Administrator are three branches—
> Analysis and Evaluation, Consumer Affairs, and Governmental
> Affairs and Public Information—and five unrelated sub-branches:
> Food Stamp Program, Financial Management, Management, Food
> and Consumer Services Regions, and Special Nutrition. Mr. Flieger
> thinks school lunch administrators are located in the Special
> Nutrition section.
>
> He declines a request to visit their offices.

Since the writer had paid his dues by scouting out all these offices,
he could end the article with a mock-hayseed head-scratching.

The whole thing is complicated. It is probably true that the Republicans' call for state block grants is just a sharp plan to garner votes from simple-minded folks who run businesses to make a profit and produce efficient results, not spend money. . . . It seems clear that this federal system of feeding local school children is just too vast to be grasped without years of bureaucratic experience—and maybe not even then.

An article of that sort is far more educationally effective than either perfervid rhetoric or a treatise by a political scientist, because readers can identify with the storyteller and see for themselves what he places before their eyes.

The same sense of being an eyewitness and then arriving at judgment informed another *World* story based in Washington—but this time the flabbergasted head-scratcher was not the writer himself but a cabdriver hired to drive to schools patronized by politicians.

Charles Boateng's Silver Cab Number 125 is a station wagon on a mission. Mr. Boateng, a 37-year-old Ghanan who moved to America 12 years ago, normally carries tourists to D.C. landmarks. Today he is escorting *World* readers toward the landmark preparatory schools of Georgetown, where many of the Democratic Party's top elected and appointed officials send their children.

The cabdriver works hard but makes only $15,000 a year and wonders why President Clinton opposes school choice: "I don't think it is fair. You are the leader of the country, right? You should set an example. If you want people to send their kids to public schools, then why are you sending yours to private schools?"

With that question in mind, the reporter and the cabbie appraise one school attended by Al Gore III and sons of other prominent Democrats who oppose letting poor parents have affordable alternatives to public schools.

The environs of the National Cathedral's rolling driveway exude an Old World aura of European stone, Gothic structures and the sort of emerald lawns that make a John Deere run and an Arnold Palmer weep. Shade trees in just the appropriate spots. Here and there, a flowering white or pink dogwood. Someone spread a cloth! . . . There she sits, sharing the Cathedral's grounds: St. Albans School for Boys, the alma mater of Al Gore. One expects the Dead Poets to convene.

In fact, here come several lads now. School is just out for the day. Most still are wearing blue blazers with slacks; one daring soul is an outrage, having matched khaki shorts with his standard coat; a few have peeled down to their white buttondowns; a shirt tail hangs out here or there. Ah, the rogues are making hay of the rules, aren't they?

Mr. Boateng is standing by his cab now. He is listening more than looking: "Where is the noise?" he asks. "If someone told me that this was a school, you wouldn't believe it. So quiet. So nice." So different from America's public schools, where the best grass often is found in sidewalk cracks or a dope dealer's pocket.

Visits to other schools were similar, and the article ended with Mr. Boateng's conclusion about President Clinton: "If he sends his daughter to private school, then you can't tell others to send theirs to public school."

REPRESENTING THE READER: SPORTS COVERAGE

The laid-back but perceptive reporting that typifies first-person accounts not only personalizes stories but shows readers that there is no need to approach every issue as if it were Armageddon. We should show readers the salient facts in Bible-based contextualization, but we also want to make the reading of our publications interesting and even fun, not an onerous duty. Sports coverage interests new readers, while providing a broad avenue for evocative discussion of basic questions affecting the culture.

Directed sports reporting, like all other kinds, requires elements of narrative, description, and observation. Here is an example depicting a good teacher (who is also a Christian) at work, from a baseball story with a theme of education.

Orioles manager Johnny Oates during a workout ranges over all the spring training complex. During four hours of practice he was almost always moving, always watching, rarely talking: "I want everyone on the team to know I may be watching them at any time," he explained later. The only thing that seemed to upset him is lack of diligence; he yelled at a rightfielder who stood absentmindedly when a coach hit a fly to the centerfielder, "Back him up. If you don't want to do it, let's go home."

Oates does take aside young players to explain probability, which is the basis of baseball strategy. When one rookie at first base seemed puzzled about why to cut off a throw from the outfield in a particular way, Oates explained patiently, "The reason is that you'll cut the ball and get the trailing runner at second much more often than you'll be able to get a runner at home. At the major league level the throw to have a chance at home has to be on a line in the air or on one bounce. That's why you're a cutoff man, not a relay man." Baseball probabilities are based on experience, and Oates is the historian, trying to convey to young men decades of observation, with one goal in mind: Old heads on young bodies.

Reporting of this kind requires you to get right up to the batting cage.

An hour standing next to Reds manager Tony Perez also shows American education as its finest, except for Perez's frequent use of obscenities. With Jamie Quirk, a marginal utility player who is trying to catch on, Perez is insistent: "Keep your body behind the ball. Use that bleeping weight you've got on you. . . . Stay behind it, get your hands in front, save your hands for the last moment. . . . Keep your body back, keep the ball in front of you. Hit the bleeper on top." And Quirk does hit the next few pitches much more sharply, with Perez giving instant reinforcement: "See what you did. See where you hit that bleeping ball. See it. Got to keep the ball in front of you."

The advantage of being up close is that you see character revealed in small ways. Instead of merely concentrating on stars, you can see how God is working on players who mostly ride the bench.

One of Oates' favorites is Tim Hulett, a marginal infielder who is also the team's Baseball Chapel leader and autographs baseballs with a citation of Romans 6:23 next to his name: "For the wages of sin is death, but the gift of God is eternal life in Christ Jesus our Lord." Hulett is practicing catching this spring so he can be a late-inning fill-in behind the plate if needed. Jerry Narron, the Baltimore catching coach, was watching as Hulett tried to catch cut fastballs and devilish curves.

"I didn't blink," Hulett reported after surviving one hard-to-handle pitch, and Narron praised him: "No blink, no cringe." Oates, a former catcher, watched as a pitch got by Hulett, and then said quietly, "Just knock it down with the big part of the glove. Stop pulling away." As Hulett listened and improved, Oates watched what he was creat ing and said, "Good, good."

The contrast between Christian perseverance and spoiled whining then became evident.

Oates watched as Paul Carey, a 25-year-old minor leaguer with a number better suited to an end in football—88—stood in the batting cage and complained about the teammate who was throwing to him, Todd Frowirth. Frowirth's unusual sidearm, almost underhand style was bothering Carey, who was muttering, "Hard to concentrate." . . . When Carey swung at and missed the next two pitches, he weakly asked another coach who had joined the observation team, "Elrod, those last two high?" Hendricks said, "Not the last one, maybe the one before." Then Carey hit two weak ground balls and said, "Not my fault. Those were balls." Hendricks replied, "You didn't have to swing at them." And Oates was there all the time, watching.

This article then presented more detail about struggling players and returned to the description of what a good teacher does.

What Perez sees is not what an ordinary observer sees. Hal Morris, the Reds' first baseman, who batted .318 in 1991 but was injured part of last year and dropped to .271, put on an impressive display of power during his first batting practice session; ball after ball went over the fence, to the delight of a teenager on the other side who had brought his glove and positioned himself well. Perez, though, thought Morris was swinging for the fences too much, and would not be able to duplicate the batting practice spectacular dur- ing a game when pitchers would be throwing him knee-high fast- balls. Perez kept telling Morris, "If the ball is low, don't try to lift it. Stay on top and see what you can do. Nice and easy. You want slow feet, quick hands."

And results can come fast.

As Morris listened carefully, adjusted, and got it, Perez was pleased: "Yes, that's a bleeping line drive. You don't have to hit bleeping flies to drive in runs; just make contact. Keep the ball in front of you, you want to see it when you hit it. Keep that bleeper in front of you, see it when you hit it, stay low." Morris confessed that he was blind but now he saw: "I wasn't seeing that low ball before, now I can."

Once you have paid your dues by providing solid reporting with specific detail, readers will indulge you in making explicit conclusions concerning your theme:

> Making the National League takes even more drill than making the National Spelling Bee, except that there is often no other activity to fall back on should a player be eliminated. Major leaguers need to be fundamentalists, with emphasis on the fundamentals of their positions: an hour of ball-blocking for catchers, bunt-defending for infielders, hitting the cutoff man for outfielders.
>
> There is constant teaching, and constant mentoring. If American education followed the baseball pattern of apprenticeship and careful attention to the basics, neither illiteracy nor the trade deficit would be growing.

Structurally, sports articles often have a three-part beginning, starting with description of the athlete in action.

> It was only a spring training workout, but Boston Red Sox pitcher Roger Clemens grunted as he threw pitch after pitch in the warm sunshine of Fort Myers, Florida. . . . He is determined to return to league-leading form this year, and also is thinking about getting back to his theological roots.

Then a quotation:

> "My father passed away when I was nine," Clemens told *World*. "When I was young going to church was like the sun coming up. You could count on it, Wednesdays and Sundays. Then when he passed away, my mom took on three jobs, raised six of us. She was the force behind us all, she still is, but that church consistency was hard. . . . I've never really had it since then . . . there's so much media and off-the-field stuff. . . ."

Finally the nut graf:

> *So much stuff.* That's the constant complaint, and plea, of conscientious baseball players now. An old Russian tale describes a chief-

tain who fought hard for the czar centuries ago and received the award of a suit of armor; the chieftain put it on and, crossing a river on his way home, fell off his horse and drowned. Today's players enjoy the money and, to a certain extent, the adulation that comes with fame, but some of the most prominent seem to yearn for a life and faith unchoked by weeds, a simpler life of bat and ball and, sometimes, Bible. That's what spring training means to sports chiefs like Clemens and Kirby Puckett: a time to touch home.

Some Christian sports profiles tend to get talky, as writers present players' testimonies. You may do that succinctly, but try to show players whenever possible displaying in action the difference in their lives that a reliance on Christ makes, rather than preaching about it.

Reynolds during batting practice says "good pitch" to the pitcher when he misses one across the plate. He says "oh, Harold" to himself when he swings at a bad one, says "get down, ball" when he hits a fly out, and laughs when he hits a series of line drives. "I'm feeling pretty good up here," he said. "Knowing about Jesus' love allows me to relax; I don't have to earn His love by what I do. Besides, reading the Bible, the sweep of history, helps to keep things in perspective."

Avoid being too quick to claim for Christ anyone who displays a nodding acquaintance with God. You should not hesitate to criticize lazy stars with jocular theology.

Spring training contains frequent lessons about the importance of glorifying God by not taking talent for granted. Kevin Mitchell, the National League's Most Valuable Player in 1989 when he led the league in homeruns (47) and runs batted in (125), reported to the Cincinnati camp in 1993 on the last possible day before incurring fines. Before going out to take his first batting practice he talked about how he "grew up in the church" under the tutelage of his mother, who is a missionary to prisons within the Church of God in Christ denomination. Mitchell said, "It really helps to believe in the Man Upstairs. You lose your sanity if you don't. When you're down He'll help you." Then, with his gut hanging out—sportswriters had asked the team's publicity director how many pounds Mitchell was overweight—the man downstairs floundered in the batting cage, popping up balls and showing all that faith without work is fat.

Mitchell would spend half the season on the disabled list. His experience contrasted with that of another player who showed discipline both in batting practice and Bible study.

Reggie Sanders came under Perez's withering examination during batting practice: "I want you to see everything you hit. See it when you hit. You want your head to stay back and your hands to cross the plate." Sanders paid rapt attention and successfully made adjustments, so he gained favor with his manager: "Good. Yes! Yes!! Yes! Keep your head down. You see how you hit the ball when you do it that way. Keep working on it!"

And off the field, sitting in the locker room, Sanders spoke of his faith: "I truly believe in the Lord. . . . If I have a good day or a bad day, I take it all the same, because I realize that whether someone is cheering me for a good play or booing me for a bad, the Lord always loves me for what I truly am. Even if no one else truly loves me, He does, and I'm always trying to learn more about him." Teammate Bip Roberts said he goes to Baseball Chapel meetings on Sunday but "during the season there's not a lot of time to do much else." Sanders, however, said, "I work at baseball and I work at my faith. On the road there's lots of time to study, so I use the NIV Study Bible and that helps me get deeper into the Word."

When doing celebrity profiles, be sure to ask the important questions that secular reporters ignore.

The Associated Press reporter hanging around the White Sox clubhouse in Sarasota on March 1 was bored. His editor, realizing that some fans mix up Michael Jordan and God, was requiring him to write a story about the deity's doings every day, but not much seemed to be happening. "Michael shagged fly balls today. . . . He took batting practice and hit 10 fly balls, 10 ground balls, and 10 line drives . . . so what? Have you run across any other angle?"

Yes. The more interesting story is not what Jordan is doing to a baseball, but what God may be doing to him. "These days I think about God a lot," Jordan told *World*." I read the Bible a lot. Of all the books I read, that's the one I do read. I see that whatever happens, happens for a reason; I wouldn't be here without the will of God. And my father's dying last year, I try to get something positive from that."

Jordan said he has been thinking about his parents, and about how he should bring up his three small children. "My mother and father used to have two jobs so they could supply us with a better life than the one they had. And we had to go to church every Sunday. I learned that God's in charge. . . ."

To conclude an article about Michael Jordan's learning about God while being treated as God by some of his fans, also interview a fan.

> After practice Jordan autographed a photo for a 35-year-old man in a wheelchair. The back of Tom Wright, from Pittsfield, Massachusetts, was broken in birth; he has spent his life since then paralyzed. Seven years ago Wright had his picture taken with Jordan before a game at the Boston Garden between the Chicago Bulls and the Boston Celtics; Wright framed the photo and hung it on his wall. He took it off the wall and out of the frame to journey to Sarasota, hoping that Jordan would autograph it. "This is a great day," Wright exulted as he stared at the signed photo. "I'll put it back on my wall. It will be there forever."
>
> No, it won't. One day it will turn to dust. And Jordan, who is worshipped by some of his fans, knows that he cannot make the lame walk.

Sports writing is not an opportunity to indulge in hero worship; directed reporting regarding sports, as in other areas, depends on an understanding of man's sinfulness but God's willingness to change his creatures. Here is an example of mixing brief descriptive detail into a discussion of character development:

> Will Clark showed total concentration in the batting cage and then went out to field over 100 ground balls to his right so he could take a split-second off his pivot when throwing back to a pitcher covering first base. Although Clark is generally regarded as one of the better-fielding first basemen, he went back for more work on defense when the official practice ended. "I got this work ethic from my parents," he said. "If kids don't develop it when they're young, it's hard to get later on. Maybe you can have them watch people who are admirable and hope they'll imitate them."

Then came the nut graf:

> Clark had hit on a question that is key not only for baseball but for the country. Issues of welfare reform, drug rehabilitation, and

prison sentencing all hinge on the teaching of responsibility and other virtues to those who often have not exercised self-control. Players and coaches agree that for both worship and work, the most effective teaching comes early . . . but there are differences of opinion about the likelihood of change among adults.

Although the article did not make the comparisons explicit, a discussion of Jewish, secular, Catholic, and evangelical emphases followed.

Theory #1 was voiced by Sandy Koufax, the great Los Angeles Dodgers pitcher of the 1960s who dropped in on the Rangers camp late in February as a favor to Texas manager Kevin Kennedy, a friend. "You can't teach character," Koufax said as he prepared to teach pitchers the technique of using their legs more to remove some of the burden from their shoulder. "It's something people develop in a thousand different ways, or they don't." Koufax, 58, who is remembered not only for his Hall of Fame performances but for refusing to pitch in the World Series on Yom Kippur, seemed pessimistic: "Players with bad traits don't change much as adults. That's the way it is now, and was when I was playing."

Dave Winfield, a future Hall-of-Famer perhaps concluding his career with the Minnesota Twins at age 42, presented Theory #2. He turned aside questions about religion but emphasized the significance of "some kind of harrowing physical experience, something that makes a player think, 'I'm not invincible, this talent came be taken away from me.'" The shock "has to be sharp," Winfield emphasized: "You don't see those changes in an adult unless there's a sharp break. By then it's usually too late."

Theory #3 is somewhat more optimistic: Players, instead of undergoing physical disaster, can pick up good habits that will change at least their surface behavior. Tom Kelly, the 43-year-old Twins manager, went to St. Mary's High School in South Amboy, New Jersey, and learned there that "players can be trained to take responsible actions." He wants players to "make a ritual out of doing it right," and mutters expletives about players who fool around. . . .

Theory #4 is the truly optimistic one. Mike Easler, the Red Sox batting coach—and a Baptist minister licensed by his home church in San Antonio—presented it while chewing on sunflower seeds before a wind-swept workout in Fort Myers. "A player doesn't have to wait for something desperately physical to knock him down. The apostle Paul didn't break a leg: God simply made him a new creature in Christ, with old things passed away. . . . My job is to mold a guy, teach him to be humble, and I pray that God will work on him so he will change not just on the outside but on the inside. . . ."

Directed sports reporting of this sort, then, displays in microcosm one of the goals of directed reporting generally: to show the nature of the world that God has made by reporting the blessings and curses that come from following or ignoring Him. The goal is not to glamorize players, but to see them as sinners who, like those not athletically gifted, need God's greatest gift.

CHAPTER TWELVE

Modern Journalism Emerges

Now we approach the time when leading American journalists forgot what their predecessors had learned about man and God, and began to contend that man could be God. The change came slowly at first: Horace Greeley's rationale remained dormant for a generation, in part because his utopianism to some degree undergirded the northern movement toward civil war and helped fuel southern reaction.

The American Civil War ended up not only as a slaughterhouse of men but a killing field of utopian thought. The blood-soaked realism that sank in and powerfully affected the politics of the 1870s and 1880s led to a concentration on individual morality that left those demanding social restructuring on the fringes of American society. By the 1890s, a new generation of reporters had arisen, and some newspapers and magazines began giving favorable publicity to the work of "Christian socialists" such as Professor Richard Ely.

Ely, founder of the American Economic Association, strove to apply principles enunciated by Brisbane and Greeley to all of American society. Demanding that all unite behind the "coercive philanthropy . . . of governments, either local, state, or national," he received favorable coverage from journalists who also fulsomely praised the gospel of salvation-through-government promoted by books such as William H.

Fremantle's *The World as the Subject of Redemption*. Government alone, Fremantle asserted, "can embrace all the wants of its members and afford them the universal instruction and elevation which they need"

Much of the new doctrine came in old wineskins. Fremantle, for example, praised the worship of governmental power as a mere further-ance of Christian worship of God, with the state taking on the church's traditional functions of charity.

> We find the Nation alone fully organized, sovereign, independent, universal, capable of giving full expression to the Christian principle. We ought, therefore, to regard the Nation as the Church, its rulers as ministers of Christ, its whole body as a Christian brotherhood, its public assemblies as amongst the highest modes of universal Christian fellowship, its dealing with material interests as Sacraments, its progressive development, especially in raising the weak, as the fullest service rendered on earth to God, the nearest thing as yet within our reach to the kingdom of heaven.

It is hard to know how much of this many journalists absorbed and believed—but these notions did begin receiving favorable press. It was easier to attribute problems to social maladjustments than to innate sin-fulness; if personality was a social product, individuals were not respon-sible for their vices. Crime reporting began to change as journalists began to attribute "antisocial action" to the stress of social factors beyond an individual's control. Editorial pages began calling for new government action not merely to redistribute income but as a means to achieve a cooperative commonwealth in which men and women could become godlike.

Joseph Pulitzer popularized such ideas in a New York newspaper, the *World*, that combined easy-to-read, gripping stories with economic envy. Typical *World* headlines were like a dragon's fire: "Death Rides the Blast," "Screaming for Mercy," "Baptized in Blood," "A Mother's Awful Crime," "A Bride but Not a Wife," and "Victims of His Passion." Readers who paid a penny in response to such appeals would encounter, on inside pages, Pulitzer's political agenda: tax large incomes, tax corporations, tax inheritances, redistribute income.

Pulitzer's *World* juxtaposed current horror with future social salva-tion; it transmitted a message of hope through science and material progress, evenly distributed by benign government agents. Features such as "Experimenting with an Electric Needle and an Ape's Brain" showed that scientific transformation of man's thought patterns was just around the corner. Stories such as "Science Can Wash Your Heart" suggested that immortality was possible. In the meantime, however, monstrous crime and terrible scandal rode mankind.

In one sense Pulitzer was merely imitating the methodology of the Puritan press two centuries before: emphasize bad news so that the need for the good news becomes even greater. But the message was totally changed: Instead of pointing readers toward man's corruption and God's grace, the *World* portrayed itself as the battler against systemic oppression, and proposed running over anyone (including business owners in America, Spaniards in Cuba, and Boers in South Africa) who stood in the way of "progress."

The *World's* circulation rose from sixty thousand in 1884 to two hundred thousand in 1886 to one million during the Spanish-American War in 1898. For journalists yearning to transform society and have fun and profit, the *World* became the New York workplace of choice, much as the *Tribune* had been at mid-century. The *World's* full-time workforce numbered thirteen hundred in the mid-1890s, and the growing arrogance of what had become a major institution soon was apparent: "The *World* should be more powerful than the President," Pulitzer argued, since presidents are stuck with four-year terms but the *World* "goes on year after year and is absolutely free to tell the truth."

Eternal life plus absolute knowledge of good and evil: Pulitzer believed he had feasted from both of Eden's trees, but he found no joy. By 1900, Pulitzer was spending most of his time on his yacht, with seventy-five employees trained to cater to his whims. As one biographer put it, "The yacht represented the logical end toward which the eccentric despot, so concerned with democracy, had been working for decades. It gave him *complete control*. It was an absolute monarchy."

The second major editor-publisher of the period, William Randolph Hearst, took Pulitzer's insights and spread them across the nation through a mighty newspaper chain. One reporter described his excitement upon going to work for Hearst.

At last I was to be the kind of journalist I had dreamed of being. I was to enlighten and uplift humanity. Unequaled newspaper enterprise, combined with a far-reaching philanthropy, was to reform . . . the whole United States. The printing press, too often used for selfish ends, had become a mighty engine for good in the world, and I was to be a part of the directing force. Proudly I was to march under the banner of William R. Hearst, helping to guide civilization's forward strides.

Hearst made the *San Francisco Examiner* profitable by adopting Pulitzer's combination of sensationalism and exposure of oppression. In 1895, he purchased the *New York Journal* and soon became famous for sending dozens of reporters to the scenes of crimes on bicycles or in carriages pulled by fire and cavalry horses; Hearst himself could be seen "leaping wild-eyed and long-legged into a carriage, to be whisked like a field marshall on the scene of battle." He loved newspapering. One reporter described how Hearst:

spread the proofs on the floor, and began a sort of tap dance around and between them. . . . The cadence of it speeded up with his reactions of disturbance and slowed down to a strolling rhythm when he approved. Between dances, he scribbled illegible corrections on the margins and finally gave the proofs back to me.

Hearst ordered his editors to "make a great and continuous noise to attract readers; denounce crooked wealth and promise better conditions for the poor to keep readers. INCREASE CIRCULATION." As one historian has noted, the "yellow journalism" pioneered by Pulitzer and Hearst was characterized not only by big headlines and exciting stories, but by "ostentatious sympathy with the underdog." Hearst's capital-S Sympathy was his first step toward making readers think he cared about them; calls for socialism came next. Hearst wrote in one signed editorial that socialistic management was the key to advancement, for:

combination and organization are necessary steps in industrial progress. We are advancing toward a complete organization in which the government will stand at the head and to be the trust of trusts. It is ridiculous to attempt to stop this development.

By 1904 Hearst was explicitly arguing that "the greatest need of this republic today is an aggressive and well organized radical party." Liberal Herbert Croly compared Hearst to Robespierre, writing that Hearst's ambition was to bring about a "socialistic millennium." Hearst evidently believed that the press had the power to "so exert the forces of publicity that public opinion" would compel such an outcome. His editorial writers worked hard to press issues into a class-struggle mold; one of the *Journal's* classic editorials portrayed:

> the horse after a hard day's work grazing in a swampy meadow. He has done his duty and is getting what he can in return. On the horse's flank you see a leech sucking blood. The leech is the trust. The horse is the labor union.

The *New York Journal* ran big cartoons showing Mark Hanna, President William McKinley's campaign manager, as a fat bully dressed in clothes filled with dollar signs, with McKinley a puppet on his lap. Hearst's viciousness seemed unlimited; as one observer noted, Hanna was depicted as "an amalgam of all sins. He was foulness compact. . . . He sent poor sailors, forced on his ships by bestial labor masters, out to sea on the wintry lakes cold and starving, unpaid and mutinous." Meanwhile, Hearst screamed that he favored the poor; such posturing was worth millions of dollars to him. Hearst sold enough newspapers to make Louis Wiley, business manager of the *Times*, cry out that crusading should be considered "a commercial trade."

Day after day, Hearst's newspapers in San Francisco, New York and then across the country, provided an artful combination of sensation and hope. On the one hand, the present was tragedy, with headlines such as "He Murdered His Friends" or "He Ran Amuck with a Hatchet." A woman already in jail for beating a man senseless with a beer bottle, stabbed her jailer with a hat pin. A maidservant poisoned her mistress' soup. In New York, a boy shot and killed his father, who was beating his mother. Another woman told "How She Horsewhipped Husband." An eleven-year-old drank a bottle of acid because she "did not want to live."

On the other hand, the future would be much better. Some day, resources now used for "barbaric" displays of wealth would fight "distress and misery." Science (actually, pseudoscience) would help: the *San*

Francisco Examiner reported that one professor had produced "solidi-fied air" and another had found out that what a woman eats determines the gender of her baby.

Hearst made an idol out of circulation, but he also tried making one out of himself. He began instructing his reporters and editors to praise him at every possibility. He posed as a benefactor of the poor, sending pale children on jaunts to the beach. A reporter sent to cover one expe-dition, however, later wrote that she was given only one container of ice cream to be dealt out on a Coney Island trip.

> When at last I placed a dab on each saucer, a little fellow in ragged knickerbockers got up and declared that the *Journal* was a fake and I thought there was going to be a riot. I took away the ice-cream from a deaf and dumb kid who couldn't holler and gave it to the malcon-tent. Then I had to write my story beginning: 'Thousands of children, pale-faced but happy, danced merrily down Coney Island's beaches yesterday and were soon sporting in the sun-lit waves shouting, 'God bless Mr. Hearst.'"

Once, when Hearst ordered all his reporters to mention his newspa-pers' "comic supplements" in their stories whenever possible, one reporter filed this report from a disaster scene.

> I was the first to reach the injured and dying. "God bless Mr. Hearst," a little child cried as I stooped to lave her brow. Then she smiled and died. I spread one of our comic supplements over the pale, still face.

Some Hearstian efforts were serious, not ludicrous. When Governor Goebel of Kentucky was assassinated early in 1901, the *Journal* printed a quatrain by reporter Ambrose Bierce: "The bullet that pierced Goebel's breast / Can not be found in all the West; / Good reason, it is speeding here / To stretch McKinley on his bier." Soon afterward the *Journal* edi-torialized that "if bad institutions and bad men can be got rid of only by killing, then the killing must be done."

When the anarchist Czolgosz assassinated President McKinley later that year, the killer was said to have been arrested with the *Journal* in his coat pocket. Hearst was hanged in effigy, circulation for a time dropped, and President Theodore Roosevelt said that Czolgosz had probably been led to his crime by "reckless utterances of those who, on the stump and in the public press, appeal to dark and evil spirits." But Hearst bounced back, changing the name of his New York morning edition to the *American*.

Hearst showed through such conduct that he was the prototypical solipsistic journalist of the twentieth century, moving around real individuals as if they were make-believe characters. Some opposed him: Congressman John A. Sullivan called Hearst the Nero of American politics for his attempts to incite class conflict; Sullivan labeled Hearst a socialist and hung his picture with red flags underneath it. For a time, Hearst was able to convince some voters to accept their role in his dreams. He used his newspaper clout to win election to Congress by a big margin, and wrote after the landslide:

> We have won a splendid victory. We are allying ourselves with the workingman, the real Americans. This is just the beginning of our political actions. Our social aspirations have a greater chance than ever to be realized.

Hearst was on his way. He was the first journalistic leader to assault regularly those who stood in his path. When Hearst could not get the Democratic presidential nomination in 1904, he called Judge Alton Parker, the party's nominee, a "living, breathing cockroach from under the sink," and labeled the party's chairman "a plague spot in the community spreading vileness." At one time, Hearst's New York newspaper had two thousand names on its S-List (persons to be mentioned only with scorn), and a reporter had to be assigned to read copy just to make sure mistakes of honesty were not made.

Through all this, Hearst retained the support of leading journalists of the left. Upton Sinclair declared in his book *The Industrial Republic* that a bright socialist future would not be far off if Hearst became president. Lincoln Steffens wrote a sympathetic profile of Hearst and explained that the publisher "was driving toward his unannounced purpose to establish some measure of democracy, with patient but ruthless force."

The movement Hearst represented was, with its newspaper base, a big-city phenomenon. The key question was whether his emphasis on oppression would spread around the country. As it turned out, it did, at least in part through the influence of national magazines such as *Munsey's, McClure's, Cosmopolitan, Everybody's*, and *The Arena*, which provided an outlet for freelancing radicals during the twentieth century's first decade. *The Arena*, for example, pushed its on hundred thousand readers to "agitate, educate, organize, and move forward, casting aside timidity and insisting that the Republic shall no longer lag behind in the march of progress."

The hopes of the radicals, although diverse in some aspects, tended often to parallel those of Horace Greeley two generations before. For example, Upton Sinclair, at first a believer in communalism, invested profits from his book *The Jungle* in a New Jersey commune, "Home Colony"; it failed, but Sinclair thought it a good try, an "industrial Republic in the making." After seeing what went into some cans of meat, Sinclair espoused another of Greeley's favorite causes, vegetarianism, and also argued that meat-eating had no place in an agricultural system managed on principles of efficiency and nutrition.

Sinclair for a time had new causes every year, but eventually, like Greeley, he became an apologist for terrorism—in this case, that of Lenin rather than John Brown. Like Greeley, Sinclair also confused holiness and hatred, eventually declaring that Jesus had been an anarchist and agitator whose vision of violent upheaval was covered up by church institutions.

Sinclair was one of the first major journalists to explicitly adopt socialism; others moved in that direction more slowly as they abandoned youthful Christian allegiances and sought a new faith. Ray Stannard Baker, after reading Bellamy's *Looking Backward* and Henry George's *Progress and Poverty*, was among those who became annoyed at the idea that God, not journalists, brought salvation; as Baker wrote in his memoirs, "I was temperamentally impatient. I wanted explanations promptly. I wanted to know what I should do to help save the world."

When Baker's father suggested other ways to save the world, the son responded, "I'm on my way up. If my strength and grit hold out I'm going to make my influence felt before I get through with it." In 1899, after two years of New York journalism, Baker wrote to his father that "The longer I am in my present work, the greater seem the responsibilities and opportunities to high grade journalism." Five years later, he was still writing that he had "a mission to perform," and felt successful: "I think we have struck the right Grail."

The most famous of the radicals, Lincoln Steffens, wrote that he began his quest as a student at the University of California during the 1880s, where professors "could not agree upon what was knowledge, nor upon what was good and what evil, nor why." To find out about good and evil, Steffens wrote that he had to become a journalist. He certainly saw evil—"graft and corruption" were everywhere—but he did not see them as coming from within.

Once, discussing the biblical Fall within the garden of Eden, Steffens said the culprit was not Adam, or Eve, or even the snake: "It was, it is, the apple." Good people were corrupted by a bad environment—and the goal of journalists, Steffens believed, was to change the environment by working to eliminate capitalism, which he saw as the twentieth-century equivalent of the apple.

Members of the media elite who learned from Pulitzer or Hearst also tended to follow them in their virulence. For example, when the United States Senate in 1906 debated the Pure Food and Drug Act, Senator Joseph W. Bailey of Texas spoke in opposition, saying:

> I believe that the man who would sell to the women and children of this country articles of food calculated to impair their health is a public enemy, and ought to be sent to prison. No senator here is more earnestly in favor of legislation against adulterated food and drink as I am . . . but I insist that such legislation belongs to the states and not to the general government. When something happens not exactly in accord with public sentiment, the people rush to Congress until it will happen after a while that Congress will have so much to do that it will do nothing well.

Muckraker David Graham Phillips ridiculed that statement. He said that Bailey opposed good food and was participating in the "treason of the Senate." Within Phillips's understanding, anyone opposing federal legislation in a good cause was corrupt and uncaring. Such blanket accusations were too much for President Theodore Roosevelt, who complained that:

> the man who in a yellow newspaper or in a yellow magazine makes a ferocious attack on good men or even attacks on bad men with exag-

geration or for things they have not done, is a potent enemy of those of us who are really striving in good faith to expose bad men and drive them from power.

Roosevelt let fly in a speech that accepted the need to expose wrongdoing but argued that:

> the attack is of use only if it is absolutely truthful. The liar is no whit better than the thief, and if his mendacity takes the form of slander, he may be worse than most thieves. It puts a premium upon knavery untruthfully to attack an honest man, or even with hysterical exaggeration to assail a bad man with untruth. An epidemic of indiscriminate assault upon character does not good, but very great harm. The soul of every scoundrel is gladdened whenever an honest man is assailed, or even when a scoundrel is untruthfully assailed.

Roosevelt called the common journalistic activity of his time "muckraking," and explained that:

> In Bunyan's *Pilgrim's Progress* you may recall the description of the Man with the Muck-rake, the man who could look no way but downward, with the muck-rake in his hand; who was offered a celestial crown for his muck-rake, but who would neither look up nor regard the crown he was offered, but continued to rake to himself the filth of the floor.
>
> In *Pilgrim's Progress* the Man with the Muck-rake is set forth as the example of him whose vision is fixed on carnal instead of on spiritual things. Yet he also typifies the man who in this life consistently refuses to see aught that is lofty, and fixes his eyes with solemn intentness only on that which is vile and debasing. Now, it is very necessary that we should not flinch from seeing what is vile and debasing. There is filth on the floor, and it must be scraped up with the muck-rake; and there are times and places where this service is the most needed of all the services that can be performed. But the man who never does anything else, who never thinks or speaks or writes, save of his feats with the muck-rake, speedily becomes, not a help to society, not an incitement to good but one of the most potent forces for evil.

Hundreds of favorable responses to Roosevelt's speech indicate that his concern about press bullying was widely shared. Protests about the media elite's ideological agenda were common.

Socialism—that's where these leaders of the magazines and newspapers are headed for. The Sentimentalist who looks to find there the Kingdom of Brotherly Love upon Earth, the honest man, hysterical with anger at the crimes of high finance, the brave fool spoiling for a fight the good citizen who says to himself, "that the evil is so great the whole must be swept away—" all alike are following the lead of the statesmen of the yellow press toward the ruinous experiment of straight-out socialism.

Such complaints, although addressed to a modern ideological development, had an old-fashioned ring to them. After all, Andrew Bradford, editor in Philadelphia of the *American Weekly Mercury* two centuries before, had opposed "that unwarrantable License which some People of much fire, but little judgment have taken of endeavouring to subvert the Fundamental Points of Religion or Morality."

A downward curve to the political prospects of William Randolph Hearst may be dated from the time of Roosevelt's speech, although other factors contributed to the failure of the publisher's ambitions. For a while, Hearst retained the support of journalists on the left, but as he lost elections, and as the sensationalism of his newspapers seemed a bit embarrassing, radicals edged away from him.

Hearst in turn lost his patience with them, and by the 1920s and 1930s was stoutly opposing governmental control of the economy. Perhaps because of Hearst's "treason" to the left after 1920, he is often regarded by journalism historians as a bad guy, and Pulitzer—who left money to found a journalism school at Columbia and to hand out prizes—is given a white hat.

Although the muckrakers abandoned their one-time standard bearer, they did not drop their "revolt against capitalism," as Upton Sinclair called it. The muckraker "as forerunner of a revolution," Sinclair concluded, "will be recognized in the future as a benefactor of his race."

Those reporters who had little thought of being benefactors—they had a job to do and a paycheck to get—might scowl at such notions. And yet, with all the cynicism that journalists love to show, the streak of pride would grudgingly show itself: One reporter reminisced of how, for a time, he had been:

battling for the people, and making tyrants quail, in a truly heroic journalistic style. I was forging shafts of ripping, tearing words that would demolish the fort of the robber chiefs who were taking unlawful tribute from the public. I called the gas company 'the Gorgon-headed monopoly,' 'the banded infamy,' and 'a greedier gorge from the public purse.' I felt myself as heroic as those who had led the crusades of old.

Top college students who enjoyed writing began gravitating more and more toward journalism; Walter Lippmann, for example, went from Harvard to an internship with Lincoln Steffens. Steffens and his associates set the standard for "the right stuff" in leading-edge journalism much as had Horace Greeley two generations before; they trained a generation of young journalists to see not only poverty and corruption as the responsibility of capitalism, but all war as the result of capitalist desires to find "a dumping ground abroad for a surplus domestic product."

Steffens, remembered by one contemporary as "talking revolution and blood and sucking the guts out of a chocolate eclair impaled on an upright fork," ended his career writing propagandistic pieces for Lenin and then Stalin. Others, such as Ray Stannard Baker, merely found themselves attracted to the Socialist Party's "high & unselfish ideals," with its "community spirit of service." But many became willing to adopt a Marxist perspective as long as it was given a spiritual gloss.

David Graham Phillips, whose attacks on the Senate justified Roosevelt's famous response, compared Karl Marx to Jesus Christ, not unfavorably. "It was three hundred years before the first Jew began to triumph," Phillips wrote. "It won't be so long before there are monuments to Marx in clean and beautiful and free cities all over the earth." Phillips anticipated the work of modern liberation theologians by writing that Christ and Marx were:

> both labor leaders—labor agitators. The first proclaimed the brotherhood of man. But he regarded this world as hopeless and called on the weary and heavyladen masses to look to the next world for the righting of their wrongs. Then—eighteen centuries after—came the second Jew—and he said "No! not in the hereafter, but in the here. Here and now, my brothers. Let us make this world a heaven. Let us redeem ourselves and destroy this devil of ignorance who is holding us in this hell!"

Most elite journalists did not embrace Communism, but were content to follow Greeley's concept of locating social problems in the environment rather than in humanity itself. One liberal journalist, Will Irwin, complained that when Americans "find any institution going wrong, we think first of individual dishonesty." Irwin's goal was to teach readers "to attribute the unfair working of social forces to faults in the system of things."

Individuals were unimportant; the system was all; progress meant changing the system. From the 1930s on, many leading American journalists applied their talents to exactly that end.

CHAPTER THIRTEEN

Overview of Start-up Considerations

I have been emphasizing writing and editing, but many other elements of a powerful publication—including photography and graphics—also deserve discussion; to do justice to those topics, this book would have to be much longer. The same goes for crucial business matters: Examinations of advertising and circulation would require a multi-volume work.

This brief chapter, however, is the consequence of the telephone calls that I have received since 1988 from those who feel called to start up Christian newspapers or magazines. I tell the callers that they need to think through principles of Bible-based journalism, but not stop there: They also need business sense and judgment. This book cannot provide that, but I can suggest a few procedures to follow before jumping in.

To start with, you should remember that directed reporting requires lots of legwork, and so does start-up or reorientation of a newspaper or magazine. Traditionally in Judaism, the youngest child at a Passover seder asks four questions so elementary that adults might be embarrassed to bring them up—but those four questions form the basis for all that comes afterward. Here are the four questions that any current or prospective Christian publisher needs to ask, and answer well, before asking anyone else to support his vision with time or money:

- Who are my current or prospective readers?
- Where do they live or work?
- What are their current information sources?
- Do they want something different?

You will have to do demographic, theological, political, and psychological research to begin answering those questions, and you will then need to assess critically the information you have gained. To see how the professionals do it, take a look at the Simmons Market Research Bureau's annual Study of Media and Markets, which includes demographic and attitudinal information on readerships of over a hundred magazines. Census Bureau and other statistics also will be helpful to you. Closer to home, you can gain information from pastors and other church leaders, and can also set up a simple focus group of Christians within your community to learn about their interests and needs.

The desire to start a Christian publication often is planted by God, but the particular way of going about it is a choice (and often a foolish choice) of man. We inevitably see heaven through a glass darkly, but there is nothing inevitable about unrealistic looks at the marketplace. Many publisher wanna-bes underestimate how much it costs to reach readers and overestimate the desirability of their publications' advertising space.

From a business standpoint, publishing is actually a subset of manufacturing, but some people mistakenly think of it as art: Those who would not merely jump in with a new type of toothpaste and expect to compete with Crest sometimes speak glibly about putting out a daily newspaper. Similarly, some who would not assume that everyone would patronize a new restaurant in their city, assume that all evangelicals will subscribe to a Christian newspaper or magazine. The rule of thumb that publishers use suggests otherwise: It is generally believed that no more than 10 percent of any demographic group will be interested enough in something to buy a magazine about it.

If you can broaden your base by bringing in conservative subscribers who may not identify with evangelical products, and do so without diluting your message, you are significantly increasing your target demographic group. Cities that sport clearly liberal newspapers and have no conservative alternative are especially good venues for Christian publications.

Wherever you are, you need to develop a publication business plan in order to work through fundamental questions and convince potential supporters that your vision has legs. The business plan should begin with a concept—a statement that summarizes in one or two sentences the essence of your publication. Under that statement should come a description of your publication and a statement of editorial need that shows why your publication is not merely an ego gratifier; this statement may include an explanation of how your publication differs from others that serve in part a similar function. (For example, if you envision a Christian magazine for your metropolitan area, you should note other magazines and news sources in your area that might appeal to some of your potential readers.)

The second section of your publication plan should be a detailed analysis of your prospective editorial content and design, with a projection of frequency of publication. You should specify here the types of articles that will appear in each issue, and give examples of each type; include columns, sections, and departments. Planning here is crucial: Without careful preparation, many dismal Christian publications have little local coverage, and rely heavily on press releases for what there is. If your goal is to put out a newspaper, you should explain here how you will cover local government, local high-school sports, local crimes and accidents, and so on.

Personnel often is policy: You should present in this second section the names and titles of your prospective editors, and you should at least list the kinds of writers you will employ; if possible, give their names and backgrounds. Many local Christian publications read very poorly; it is apparent that they are advertising vehicles, with editorial content almost an afterthought. The second section also should provide a sense of what your publication will look like. You should be able to describe the kinds of photographs, drawings, or other illustrations you plan to use, and the kinds of headlines you envision, with specific fonts and type sizes. You should note here the name of your art director, and mention others who will be involved in design and layout. The typical local Christian publication looks terrible; many who start one give no thought to questions such as these.

The third part of the editorial plan should provide detailed information about production. List here the computer hardware and software that you will be using. Show who will handle printing and production, and give specific detail about how many pages your initial issue will contain, and whether they will be in color or black and white. Note the type of paper you will use and list printing costs. Finally, include information on who will print the first issue, and on what type of press.

Part four of the plan should stress circulation issues. This section should begin with a detailed analysis of your market that will address questions such as: Is your good idea economically feasible? How many potential readers do you have? What is their income, educational background, marital status, and so forth? You should consult census data and then gain information on churches in your area.

Then, you should say whether you will sell your publication, or give it away and depend on the advertising revenue that a larger circulation can bring. Some technical (but important) questions related to circulation can be answered down the road: For example, if you are publishing a magazine, will you use blow-in subscription cards, and will you send reduced-price renewal notices to unresponsive subscribers? (*Architectural Record* was known for sending out nine; the first three or four asked for full price, and subsequent notices dropped the price.) But you must address in your publication plan the basic issue of pricing your product, because if you start out with free distribution it will be hard to switch to paid subscriptions.

In making this decision, pay close attention to the history of other publications in your area, and other Christian publications in similar areas. To answer the big question, you will also have to think through a host of smaller questions: If your publication has a price on its head, will it be sold largely through subscriptions, or at single-copy sales points? (Newsstands and their modern equivalents, or Christian bookstores?) If you rely on free distribution (the trade name is "controlled circulation"), will you work through churches or other outlets? Will you have your circulation audited, so that advertisers can rely on your figures?

You may have to develop this section of your publication plan at the same time you develop part five, which should be a summary of your advertising potential. Advertising is essential to journalistic survival: Newspapers and magazines rarely make much money from subscription sales, but instead use their circulation to attract advertising. Today, there are so many different ways for advertisers to get across their messages that the environment is very competitive. You should indicate in the plan your awareness of potential competitors for advertising dollars, and you should then explain why your publication will be a good buy for advertisers.

To develop this section it will be important once again to look at the experience of Christian publications in communities similar to yours, and of other publications in your area. See how many ads, and of what type, they carry per issue; note their ratio of advertising to editorial matter; study their rates, and find out all you can about (or estimate from their ad space and rates) their billings per issue and annually. Then, make your projections, and include with this section a prospective, basic-rate card.

It will be important for you to consult with those who are knowledgeable about advertising: You do not have to be a rocket scientist to determine advertising rates, but they do have to be structured carefully so that revenue from the most popular sizes of ads (often 1/8- and 1/4-page) can be maximized, with repeat advertisers encouraged by reduced rates. (Rates need to encourage both size and frequency, so that an every-issue, full-page ad rate has the lowest cost per square inch, and the one-time, 1/16th page ad has the highest cost per square inch.)

You can put off decisions on some of the details—agency rates, camera-ready discounts, discounts for multiple runs, and so forth—but you do need to have a rough sense of what revenue and advertising ratio (ad pages to all pages) to expect. In making that determination, look at the ratios of competitors in your community and parallel publications in others; it is improbable that you will be able to beat their ratios during the first year.

Part six of your publication plan should major in the financial, providing estimates for the first three years of operation. You should include costs in four areas (editorial, production, circulation, and advertising), including costs of office space, insurance, utilities, and telephones; do not forget start-up costs, including those for direct mail for test marketing. Then, after you add up how much money you need, you should show where you plan to look for it. Are there potential underwriters? (They will be looking very closely at this business plan.) Show whether you will have to borrow money, and if so, from whom, and at what cost, both for paying back monthly principal and taking care of interest payments.

Realism is needed here. Christian publication start-ups have a history of undercapitalization, and revenue during the first two years of publication often is hard to come by: The first year is speculative, with new subscriptions rarely taking in much over what it costs to get them, and the second year can be particularly difficult because cash requirements to service the new readers are high. Successful magazines take at least three years to break even; *Sports Illustrated* lost money for thirteen years.

Part seven of your publication plan should include a prototype cover and table of contents; if you are ambitious and need to impress investors, you might even have a dummy issue. Since a fully worked out plan can run to a lot of text—forty double-spaced pages, or ten thousand words, is not unusual—once you complete all seven sections you should also write an executive summary of not more than two pages, or five hundred words.

Going through this type of planning and being able to put your vision on paper is complicated but essential. The process will help you think through your goals and come to understand intimately that if God is calling you to start a publication, it does not glorify Him for you to fail abjectly. And yet, many people write out, at best, a vague summary of their idea and call it a business plan. Some get nods from their friends when they ask whether putting out a publication is a good idea, and they call that research.

It is a fearsome thing to have good intentions but to fall into a financial squeeze that can quickly devour both cash and spirit. One intelligent and well-intentioned young man with $100,000 (left to him by grandparents, plus some other funds) read a book that made the high-wire act of publication start-up seem like a piece of cake upside down. As he later wrote me (names are changed to protect the enthusiastic), "I decided to launch the *Call* after reading *Publish Your Own Newspaper in Ten Easy Steps Without Losing a Dime*, a simple little paperback by a retired journalism professor from Samson College. He made it sound so simple. I badgered the Lord for wisdom and guidance, and He told me to launch a newspaper here in my hometown."

The monthly newspaper, launched in November 1992, was traditionalist in orientation but not clearly Christian. It initially grew in circulation; its largest issue was published in June 1993. Salaried advertising solicitors were hired, but they were unable to pull their weight as circulation stopped growing. For a year beginning in July 1993, publication revenue declined so that during the spring and summer of 1994 the newspaper, with a circulation of 11,000, was losing $5,000 each month.

Why did the publication not find more of an audience, so that it became an advertising imperative? A basic problem was its dullness. The publication called itself a local newspaper, but much of its material was not written locally. It had flaccid writing. It ran press releases. It did not contain coverage of local government, high-school sports, or other high-interest, local events. It did not run investigative stories that could have slayed local dragons and given the newspaper a must-read quality.

The news pages suffered from the *bland is beautiful* aesthetic that typifies both Associated Press style and the articles of Christians who are afraid of giving offense. The young publisher then tried to compensate for the blandness of his news pages by occasionally running columnists who preferred hysteria to historia.

The formula did not work. "I moved out in faith," he wrote in one letter, "knowing that my goals were good and God would bless the attempt. It seems almost unbelievable to me that I've gone through that much money, but indeed I have." In the fall of 1994, a phone call came. It was the publisher, saying in a disconsolate voice, "We went belly-up."

This publisher's sad experience exemplifies some hard truths. First, most publication start-ups fail. Second, Christian publication start-ups have an advantage in that their principles tend to be sober. Third, they have a disadvantage in that many Christians believe the so-called gospel according to Charlie Brown, which states that sincerity outweighs sense. Overall, the pluses and minuses seem to balance out.

Compare the failure just discussed with the history of a publication that by the summer of 1995 was modestly but solidly established: *The Dallas Christian Heritage*. The entrepreneur here, John Dwyer, received a degree in journalism in 1978 and had a variety of business experiences through most of the 1980s: selling business machines, working as an insurance agent, heading a company selling and leasing copying machines, and starting an insurance company. By 1990, after seminary study, he was ready to look into the possibility of starting a Christian community newspaper.

Dwyer systemically assessed the Dallas metropolitan area in 1990 and 1991 and came to a thumbs-down decision; capital seemed insufficient, and Dallas in any event was one of the rare cities that had two competing daily newspapers, the *Morning News* and the *Times-Herald*, as well as a great expanse of local magazines and suburban newspapers. At the end of 1991, however, the *Times-Herald* folded; even though Dwyer was not planning to compete with the big boys, the media environment seemed a bit less crowded. After taking another look, and knowing that he had savings from previous work to keep his family afloat during a no-return start-up period, Dwyer in March 1991 began to work full time to realize his vision.

He began with realistic expectations: "Christian newspaper publishing is not normally a profitable business . . . typically, it's a very labor-intensive, low-profit operation." He examined the experience of others, including a Dallas predecessor who borrowed $40,000 from the bank, hired a full-time advertising manager, and soon stopped publication, the money gone. "If you staff up," Dwyer learned, "you'll lose your shirt before you even know it's on. So I decided to be my own advertising manager. Not everyone wants to advertise in a Christian newspaper; I decided that I wanted to know who those people are."

Dwyer also analyzed circulation needs and "decided to distribute the newspaper free through churches, but to do it the right way. It's easy to throw out a bundle of papers at a church, but if you don't have personal contact and keep checking back then you find out that six months worth of papers have been thrown into the closet." From March through June 1992, anticipating a July 1992 start-up date, Dwyer contacted Dallas area churches and worked on distribution mechanisms.

Once publication began, Dwyer continued to keep personnel expenses low: "I'm the only full-time employee. I have now hired a distributer who works on both primary and secondary accounts, revisiting the racks. There are half a dozen freelance writers, and I pay them by the job. I edit and direct them." The newspaper in 1995 had a distribution of twenty-five thousand and was available at nine hundred locations, half of them churches and the other half largely restaurants, libraries, and Christian schools.

Dwyer's experience in Dallas shows that careful planning plus continued commitment to a project that becomes not a job but a calling— "it doesn't work unless you care deeply about it," he says—can overcome some hazards. Common factors in successful start-ups include: The principals have spent time as disciples before becoming leaders; they have test-marketed their ideas before making an overall commitment to them; they have learned about all aspects of the business.

There are also examples of publications that have gained financial solvency but have lost their souls in the process.

Staying afloat financially is a means to an end: Your goal should always be to communicate God's truth. Thriving as a Christian publisher requires boldness: In almost any venue, you will be facing entrenched organizations that often have built broad support by trying to be all things to all people. Christians who play that game lose. Courage is not only biblically correct, but a quality conducive to survival in a competitive environment.

To survive, in other words, new publications need not only breadth of readership but depth, a core of readers who care so much about the publication that they will not only subscribe but contribute to keep it alive. Those committed readers will promote your publication because they believe in its message; if your publication becomes vanilla, their support will liquefy.

Newspaper and magazine publishers are sometimes advised to downplay Christian conservative content for fear that it will scare away potential advertisers. It may have that effect on some, but smart advertisers will not care about the content as long as the ads are getting a good response: Building up circulation by getting people to want to read your publication is crucial. (Also, if anti-Christian groups attack and threaten boycott, it's important to have allies who will rush to your support—and that will happen only if you do not cravenly offer to compromise with ungodly forces.)

Sometimes, sadly, Christian publications show no boldness, because their owners see them as promotional pieces, not as necessary communications links for people under attack. One printing company looking for customers had some success in asking Christian radio stations to set up local newspapers in order to promote "local concerts, station events and community activities. . . . You can have all the benefits of a monthly printed promotional piece, for a lot less than you thought."

When the business sense is missing from a publication, problems quickly pile up. But when publishers and editors are content to be in the business of delivering product and delivering customers to advertisers, then they should be in some other business.

The journalist's calling is truth-telling, and his primary means of support are circulation and advertising; the heart and the rib cage are both essential, but their functions should not be confused. When a publication is looked upon as promotional, little honest news can be expected from it. Journalism worth honoring requires good business sense, but it needs more than that: It needs the mind and the arm of crusaders.

CHAPTER FOURTEEN

Journalistic Ethics in an Era of Subjectivity

W e have covered much terrain in the first thirteen chapters, and have touched on some ethical problems—more are dealt with in a previous book of mine, *Prodigal Press*—but the battle against propaganda requires additional emphasis in this last chapter. Christians need to distinguish between being on the Lord's side, by sticking as closely as we can to His revealed Word, and being the servant of any person or group of people, no matter how distinguished. Put no confidence in princes (Psalm 118:9) is good advice for everyone and *especially* for journalists, whom princes readily try to influence.

And yet, the tendency to confuse journalism with public relations is a common failing among Christian magazines and newspapers. God-respecting and self-respecting editors should not run pieces puffing particular organizations, *especially* those that offer incentives to do so. One of the most telling signs of the generally low level of Christian journalism at the end of the twentieth century is the expectation of many publicists that Christian magazines and newspapers will do their bidding. Some Christian groups express irritation at *World* for publishing anything negative about them, even generally positive reports that contain a critical paragraph.

Sometimes, organizations tell us not that the material we have gathered about them is inaccurate, but that we should drop an inquiry because its results could embarrass them. Allies also propose to us what appear to be the customary deals of our era: You publish a favorable piece about us, and we will be of special help to you. A firm NO surprises them. Given the pressures to puff, it is no surprise that journalists are bought and sold, and that many Christian publications act in worldly ways. But Christians have already been bought with a price far greater than anything cash can match.

Ideological pressures may also pile up. Some readers want Christian conservative magazines to be hard-nosed about liberal hypocrisy but blind to that among some conservatives. The temptation to have a double standard is present because, as noted in an early chapter, biblical Christians are fighting alongside conservatives on many issues—but a publication, to receive (and be worthy of) reader trust, should treat facts as facts. Early Christian journalists such as Marchamont Nedham emphasized the importance of covering the defeats of our own side.

In this connection, there is no conflict of interest for a Christian publication staffer to be engaged in pro-life work on the side: Every Christian should be strongly pro-life. However, if you are reporting on political candidates, you should not be writing materials for a particular candidate, even if he embraces pro-life principles: Putting no confidence in princes, you need to be free to report the failures of all candidates, including your favorite.

The fear of the Lord and of violating God's law by lying (even in a good cause) is the beginning of good reporting. Accuracy, accuracy, accuracy: Observing God's world lackadaisically shows disrespect for his creation. This is the world that God has made; rejoicing and being glad in it means not coveting an alternative world.

An editor's demand for specific detail should also be more than a utilitarian cry to increase reader interest. Just as Rembrandt, Franz Hals, and other great Dutch painters of their era showed Reformational understanding by painstakingly portraying humans on earth, not floating off the ground, so a search for descriptive material is moral as well as mechanical.

A lack of precise detail often reflects a murkiness of observation and thought, but it also contributes to a tendency to scream. *World* has never run anything as loaded as the following, but here is the beginning of one lead story from a Christian newspaper:

> Ordinary Americans are increasingly living in a fantasy world created by a mendacious and cavalier oligarchy of would-be rulers . . . a haughty association of self-proclaimed demigods whose control of great wealth has provided them the means to suborn, use and manipulate morally weak human beings. Through these chattels they are creating a never-never world of Alice in Wonderland mind-boggling madness where down is up, no is yes and wrong is right. . . .

That is an extreme example, but it is easy to fall into the trap of offering hysteria, not history. As you research and write a story, you should ask yourself: Am I teaching readers to be resolute in biblical application but calm in the face of anti-Christian aggression, or am I fostering panic? For example, a story on the homosexual lifestyle could inspire us to fiery denunciations—but better to keep a grip on our feelings and present the facts of the hunt for stimulation, as the San Francisco article excerpt earlier did. Sentences like, "Dan White sated the gay community's demand for blood by killing himself in 1985," should be deleted.

You need to exercise special caution when sensational facts that fit well with your political attitudes are revealed. For example, since the editors of *World* are not fans of Bill Clinton, coverage of the Paula Jones accusations that surfaced early in 1994 posed challenges. Biblical accusations demand the testimony of at least two witnesses, but Ms. Jones and Mr. Clinton were the only two individuals in the room when the alleged sexual harassment took place. Ms. Jones did tell a half-dozen people about the incident shortly after it occurred, but she did not cry out during the event and physical evidence was lacking—so there was only one witness on the record, and we did not run a story.

What became interesting after that was the difference between media handling of Ms. Jones's accusations and those made by Anita Hill. Ms. Hill's complaint concerned words, not physical exposure, and was not made until a decade had gone by. Yet the *Washington Post* and other mainline media outlets that had lionized Ms. Hill ignored Ms. Jones; the *Post* even suspended without pay for two weeks a reporter who wrote a story about the harassment charge and was angry when the *Post* refused to publish it.

When feminist groups that had supported Anita Hill sneered at Paula Jones, and when the *Post*'s suppression of the story became an issue, *World* assigned a reporter to write a cover story not so much on Paula Jones's allegations as on the media and feminist inconsistencies. The article, which ran on April 30, 1994 (the Post finally ran a story on May 4, and other media came through on May 6 when Ms. Jones filed a sexual-harassment lawsuit), also had to be sensitive to reader sensitivities concerning sexual explicitness.

> Paula Jones was 23 years old in May 1991, working at a conference Gov. Clinton was attending; according to her sworn testimony, a state trooper approached her and said the governor wanted to see her in his room. Being a new state employee, she complied. She entered the room and found him alone, she attests, and he began making sexual advances. He asked her to perform a sex act that wouldn't require her to remove her clothes, she says. She left the room, shocked and crying, and immediately told a co-worker, her mother, her fiancee, her two sisters, and a close friend.

Reporting such charges and others does not show a lack of respect for those in authority: The only way to maintain respect for the presidency may be to disrespect pretenders in the Oval Office. "Honoring the king" means honoring Richard the Lion-Hearted, not John who usurped the throne; in 1776, Americans realized that they could no longer obey a king, George III, who acted like a dog. Compassion does not mean overlooking the sins of others, but confronting them and suffering with them as they struggle to change—and confronting our own sins as well.

Overall, Christian publications that wish to practice biblically directed journalism should stand firm against propaganda in five ways: They should not pretend that all is well with Christian organizations that are having problems; they should be willing to criticize political allies; they should be willing to praise opponents who act rightly in particular circumstances; they should not place above criticism even great church leaders; and they should not cover up embarrassments that befall even strong organizations.

Let us look briefly at some examples of those practices of nonpropagandistic journalism. First, an honest publication needs to be willing to report on hard times for allies, as in a *World* story headlined, "Rescue Me," and subtitled, "Stung by Federal Law and the High Court, 'Operation Rescue' Is in Need of Rescue—or Reinvention":

> By the time Operation Rescue National director Flip Benham and Wendy Wright, ORN communications director, arrived at the Little Rock "com center" the day after the Fourth of July, they had been beaten up by the media's questions and by the oppressive 100-degree heat, and beaten down by the reception the group had received so far in the Arkansas capital.
>
> Com centers in operations past have been wide, busy rooms filled with phone banks and volunteers and a sense of carefully aimed anarchy. The Little Rock com center was an empty office, 8-feet-by-20-feet, with an answering machine and only one telephone that seemed to work. . . .
>
> By Wednesday afternoon hardcore activists from the three participating groups (ORN, Rescue America, and the Pro-Life Action Network) were showing up for the three-day "Summer of Justice" event, but whether any Arkansans would turn out remained to be seen. Miss Wright said she was keeping her expectations low; "Maybe I'll be surprised."
>
> She wasn't. . . .

Second, there should be a willingness to oppose associates when biblical principles warrant. For example, *World* favored most of Newt Gingrich's agenda in 1995, but still was critical at times.

> Achilles' heel number one is the tendency of the new leadership to imply that economic issues are the only ones that really matter in America today. No better proof of that has been offered than the decision by Mr. Gingrich to select New Jersey Gov. Christine Todd Whitman for the high profile job of responding to President Clinton's State of the Union address last week.
>
> Economics is about the only thing Gov. Whitman has in common with the highly energized Republican masses who rose up on Nov. 8 to call for new directions in Washington and throughout the country. Granted, economics is a big part of that call—and was a dominant theme in the "Contract with America" that propelled Mr. Gingrich to the Speaker's chair and so many of his Republican majority into office. But economics was by no means the only fuel in that noisy engine.

Mrs. Whitman is little more than a Democrat in Republican's clothing—and the disguise is shabby at that. Beyond her Johnny-come-lately commitment to tax-cutting, she shares little with the Republican platform of recent years. . . . She favored abortionists by proclaiming Freedom of Choice Day in New Jersey; she endorsed condom distribution in the schools; and she wrote an open letter praising the state's "gay, lesbian, and bisexual community."

The point is that Speaker Gingrich reached all too deliberately in Gov. Whitman's direction. "We want to show how broad a base the Republican Party has," he explained pointedly when he asked Mrs. Whitman to take the important speaking job. How could Mr. Gingrich have said more specifically that the economic revolution matters, but the social revolution doesn't?

For tens of thousands of footsoldiers, that message doesn't settle in very comfortably. If the new Republican leadership thinks it can reshape America simply by restructuring fiscal issues, just by realigning taxes and downloading some tasks to the states, then its analysis of things isn't ultimately much different from Marxism. Its methods are different—and far preferable—to those of Marx, but its bottom-line message is that human beings will in the end respond to economic factors more than to any other. Such an analysis is repulsive to earnest Christians.

Third, a publication that hopes to report and teach rather than propagandize is always aware that leaders who consistently have done evil can do good once in a while. Such surprises need to be reported, in the way that *World* reported favorably the initiative of one ardently liberal senator.

Sen. Howard Metzenbaum (D-Ohio) reportedly was infuriated in 1989 by a Cincinnati, Ohio, case in which a black child was quickly taken from white, Christian, foster parents after they expressed a desire to adopt. The reason: The child allegedly needed a black home. The child was killed not long after by an abusive black adoptive couple in upstate New York.

As a result, Metzenbaum last summer crafted the Multiethnic Adoption Act, which originally was designed to fight discrimination against couples seeking to adopt transracially. . . .

Fourth, an honest publication should be willing to criticize even great church leaders, for all have sinned and fallen short of the glory of God.

One *World* article that generated considerable comment, pro and con, was the cover story headlined, "Silence of the Shepherds," and subtitled, "As the Preborn Death Toll Mounts, Pro-lifers Are Asking: Where Is the Pastoral Leadership in Opposition to Abortion?" The article, as noted in chapter 4, supportively quoted pro-life leaders who criticized Billy Graham's quiet concerning abortion. Some readers were shocked by *World's* implicit critique of a tremendous leader, even though it was respectfully couched. And yet, Christian journalists should always be willing to speak up sadly if the facts warrant.

Fifth, embarrassments must not be covered up, or else Christian journalism is embarrassed. The New Era foundation scandal in 1995 was big news, but one Christian news organization did not publish any stories about the affair because its parent organization was itself involved in the financial collapse, and the parents did not want bad publicity. Here, once again, it is important to remember the great cloud of Christian journalistic witnesses: Were some of our predecessors tortured and killed so that we can live lives of fear under much less intimidating circumstances?

A commitment to avoid covering up mistakes should begin in a publication's own letters-to-the-editor page. Some publications fill such pages with letters praising their efforts or offering minor additions to stories, but a Christian publication with spunk will receive letters that strongly criticize its stands; the publication should print them even when all the staffers believe that the letters are misguided. There is even an ulterior motive in doing so; as publisher Joel Belz wrote in *World*:

> We aren't thrilled when people point out that we dropped the ball in a certain instance. But we still are committed to provide a regular opportunity for people to make just those points for a very simple reason: It adds to our overall credibility.
>
> Oddly, many Christians (and the leaders of too many Christian organizations) believe an open forum for criticism injures their credibility. So they sit on the facts and suppress discussion. They clam up and shut off the information flow.
>
> Such folks forget, however, that light always trumps darkness. Truth, by God's order of things, always beats out ignorance.

That tendency toward occasional self-examination, combined with a confidence in God's providence, is not found in the liberal press these days, particularly as pressure toward political correctness makes deviations career-shortening. God saves [sinners, but] for many leaders of the liberal press there is no sin, just faults in the system of things. For many there is no personal salvation, just social restructuring. Maybe there could be a God in such a system, but he would have nothing to do.

Chapter Twelve brought our brief look at journalism history to the early twentieth century. The technological change since then has been so remarkable that there is no need to remark on it here. What is striking, though, is that amidst all the material upsurge the spiritual draught has remained. The essential combination of ideas in place among intellectual and media leaders ever since the progressive upsurge early in this century—a new, government-centered gospel—has remained standard.

Muckraker Lincoln Steffens was one of the prime molders in this regard. Modern journalism began in 1517 with the sound of Martin Luther's hammering on the cathedral door, but in 1917 Steffens baptized the newborn Russian Revolution, writing of how Petrograd mobs made him "think of the mobs that followed Jesus about." For centuries much of American journalism had emphasized *restraint*, but Steffens set the tone for twentieth-century journalism by praising radicals who were willing to "lay out consciously and carry through ruthlessly [a program] to arrange the conditions of social living . . . to adjust the forces of economic life."*

Other journalists have shied away from the extremes of ruthlessness, but the emphasis on using government power to adjust economic forces has been a constant. Earlier journalists had pointed readers to the Bible, but after 1917 leading editors such as Oswald Garrison Villard argued that, "There are plain masses seeking a journalistic Moses to clarify their minds, to give them a program of reconstruction." Decade after decade, in line with such thinking, leading newspapers and magazines from the 1920s to the present have portrayed man as possessing unlimited potential that a strong and benevolent state could help to liberate, if only journalistic influence were brought to bear on the side of perceived righteousness.

The story of the past seven decades is one of muckraking become

---

* For more information on journalism in the Progressive era, and full footnoting, see Chapter Nine of *Central Ideas in the Development of American Journalism.*

common, and mainstream journalists claiming that they are for liberty but in practice promoting new forms of oppression. In doing so, they often neglected the sacrifices of their courageous predecessors and genuflected before a future that claimed to work. American journalism, which had developed as an antiestablishment force, became part of a new establishment that did not have the self-understanding to recognize itself as one.

Mainline journalists considered themselves the watchdogs of government, but many went from keeping watch over government to keeping watch over their ideological interests. In the 1920s, when liberal educators tried to install evolution as the established religion in public schools, reporters at the Scopes trial in Tennessee refused to take seriously opposing views and cast William Jennings Bryan as a redneck menace. In the 1930s, many correspondents in Moscow, believing that they had a greater purpose than accurate reporting, became shills for Stalin and launched scurrilous attacks against those few who were determined to tell the truth.

Every decade has brought with it notorious examples not only of journalistic intolerance but also heroism: There always will be members of the great cloud of journalistic witnesses. Perhaps the most outstanding of these in twentieth-century America was Whittaker Chambers, a Communist Party member and spy during the 1930s who went through two major life changes at the end of that decade and the beginning of the next: He became a Christian, and he became a superb writer for *Time* magazine at a time when it was not the vehicle for the left that it has since become.

In the late 1940s, with the cold war and concern about Soviet espionage growing, Chambers was called to testify about the Communist Party's work for the Soviet Union and did so, bringing out facts about former State Department official Alger Hiss that Hiss denied. A jury eventually found Hiss guilty of perjury, but newspapers such as the *Washington Post* were not happy. (One reporter told Hiss, "Do you want to know the verdict of the press? Not guilty—in fifteen minutes.") Chambers received extreme abuse, but his Christian faith enabled him to persevere; in 1951 he wrote a best-selling book, *Witness*, that is still well worth reading. He died ten years later. Archives from the former Soviet Union support Chambers's reports and suggest Hiss's guilt.

The courage of Chambers and others slowed down the journalistic rush to the left, and during the 1950s the press bent to a generally conservative era; during the 1960s, however, a new stampede began. Pride in shaping the news was everywhere; by 1965, correspondents were noting that they did not write stories unless they could include "analysis and interpretation." For a long time newspaper home offices had held the reins on Washington reporters who tended to favor more centralized power, but by the mid-1960s a typical correspondent was able to say, concerning his relationship with editors, "I make a hundred decisions where they make one."

The long-range journalistic triumph of Horace Greeley and Lincoln Steffens became evident in many areas of coverage; for example, as reporter Robert Elegant has noted, his colleagues in Vietnam during the 1960s overlooked the record of Communism and, attracted by the vision, saw the North Vietamese as "righteous, magnanimous, and just." The herd mentality was in evidence as most correspondents spent most of their time at a comfortable Saigon hotel and, in Elegant's words, talked "chiefly to other correspondents to confirm their own mythical vision of the war."

Some reporters did get out in the field, where they practiced a new objectivity. *New York Times* correspondent Gloria Emerson has written about how she accompanied four Vietnamese "students" on their mission to firebomb an American vehicle and burn to death the American soldiers inside; she figured that since she had gone along on U.S. patrols she should go with the other side as well. The plan was for one member of the ambush team to race into a busy intersection and wave his arms until a jeep stopped; then a second member would throw in a plastic bag full of gasoline, and a third member would toss in a lit match.

Emerson and the ambushers waited for twenty minutes; in an autobiographical account, *Winners and Losers*, she wrote about "warning myself over and over again to stay out of it and not to interfere, not to remember the crusts and the smell of burned men I had already seen in hospitals." When an American jeep came by, "There was that second when I could have screamed, yelled, rushed forward to warn him, given the plan away." But she did not. Providentially, one of the "students" had bad aim: His bag of gasoline splashed against the windshield, and the

GI escaped. But the incident nevertheless was a defining moment for a new journalistic ethic: Since reporters had gone out on ambush-setting by U.S. soldiers, not to go to the other side's ambush would be a biased act. American reporters were not Americans but citizens of the world, superior to the morality by which their fellow citizens lived.

William Randolph Hearst in 1898 succeeded in his plan to use press sensationalism to push the United States into conflict with Spain. He had sent Frederick Remington to Cuba to draw victims of Spanish atrocities; when Remington cabled from Havana that he could not fulfill the assignment because the facts did not support the allegations, Hearst purportedly cabled back, "You furnish the pictures, I'll furnish the war." In Vietnam, reporters tried to sucker servicemen into incidents that would show American brutality, such as cutting the ears off of a corpse or throwing a body from a plane.

Journalists learned to "falsify with credibility," according to Elegant. They furnished the pictures, and America abandoned Indochina.

The result was truly gruesome, and unexpected by reporters who, brought up to believe in the natural goodness of man, found it difficult to gauge depths of depravity. Sydney Schanberg of the *New York Times* wrote from Cambodia in 1975, just before the Khmer Rouge took power, that for "the ordinary people of Indochina . . . [it] is difficult to imagine how their lives could be anything but better with the Americans gone." His failure of imagination was corrected too late: On May 9, 1975, he wrote about the "maniacal behavior" of the Khmer Rouge, but by then there was nothing the United States could do to save several million Cambodians from execution. On May 3, 1976, Schanberg received the Pulitzer Prize for international reporting.

The search for foreign heroes of the left continued into the 1980s. Karen de Young, foreign editor of the *Washington Post*, acknowledged that "Most journalists now, most Western journalists at least, are very eager to seek out guerilla groups, leftist groups, because you assume they must be the good guys." In Nicaragua, *La Prensa* editor Pablo Antonio Cuadra wrote that he was "forced to endure for nine years of the Sandinista regime the almost daily visits of American journalists. They always ask the same questions—almost all of them fervent admirers of what the Sandinistas have told them . . . after the questions and answers, the result is always the same: a total lack of comprehension."

In domestic politics as well, reporters over time (as journalist-professor William Rivers noted) became "prime promoters or offstage prompters of the Congressional hearings, legislative battles and other events they are chronicling, theoretically with detachment." One *Washington Post* editor described the practice of "not only getting it from the horse's mouth but being inside his mouth." Another *Post* editor, Philip Foisie, described how staffers at meetings had agreed on the key issues for the 1970s and 1980s—establishing limits on resources and growth, and other aspects of the liberal agenda—and would "use these trends more methodically to line up our sights on the news. We should reach out more for the news, and not wait until it comes to our doorstep, until it 'happens.' . . ."

That degree of editorial self-consciousness was unusual; most journalists simply and unthinkingly fit the bits and pieces of daily events into a grid that excludes God. Benjamin Harris in 1690 saw every story as a piece of the heaven-designed quilt; latter-day liberal reporters of 1995 see a feminist triumph in Vermont or the establishment of a day-care center in Texas as part of a progressive etching-in-progress. Cotton Mather's report on a New England earthquake in the 1720s began, "The glorious God has roared out of Zion." Mather surely did not have to ask himself, before composing his report, how the earthquake fit into his worldview. Similarly, experienced reporters rarely stop to think about the way a particular event fits within their larger understanding; they know that it does.

If mainline (or should they be called oldline?) newspapers continue in their ideological cheerleading, the function of biblically directed journalists will become even more significant—and not just for Christians, but for any who desire alternative voices. Twenty years ago many cities boasted feisty "alternative" news voices: They were criticizing liberalism from the left, but at least they were able to perceive some of the emperor's nakedness. In 1994, however, the *Washington Post* reported that, "what began as the alternative press has been completely assimilated now."

Christians have always resisted assimilation. Today, those who are bold and courageous can stand with the great cloud of witnesses, made up of Christians who spent their lives—and sometimes gave them up—in the pursuit of God-directed writing and teaching. Directed reporting, based on faith in the Triune God and not in man, is a lever for toppling modern journalism's idols and bringing readers back to a Christ-centered press. Every Christian journalist should look in the mirror and ask: Will I stand with John Foxe, John Stubbes, Alexander Leighton, John Twyn, Increase Mather, John Peter Zenger, Samuel Adams, and many more, or will I follow the ways of the world?

There will be opposition, but—as the writer of Hebrews begins chapter 12—"Therefore, since we are surrounded by such a great cloud of witnesses, let us throw off everything that hinders and the sin that so easily entangles, and let us run with perseverance the race marked out for us. Let us fix our eyes on Jesus, the author and perfecter of our faith, who for the joy set before him endured the cross, scorning its shame, and sat down at the right hand of the throne of God. Consider him who endured such opposition from sinful men, so that you will not grow weary and lose heart" (vv. 1–3 NIV).

The *Washington Post* article on the seventeenth annual convention of the Association of Alternative Newsweeklies was filled with mournful quotations. "I look at these papers and detect a lack of passion," one radical editor commented. "No one is on the ramparts because they're not sure what they should be fighting for. Do we have an ideology other than being pro-choice, pro-gay rights and pro-Grateful Dead?"

No, the passionless alternatives do not, but passionate disciples of Christ's passion do, out of gratitude for the sacrifice that transcends the daily news, because it lasts for eternity.

Line-by-Line Editing: Example

Thorough "line editing" means examining every detail in a story and raising questions. The following is an article submitted by a World *writer and the questions about it raised by managing editor Nick Eicher.*

Country music was once the soul of the blue-collar, pick-up driving, tobacco-spitting,[1] mostly rural segment of our society. Or at least that was the way it was portrayed. There have been songs within country music that have poked fun at the stereotype of "I wound up in prison and my mom got hit by a train on Christmas day" type[2] of song that typified the genre.

Now country music has more of a polish to it.[3] And the sound has

---

[1] tobacco-chewing, sted tobacco-spitting

[2] Is that line from an actual song? If not, find one and use it. Overall, for the lead graf, I would suggest starting with a quote from one of those ridiculous songs, then picking up with "Country music was once the soul of . . ." and reworking the last sentence along these lines: Some country songs have even parodied the divorcin', boozin' [or whatever is appropriate from the actual song you quote above] type of lyrics that typified the genre.

[3] Now country music is more polished.

changed. Gone, for the most part, is the twang. In its place are bands and artists that sound more like Eagles or James Taylor. In fact, if those artists were to have emerged today, they would most likely have been signed by a country label rather than a pop/rock one.[4]

And for the Christians that[5] listen to the radio shows besides Rush and Dobson, country music offers an alternative to Christian music that often promotes family values and can even sometimes praise our God outright.

Not that honky-tonks have been abolished from country lyrics, but a significant number of artists are now releasing music classified[6] as "positive country." And within that are several Christians that[7] are taking uncompromised Christian lyrics to a mass audience and going all the way to the top of the charts with it.

[8]Many country artists will claim a relationship of some sort with God. It is more common than not at the country awards shows to hear an artist give his creator credit. And most of those will release a song here and there that Christians go crazy about. But few of those artists actually make it a consistent part of their music. Except, that is, for Paul Overstreet.

Overstreet has released three albums over the last five years on country labels that have all been picked up by Word Records to release to the Christian market as well. And while Overstreet is a country artist, his faith in God pervades all that he writes. And that is, very consciously, his desire.[9]

He has been asked by country record labels, "Is this country music, or is this Christian?" His response, "I don't separate the two. I create country music. That's what I do. But my faith comes before that, so any music I do would have to be under the person of Jesus Christ."

---

[4] Can you attribute that statement to someone? How do you know?

[5] who, sted that.

[6] Who does this classifying?

[7] Who, sted that.

[8] I would reverse the order of the two paragraphs beginning "Not that honky-tonks . . ." and "Many country artists . . .", and moving the reference to Paul Overstreet to the "honky-tonks" graf: " . . . to the top of the charts with it. Paul Overstreet is one of those who's made it to the top."

[9] Delete the whole sentence.

One result of this is that Overstreet fills a niche that other Christian artists have so far not been able to touch. He has considered signing with Christian labels in the past, but has found that God has placed him where he is for a very specific purpose. If he were on a Christian label, he'd be just another Christian artist, probably just reaching a Christian audience.[10] Looking at Paul Overstreet's career today, it seems very clear why God chose him[11] as his messenger. Overstreet is one of the most successful song-writers in country music history. Before releasing his own albums, he wrote smash hits like "Forever and Ever," "Amen" and "Deeper than the Holler" for Randy Travis, "Love Can Build a Bridge" for the Judds, and "The Battle Hymn of Love" for Kathy Matea. He has a total of 13 songs that have made it to #1 on the charts[12] and many more that have made it to the top ten.

In reality, his career has been a long road and God's hand is evident[13] on the life of this songwriter in many different ways.

He moved to Nashville from Mississippi in 1973 to try to make it in the music business. His first desire was to be a performer and not a writer, though. He played in bands for several[14] years, spending many nights out on the road[15] playing at bar after bar. That lifestyle got old quick for Overstreet. "I just couldn't stand to be there unless I was drunk. So I drank a lot. And I knew that was pretty rough on me." Finally Overstreet got to the point one night in a club that he prayed, "Lord, if you'll get me out of these clubs, I'll quit drinking."

A few months later, Paul[16] got a job as a writer for one of the music publishing companies. Later he would see that God was answering his prayer. But he didn't stop drinking at the time. If anything, it got heavier.[17]

---

[10] Overstreet's statement or yours? It's better if it's his. If it's yours, delete it.

[11] Who's your source for this statement?

[12] Which charts? Billboard?

[13] Does Overstreet acknowledge this? If so, say so.

[14] How many?

[15] Was he married at this point? (Overstreet's wife is mentioned only in the last paragraph. Did he not talk about her and her influence on his life? If there is information about her, I think that's important to the development of this story.)

[16] Always use "Overstreet," not "Paul."

[17] Why? Needs more specific detail.

One day[18] Paul found himself in a deep conversation with some of the guys[19] he worked with. He wanted to know if they believed in God. Most of them didn't. But, he says, "I did believe in God. At least I said I did. And in my heart, somewhere way back in there, I still did believe, and I told them that. I said, 'I believe that Jesus Christ is the son of God, and that he came to die for my sins.' And I'm saying this, but life is like this. And I heard this guy[20] going, 'Well, I believe that this life is all there is.' And that caused me to examine my life, I looked at this other guy's life, and my life was in worse shape than his!"

That was when a big change took place in Overstreet's life.[21]He went to a store[22] and bought a Bible and started to read—from the beginning. "I thought, if I get through Genesis, I'll have it made! And I did."

Eventually,[23] in 1984, Overstreet committed his life to Christ. "I laid it all on the altar. I was ready to give up music if that's what He wanted. And that was a major step for me. Up until then, I would never have been able to do that. It was a sacrifice—like Abraham and Isaac."[24]

Another issue Overstreet confronted was alcohol. He had never given up drinking. "Then I remembered that promise I had made God, in that nightclub. And I read somewhere in the Bible that it is better to not make a promise to God than to make a promise and break it. And when I read that, it scared me to death."

When he gave up alcohol, he found a renewed energy to write.[25] And that's when the career took off. He had had one hit record, "Same Old

---

[18] Where are we in the chronology?

[19] Who? Where did he work?

[20] Who?

[21] Does Overstreet acknowledge that conversation as the turning point in his life?

[22] Which store? If you don't know, delete the reference and just say, "He bought a Bible and started to read . . ."

[23] About how much time elapsed between the purchase of the Bible and his acceptance of Christ?

[24] How did he know God didn't want him to give up music?

[25] How long did it take to go from alcoholic stupor to renewed energy? How long from renewed energy to career taking off?

Me," by George Jones, up to this point.[26] Since 1985, there are few that can claim success equal to Overstreets.[27]

Despite all of his success,[28] Overstreet can tell you a lot about the struggle of being a Christian in a secular industry. Just after becoming a Christian, he started playing in a group called SKO, which stands for the last names of the members of the group, Thom Schuyler, Fred Knocbloch and Overstreet. This soon became difficult. Overstreet explains, "As a group, in country music, we were going this way, which was the way of country music.[29] But my heart was being pulled over to do something a little different, something that had a witness to it." So he left that group to try to find his version of something "different."

He went to several[30] of the Christian labels to talk to them about doing an album. But none were[31] interested. And during the meantime, his writing career was flourishing[32] in country music. So Overstreet finally made a realization: Stay in country music, change the way you write.

"I used to write all sad songs. And then I realized that the Scripture says, 'As a man thinketh in his heart, so is he,' and 'Woe to him who sings a sad heart a sad song.' So I said, 'Well, there's two good reasons to try to write something different.'"

Shortly after this, Overstreet launched his own solo country career with the album, *Sowin' Love*. This seems to be when everything finally clicked[33] for him. He had struggled to find a voice for his message. With *Sowin' Love*, "I found that a lot of people got encouraged by that album.

---

[26] Put a date on "this point."

[27] Overstreet's. Name a few of those who can claim success equal to Overstreet's, i.e. "Only Johnny Cash and the Judds can claim success equal to Overstreet's." Then, quantify his success.

[28] What success? You've only mentioned one hit record.

[29] What is "the way of country music"? That needs to be explained.

[30] Which labels?

[31] was, sted were.

[32] Specific detail needed. Specify what you mean by "flourishing."

[33] Does Overstreet acknowledge this? Attribute it to him, if that is the case.

And it really touched a lot of people. Because the songs were real. They were things that my heart felt."[34]

To some extent, Overstreet's struggle had found a resting place. But that didn't last for long. His label, MTM, sold his contract[35] to RCA, and the struggle began once again.

Many[36] in radio told him, "We love the kind of stuff you're doing, we want to play it." But others were "not compassionate towards my faith. There are people that just don't want anything that's going to be preachy or a message or anything. Just give us some partying kind of music." Unfortunately, that is the stance RCA took.

"They were trying to change me.[37] [That] takes some of the message out of my songs, and that ruins me. If I take away the message and songs that I think encourage people who are trying to live a life that's godly, then it's like trying to take the salty taste out of salt. What good is it? And that's what I felt was happening. I felt like I was having to become a man pleaser more than doing what God was telling me."

After recording two more albums[38] with RCA, Overstreet finally decided to leave. He had been pulled away from the direction he had with *Sowin' Love*, and now wants to get back to that.[39]

He explains his decision like this: "Radio can do what they want to. They can quit playing your records or they can play them, but I think you're going to be better off as long as you are true to your heart. If you are true to your heart and they don't play the records, then there is still something there to rejoice about. But if you compromise what's in your heart, and they still don't play your records, oh, then, you can really kick yourself around awhile." He says this painfully, with a clear impression[40] that he has walked that road.

---

[34] Quote from some of the lyrics to the songs in order to show his writing style, how his faith in Christ transformed his ability to write.

[35] Why?

[36] Who? Which stations?

[37] How? What did RCA do or say?

[38] Did those albums reflect man-pleasing lyrics? Quote some to show the difference.

[39] What's his plan to "get back to that"?

[40] Specific detail.

It is difficult to understand why any label would have a problem with the result Overstreet had from *Sowin' Love*.[41] The album had four songs reach the top 5 on the country charts.

Either way, Overstreet doesn't fault RCA. He faults only himself for ever agreeing to change at all.

Now Overstreet has a clear understanding of exactly what he wants to do. He doesn't have a label right now, but expects to sign with one by the end of the year[42] and turn out another album shortly after that. When he does sign, one thing is clear, "I'm not going to sign with a label that is afraid for me to have serious songs."

In the meantime, Paul and his wife Julie have their hands full with their five kids, all of whom they are homeschooling.[43] Overstreet didn't go to the Dove Awards last month, where he won best country song of the year, because he wanted to be at his kid's[44] T-ball game.

---

[41] Too much editorializing.

[42] What is the basis for his confidence in that assertion?

[43] Any details of Overstreet's home life? Does Overstreet teach the children? Which subjects? What are the ages of the children? What are his convictions on home education?

[44] Which kid?

McDowall's Defense of Biblical Sensationalism

Journalists who exposed corruption sometimes had to defend themselves against arguments that exposure of wrong-doing would
increase its incidence or corrupt general discourse. In August 1834,
the Reverend J. R. McDowall, editor of a hard-hitting New York
monthly appropriately titled *McDowall's Journal*—his motto was, "The
world is our field, prevention is our aim"—printed a spirited justification of the biblical sensationalism he practiced. McDowall's discussion,
more thorough than any others I have seen, provides valuable insights
into the logic of some early crusading journalists, but to my knowledge
it has never been reprinted. A few excerpts follow; for easier modern
reading I have re-paragraphed some of McDowall's material and deleted
some italics and other overly used attention-getting devices of the time.

SHALL LICENTIOUSNESS BE CONCEALED, OR EXPOSED?

This I apprehend is one great question before the community; and the
final decision of it will doubtless constitute an interesting and important
era in the history of this vice. It is assumed that the Bible is our only rule
of Faith and Practice, and is a competent arbiter of the question.

    First,—I propose for decision the general questions: *Shall Vice and*

Sin be concealed, or exposed? In deciding this question, I inquire, What
does the Bible TEACH? and What does the Bible PRACTICE?

What does the Bible TEACH?

(1) Cry aloud and spare not; lift up thy voice like a trumpet, and SHOW
MY PEOPLE THEIR TRANSGRESSIONS, AND THE HOUSE OF
JACOB THEIR SINS (Isaiah 58:1). *Show my people their transgressions.*—He must tell them how very bad they really were . . . He must
deal faithfully and plainly with them . . . God sees sin in his people, in
the house of Jacob, and is displeased with it. They are often unapt and
unwilling to see their own sins, and need to have them showed them, and
to be told, *Thus and thus thou hast done.*

He must be vehement and in good earnest herein, must cry *aloud, and
not spare;* not spare them, nor touch them with his reproofs, as if he were
afraid of hurting them, but search the wound to the bottom, lay it bare to
the bone; not spare himself or his own pains, but cry as loud as he can;
though he spend his strength, and waste his spirits, though he get their ill
will by it, and get himself into an ill name; yet he must not spare . . .

(2) Son of Man, CAUSE JERUSALEM TO KNOW HER ABOMI-
NATIONS (Ezekiel 16:2). God not only commands Ezekiel to expose
abominations, but details minutely the abominations to be made known.
It will be recollected that we are now investigating the *general* precept
of the Bible in regard to concealing, or exposing vice and sin. . . .

(5) The Lord said moreover unto me, son of many wilt though judge
[plead for] Aholah and Aholiba? Yea, DECLARE UNTO THEM THEIR
ABOMINATIONS (Ezekiel 23:36). Please examine the whole chapter.
In the 33d Chapter of Ezekiel is pointed out the duty of watchmen to
blow the trumpet and warn the people of approaching danger. But is it
in vain for a watchman to shout "Danger!" unless the people are dis-
tinctly told what the danger is? Certainly that was the uniform practice
of the ancient prophets. . . .

(6) "If thy brother, son of thy mother, or thy son or thy daughter, or
the wife of thy bosom, or thy friend, which is as thine own soul, entice
thee secretly, saying Let us go and serve other gods . . . neither shalt thou
spare, neither shalt thou CONCEAL him . . . And all Israel shall hear, and
fear and shall do no more any such wickedness as this is among you"

(Deuteronomy 13:6–11). Hence it appears such idolators were to be made *public examples*, for the good of all.

(7) *And have no fellowship with the unfruitful works of darkness, but rather reprove them* (Ephesians 5:11). . . . . Endeavor to expose their wickedness, and make the perpetrators *ashamed* of them . . . If it should be said that the perceptive duties that have been cited to expose vice and sin have special or sole reference to the sins of the *church*, and not to those of the world, then I reply both the church and the world are under the same moral government of God—both are amenable to the same laws—both will stand at the same final Tribunal—and both will be either condemned or acquitted by the same general principles.

Moreover, St. Paul, particularly in the first chapter of the Romans, and the other apostles did expose and denounce the sins and vices of the *gentiles* as well as those of the *church*. And finally, it would be hard indeed to charge upon the church all the sins, and vices, and abominations that are exposed and condemned in the Bible. The precept therefore, has as much respect to the abominations of the *world*, as to those of the *church*. And as there is nothing in the Scriptures of an opposite spirit and import to the general scope of the passages quoted, we are forced to the conclusion that the BIBLE PRECEPT is, to DETECT, EXPOSE, and PUNISH VICE and SIN.

What does the Bible PRACTICE?

When Adam and Eve had eaten of the forbidden fruit and thus transgressed the commands of God, *they hid themselves, as vice and sin are wont to do*. Then what did God do? He went into the garden and sought for them saying, "Adam where art thou?" And *detected, exposed,* and punished them.

(2) When Cain committed fratricide, the Lord suffered him not to escape, but detected him, saying unto Cain, "Where is Abel thy brother?" "What has thou done?" And thus did the Lord expose and severely punish Cain. Genesis 4:8–14.

(3) In like manner, was the wickedness done by Jacob's sons to their brother Joseph in selling him into Egypt, and then in lying to their father about his death—*detected and exposed*.

(4) Another interesting illustration of the Bible practice is found in the case of Achan, whose theft so seriously troubled the armies of Israel.

Showing very clearly God's utter abhorrence of concealed vice and sin, and his determination to have it detected, exposed, and punished. . . .

(20) In the book of Esther is a very interesting narrative of Haman's wicked devices against the Jews, and of his detection, exposure and punishment. "And when Haman saw that Mordecai: wherefore Haman sought to destroy all the Jews that were throughout the whole kingdom of Ahasuerus, even the people of Mordecai." (Esther 3:5, 6) But when the plot had advanced so far that the destruction of the people of Mordecai seemed inevitable, then the Lord saw fit to detect and expose the machinations of Haman. And cold indeed must be the heart that can read this story and not rejoice at the developments of the 7th chapter. And colder and harder still must be the heart that would advocate the concealment and protection of vice and crime, and sin. . . .

(27) The 16th of Ezekiel is not the only chapter that exposes vice and sin. Among other chapters of the *same character*, we may mention—the fifty-ninth of Isaiah, the fourth of Hosea—see also the 1st, 2d and 3d.), the twenty-second of Ezekiel, and the Prophets generally, the twenty-third of Matthew, the first of Romans.

Ezekiel was among the Jews, what *Juvenal* was among the Romans; a ROUGH REPROVER OF THE MOST ABOMINABLE VICES. THEY BOTH SPOKE OF THINGS AS THEY FOUND THEM; STRIPPED VICE NAKED, AND SCOURGED IT PUBLICALY. THE ORIGINAL IS STILL MORE ROUGH THAN THE TRANSLATION.

(29) See how God speaks of Licentiousness.—Will you denounce God as indecent? As collateral evidence and illustration of the Bible method of dealing with vice and sin, especially of *speaking* upon the subject of Licentiousness, let us examine some of the laws which God gave to Israel . . . "Moreover thou shalt not lie carnally with thy neighbor's wife to defile thyself with her. And thou shalt not let any of thy seed pass through the fire to Molech, neither shalt thou profane the name of they God: I am the LORD. Thou shalt not lie with mankind, as with womankind; it is abomination. Neither shalt thou lie with any beast to defile thyself therewith . . ."

At this time when so many honest Christians are anxiously inquiring and seeking for light, and truth, and correct principles, and for the proper mode of speaking and conversing upon the subject of licentiousness, it is peculiarly interesting and important to know how God spake upon this subject: for true Christians will never hesitate to follow an example set by their Father in heaven. God's mode and style of speaking upon the subject I have exhibited in the selections indiscriminately made from all the sacred writings . . . It would be well for us not to become "wise above what is written." Shall we be "wiser than God?" "Shall any teach God knowledge?" (Job 21:22)

TAKE NOTICE: Not only did the allwise Jehovah speak in this style, and give these laws and statutes on the subject of Licentiousness, but he gave commandment, saying "Thou shalt teach them diligently unto thy children, and shalt talk of them when thou sittest in thy house, and when thou walkest by the way, and when thou liest down, and when thou risest up." (Deuteronomy 6:6–9) . . .

And thou shalt teach them diligently unto thy children. Under all the Divine dispensations from the beginning, no duty is set higher, or more insisted on, than that of instructing children in the knowledge of religion. [and what is "the knowledge of religion," but the knowledge of vice and virtue, of sin and holiness, of evil and good, of wrong, and right?] . . . Christian parents are most expressly enjoined to "bring up their child in the nature and admonition of the Lord"; and to the praise of young Timothy, as well as of those relations who had been his instructors, it is said, "that from a child he had known the Holy Scriptures, able to make him wise unto salvation, through faith which is in Jesus Christ."

Now is it to be supposed that "young Timothy" was taught to omit, in his reading of the Scriptures, all those chapters that relate to licentiousness? Must "young Timothy" be kept in profound ignorance of this vice against which the Bible thunders so loudly? Is only a part of the Bible "profitable for doctrine, for reproof and for instructions in righteousness?" . . .

No concealment of vice at the final Judgment . . . O, the developments and disclosures of that awful day! "When God shall judge the SECRETS of men." (Romans 2:16) When every disgusting abomination shall be stripped naked, and vice in all its horrid deformity and odiousness shall be exposed to the assembled universe! Ah! whither will fastidiousness then flee—and how shall squeamishness veil her face? Will the rocks and mountains afford a hiding place?

Let us think, speak, and act with sole reference to our final account. We are to give account of ourselves to God, and not to man. If duty requires the detection, exposure, and punishment of vice, we are not to inquire or regard what the world will say; our only concern is to know what God thinks, and what he will say. Hear the Lord Jesus—"What I tell you in darkness, that speak ye in light: and what ye hear in the ear, that preach ye upon the housetops. And fear not them that kill the body, but are not able to kill the soul; but rather fear him that is able to destroy both soul and body in hell." (Matthew 10:27, 28)

CONCLUSION OF THE ARGUMENT

Having adopted the Bible as our only Rule of Faith and Practice, and having ascertained that it is both the Doctrine and Practice of the Bible to expose vice and sin, and having also ascertained that licentiousness, which is one of the most flagrant and abominable of all vices, is not recognized by the Bible as an exception to the general rule of exposing vice and sin—It necessarily follows, THAT IT IS OUR DUTY TO EXPOSE LICENTIOUSNESS.

The code of criminal law proscribed by every civilized and Christian government, requires the most diligent and energetic efforts to *detect, expose, and punish vice.* Look at all the combination of wisdoms and power in the Legislative, the Judicial and the Executive departments of all our governments, both superior and subordinate, to effect these objects. It is only upon the detection and punishment of vice, that the peace and safety of society depend. Banish from the community the vigilance of a Police by day, and of a Watch by night—Deprive the constable of his staff, and the sheriff of his power—Demolish Bridewell and Jail, Penitentiary and Prison—Paralyze the strong arm of the law—Close every court of Judicature—in short, abolish the whole system of means and measures, or powers and function, organized for the *detection, exposure, and punishment of vice*—And then shall you see commence the Reign of Terror and the Misrule of Anarchy. Then shall the assassin plunge the dirk and the dagger at noon-day, and blood shall deluge the land. . . .

Burglary and Burning, Riot and Rain, Pillage and Plunder, Death and Destruction shall become the watchwords of an infuriated mob. The domestic fireside, that sacred retreat of innocence and virtue, shall be invaded by *Lust and Rape*, and the dwelling place of a mother's purity and of a daughter's chastity, shall be converted into the Brothel and the House of Death. Order, Temperance, and Sobriety, shall be ingulfed in the whirlpool and confusion of bachanalian revelry, and midnight debauchery. The Sabbath shall no longer be sanctified by the church-going bell, by the prayers, and praises, and precepts of God's Holy Sanctuary, by the quiet devotions of the social circle, or the aspirations of calm retirement: but the Lord's Day shall become the grand Jubilee of Tumult and Banqueting, of Horse-racing and Gambling, of the Parade of Military and the Pageantry of Pride and Folly, of the Desolation of Error and the Havoc of Infidelity.

And yet all these horrors are but the inauspicious beginning of that Reign of Terror, and the Misrule of Anarchy, consequent upon the abolition of Penal Law, and the concealment and protection of vice. Those therefore who oppose the detection and exposure of vice, must see that they are acting in opposition to the best interests of society, and to the collective wisdom and experience of legislators in every age of the world, *But this is not all:* Such opposers must find themselves acting in fearful opposition to the Precept and Practice of the Bible, and of the Bible's God.

The Decline of American Journalism

[Chapter One of *Prodigal Press*]

A recent study by New York University Professor Paul Vitz found that the vast majority of elementary and high school textbooks go to great lengths to avoid reference to religion. Vitz found American history textbooks defining pilgrims as "people who make long trips" and fundamentalists as rural people who "follow the values or traditions of an earlier period." One textbook listed three hundred important events in American history, but only three of the three hundred had anything to do with religion. A world history textbook left out any mention of the Protestant Reformation. A literature textbook changed a sentence by Nobel Prize laureate Isaac Bashevis Singer from "Thank God" to "Thank goodness."[1]

Standard journalism history textbooks provide similar distortions in their accounts of early nineteenth-century newspapers. Two chapters in the most-used textbook, Emery and Emery's *The Press and America*, deal with the 1800-1833 era of American journalism without once mentioning the Christian worldview that then characterized many major American newspapers and magazines.[2] The textbook does not even mention the *New York Christian Advocate*, in 1830 the weekly with the largest circulation in the country, or the *Boston Recorder*, which had the second largest circulation in that city.[3]

Other twentieth-century textbooks have similar blinders.[4] They ignore comments by early nineteenth-century press-watchers who noted, "Of all the reading of the people three-fourths is religious . . . of all the issues of the press three-fourths are theological, ethical and devotional." They do not mention that New York City alone boasted fifty-two magazines and newspapers that called themselves Christian, or that from 1825 to 1845 over one hundred cities and towns had explicitly Christian newspapers.[5] The facts, though, are irrefutable, once they are dug up: In the early nineteenth century, American journalism often was Christian journalism.

In those days, many Christian newspapers covered everything from neighborhood disputes to foreign affairs. They did not restrict themselves to church activities. The *Boston Recorder*, for example, included news of everyday accidents, crimes, and political campaigns. Its circulation success allowed one editor to conclude that the *Recorder* had gained "the attention of the public" and "stirred up the minds of Christians to duty"[6]

Recorder cofounder Nathaniel Willis was an experienced journalist. Born in 1780, he edited the *Eastern Argus*, a partisan newspaper in Maine, during the early years of the new century. In 1807, though, Willis' life changed. He went to hear what he thought would be a political speech by a minister, but the minister went back to biblical basics. Willis, in his own words, "was much interested, and became a constant hearer. The Holy Spirit led me to see . . . that the Bible is the Word of God—that Christ is the only Saviour, and that it is by grace we are saved, through faith."[7]

The new vision changed Willis' life. First he "began to moderate the severity of party spirit in the *Argus*, and extracted from other papers short articles on religious subjects." He wanted to make the *Ads* an explicitly Christian newspaper, but local politicians who had backed the newspaper were opposed. Willis gave up the *Ads* and moved to Boston. He opened up a print shop there and investigated the journalistic marketplace.

Some newspapers, Willis found, were largely political and commercial, others largely church public-relations organs specializing in ecclesiastical news. Willis closely analyzed three religious weeklies in particular and would not even count them as newspapers, for "A proper newspaper . . . contains secular news, foreign and domestic, and advertisements." With coeditor Sidney Morse, Willis then produced the first issue of the *Boston Recorder* on January 3, 1816. According to the Prospectus published that day, the *Recorder* was to be a newspaper with "the earliest information of all such events as mankind usually deem important," rather than a set of abstract sermonettes.[8]

Willis stuck to his plan, and did not consider it lacking in piety. He knew that news stories could be written in a way showing the consequences of sin and the need for Christ. For example, an article in 1819 headlined "Shocking Homicide" reported that a man had killed his own son after being "for a long time troubled with irreligious fears, and a belief that his sins were too numerous to be pardoned."[9] An 1820 article criticized Admiral Stephen Decatur for fighting a duel for fear of being declared a coward: He forgot "that there is no honor, which is valuable and durable, save that which comes from God."[10]

For Willis, in his own words, all kinds of stories provided "occasion to record many signal triumphs of divine grace over the obduracy of the human heart, and over the prejudices of the unenlightened mind." The *Recorder*, he wrote, was a record of "these quickening influences of the Holy Spirit."[11]

Christian-run newspapers in other cities had similar formats and success. The *Baltimore Chronicle*, in its international coverage, described the troubles of one king: "A bloody cloud now swims before his vision, distilling blood instead of rain; the agitated monarch sees nothing but mangled limbs and bleeding bodies . . . If Divine Providence had intended to have produced a living instance of the worthlessness of human grandeur, could a more awful example have been afforded?" The *Portland Gazette*, for its local coverage, described how two persons were killed by lightning within a house, for want of a lightning rod. It then concluded, "By such events, as well as by a multitude of electrical experiments, Providence is teaching us."[12]

Christian newspapers through the mid-nineteenth century attempted to provide a biblical worldview on all aspects of life. One Ohio newspaper declared in 1858 that the Christian newspaper should be a provider of not "merely religious intelligence, but a *news* paper, complete in every department of general news, yet upon a religious, instead of a political or literary basis." Another, the *Northwestern Christian Advocate*, proclaimed in 1860, "Let theology, law, medicine, politics, literature, art, science, commerce, trade, architecture, agriculture—in fine, all questions which concern and secure the welfare of a people—be freely discussed and treated, and this, too, for God, for Jesus Christ, and the advancement of the Redeemer's kingdom among men."[13]

Overall, many early Christian journalists showed an awareness of how the Bible uses bad news to show us the wages of sin and to prepare us for understanding the necessity of the Good News. The journalists knew that general statements about man's corruption were far less gripping than coverage with specific detail of the results of sin and misery

A GREAT CHRISTIAN NEWSPAPER:
THE NEW YORK TIMES

Harvard, Yale and other universities founded by Christians now preach an atheistic gospel. A similar story could be told of some of the great newspapers of the land, including the *New York Times*, established in 1851 by Henry Raymond, a Bible-believing Presbyterian.[14] The *Times* became known for its accurate news coverage and for its exposure in 1871 of both political corruption (the "Tweed Ring") and abortion practices. Tales of the *Times'* political exposés may be found in journalism history textbooks.[15] The abortion story is ignored, but it had a far greater long-range impact, one that shows how significant Christian journalism could be.[16]

Abortion was officially illegal but nevertheless rampant in New York City from the 1840s through the 1860s. *Times* editorials complained that the "perpetration of infant murder . . . is rank and smells to heaven."[17] But little was being done about it until the *Times* sent one of its reporters, Augustus St. Clair, to carry on an undercover investigation of Manhattan's abortion businesses. For several weeks St. Clair and "a lady friend" visited the most-advertised abortionists in New York, posing as a couple in need of professional services. The result was an August 23, 1871, story headlined "The Evil of the Age."[18]

The story began on a solemn note: "Thousands of human beings are murdered before they have seen the light of this world, and thousands upon thousands more adults are irremediably robbed in constitution, health, and happiness." St. Clair then skillfully contrasted powerlessness and power. He described the back of one abortionist's office: "Human flesh, supposed to have been the remains of infants, was found in barrels

of lime and acids, undergoing decomposition." He described the afflu-
ence of a typical abortionist: "The parlors are spacious, and contain all
the decorations, upholstery, cabinetware, piano, book case, etc., that is
found in a respectable home."[19]

St. Clair also listed leading abortionists by name and noted their
political connections: "You have no idea of the class of people that come
to us," one abortionist said. "We have had Senators, Congressmen and all
sorts of politicians, bring some of the first women in the land here." St.
Clair concluded with a call for change: "The facts herein set forth are but
a fraction of a greater mass that cannot be published with propriety.
Certainly enough is here given to arouse the general public sentiment to
the necessity of taking some decided and effectual action."[20]

When the *Times* laid out the basic facts public interest evidently was
aroused, but a specific incident still was needed to galvanize readers.
Tragically for a young woman, providentially for the anti-abortion effort,
an ideal story of horror arrived within the week. St. Clair published his
exposé on August 23; on August 27 a *Times* headline at the top of page
1 read: "A Terrible Mystery."

General facts of the story were miserable enough: The nude body of
a young woman was found inside a trunk in a railway station baggage
room. An autopsy showed her death had been caused by an abortion. The
Times, though, provided evocative specific detail: "This woman, full five
feet in height, had been crammed into a trunk two feet six inches long.
. . . Seen even in this position and rigid in death, the young girl, for she
could not have been more than eighteen, had a face of singular loveliness.
But her chief beauty was her great profusion of golden hair, that hung in
heavy folds over her shoulders, partly shrouding the face. . . . There was
some discoloration and decomposition about the pelvic region. It was
apparent that here was a new victim of man's lust, and the life-destroy-
ing arts of those abortionists."[21]

Details of the exciting "trunk murder" detective story were played
out in the *Times* during the next several days, as police searched for the
perpetrator. Meanwhile, the *Times* reminded readers every day that this
particular incident showed what went on "in one of the many abortion
dens that disgrace New York, and which the *Times* had just exposed as
'The Evil of the Age.'"[22] The police arrested one of the abortionists
whose advertisements had been quoted in St. Clair's story, and the *Times*

followed with an editorial, "Advertising Facilities for Murder." An editorial quoted St. Clair's article, discussed the death of the "golden-haired unfortunate," and asked whether "the lives of babes are of less account than a few ounces of precious metal, or a roll of greenbacks?"[23]

The *Times* also printed a superbly written follow-up by St. Clair. "A Terrible Story from Our Reporter's Note-Book" revealed how St. Clair, in his undercover research for the exposé, had visited several weeks earlier the accused abortionist's Fifth Avenue office, with its "fine tapestry carpet" and "elegant mahogany desk." St. Clair described one of the patients he had seen: "She seemed to be about twenty years of age, a little more than five feet in height, of slender build, having blue eyes, and a clear, alabaster complexion. Long blonde curls, tinted with gold, drooped upon her shoulders, and her face wore an expression of embarrassment at the presence of strangers."[24]

St. Clair then quoted the abortionist's reply when St. Clair asked what would happen to the aborted infant: "Don't worry about that, my dear Sir. I will take care of the *result*. A newspaper bundle, a basket, a pail, a resort to the sewer, or the river at night? Who is the wiser?" On his way out, St. Clair glimpsed once again the beautiful young woman he had seen on his way in. This time, as a fitting conclusion to his story, he drove the point home: "She was standing on the stairs, and *it was the same face I saw afterward at the Morgue*."[25]

The abortionist was convicted and sentenced to seven years in prison. The *Times* insisted, though, that legal action by itself was not enough; only a change of heart among New Yorkers would bury the abortion business for several generations. Providentially, New Yorkers had been "grievously shocked by the terrible deeds of the abortionists," the *Times* could report, and it was clear that abortion would no longer receive approval.[26] Abortion continued to be considered disgraceful until the 1960s, when a much-changed *New York Times* and other newspapers began pushing pro-abortion positions.

A reading of the *New York Times* through the mid-1870s shows that editors and reporters wanted to glorify God by making a difference in this world. They did not believe it inevitable that sin should dominate New York City or any other city. They were willing to be controversial. One *Times* anti-abortion editorial stated, "It is useless to talk of such matters with bated breath, or to seek to cover such terrible realities with the veil of a false delicacy . . . From a lethargy like this it is time to rouse our-selves. The evil that is tolerated is aggressive."

The editorial concluded that "the good . . . must be aggressive too."[27]

SUNSET FOR CHRISTIAN JOURNALISM

Aggressive journalism by Christians disappeared soon after one of its major successes, for four particular reasons and two underlying causes.

First, looking at the *New York Times* specifically, one generation died or departed. Owners and editors who knew not Joseph emerged. The newspaper's slogans became "It Does Not Soil the Breakfast Cloth" and "All the News That's Fit to Print." Evil unfit for breakfast table discussion or considered unfit to print was ignored and thereby tolerated. Several generations later, it was embraced.[28]

Second, many Christian publications began to prefer "happy talk" journalism. They ran stories about individuals who seemed overwhelmingly decent, cooperative, responsible, and benevolent. Such coverage hardly left the impression that man is a fallen creature desperately in need of Christ. The refusal to cover evil also led to a certain dullness of copy, because without real villains there is little real drama. The *Central Christian Herald* once ran the following news report: "There is literally nothing stirring."[29]

Third, many Christian publications refused to meet the communication demands of an increasingly fast-paced marketplace. There is a place for both popular and elite publications, and there is always a need for careful scholarship, even when short attention spans become typical. Some Christian magazines, though, seemed to pride themselves on unnecessary verbiage. The classic statement of literary arrogance was offered by the editor of one very dull magazine, *Spirit of the Pilgrims*, when he announced that "extended and labored articles" were the best kind. Readers who "are uninterested in communications of this nature," the editor wrote, "may as well give up their subscription and proceed no farther with us." *Spirit of the Pilgrims* soon went out of business.[30]

Fourth, denominational infighting was on the rise. Some newspapers spent much of their space attacking their brethren. Other newspapers, noting that splits had resulted from differences on key issues such as slavery, thought that divisions could be resolved if Christian newspapers steered away from controversial issues.

Overall, however, the problem was not particular villains, but two underlying theological trends. One was anti-Christian, one operated within Christendom; but they worked together to provoke journalistic retreat.

The outside trend is obvious: During the last two-thirds of the nineteenth century, American society generally was casting aside the Christian principles on which it had been founded. Every area of American life was affected by this shift.

The *Boston Recorder*, located in the New England cockpit of theological liberalism, was hit very early by the great slide. It held its own against Unitarianism, which had captured Harvard College. *Recorder* editorials frequently explained the fallacy of believing in man's natural goodness, and complemented those editorials with stories showing the outworkings of original sin.[31] But in the mid-1830s, a new attack emerged from a peculiar merger of materialism and pantheism.

The threat had been building for a long time. Rousseau, Kant and other purveyors of intellectual romanticism—the idea that man's reason did not have to operate within God's revelation, but could actually *create* truth out of its own resources—had long been read at Harvard and absorbed by Unitarian ministers. But Harvard's alternative to Christianity seemed cold until 1836. In that year Ralph Waldo Emerson's essay "Nature" appeared, and the Transcendental Club, composed of young Unitarian preachers, began meeting at the parsonage of George Ripley, who later became an editor of the *New York Tribune*.

Emerson laid out the Transcendentalist challenge in "Nature," and more precisely in his 1838 speech at the Harvard Divinity School. Christianity, he said, speaks "with noxious exaggeration about the person of Jesus," instead of emphasizing "the moral nature of man, where the sublime is." Humanity, Emerson proclaimed, "is drinking forever the soul of God" and becoming Godlike itself. Speak no further of man's sin and his responsibility before God, Emerson suggested: Man is God, or at least part of God, because a little bit of godstuff is sprinkled everywhere.[32]

If God is pantheisically everywhere, though, God is nowhere. Theoretical pantheism could merge nicely with practical materialism. Transcendental thinking was spread in magazines such as *The Dial* and then popularized through non-Christian newspapers and the new public school systems set up by Unitarian Horace Mann and his disciples. There was no need to report on "God's providence" if news events arose from a combination of natural chance and man's godlike skill. The movement away from Christianity was heightened after midcentury when Charles Darwin provided a convenient way to satisfy the long-felt desire of haughty hearts.[33]

Following the traumatic Civil War, even editors of some Christian publications succumbed to intellectual trendiness. For example, editor Lyman Abbott of the *Christian Union*, a large-circulation weekly newspaper of the 1870s, decided that the Bible was fable rather than fact. He became known for attacking God's sovereignty in the name of Darwin. With the support of others who were similarly swayed, Abbott eventually took Christianity out of the magazine's title as well as its pages, with the name becoming *Outlook* in 1893. By that time, other anti-Christian doctrines—Marxism, Freudianism, and a general emphasis on "science" as mankind's savior—had kicked in also, or soon would.[34]

And yet, just as those trends were gaining power, a counterinfluence was developing. The period of great advances for anti-Christian thought also was a great era of revivals. During the last two-thirds of the nineteenth century God used great evangelists such as Charles Finney and Dwight Moody to expound the gospel of grace to millions. Many were saved through their preaching. Many also learned, as Proverbs 1:7 notes, that "the fear of the Lord is the beginning of knowledge" and wisdom. They thus were kept from believing in evolutionary or Marxist scriptures.[35]

Revivalism, though, did not particularly help those Christian newspapers that were endeavoring to cover every aspect of God's creation and perhaps "stir up the mind of Christians to duty" The great revivalists' focus on evangelism tended to be specifically individualistic: Worldview was not stressed. Furthermore, many Christians began to believe that the general culture inevitably would become worse and worse. They thought that little could be done to stay the downward drift. Christian publications should cover church news, they thought, and ignore the rest of the world.[36]

The anti-Christian trend and separatistic Christian reaction combined to end the Christian presence in newsrooms. As journalists who had embraced materialism and/or pantheism advanced in newspaper and magazine work, Christians who embraced separatistic revivalism retreated. Some Christian newspapers may have died after being over-run, but many evacuated the social realm without ever engaging the invading forces.

The general result of the two underlying movements was that the Reformational idea of Christ as Lord of all of life was neglected. Relations of ministry and laity, and of sabbatical and general church activities, also were affected. Calvin and other leaders of the Protestant Reformation had argued that good work outside the pulpit glorified God as much as the activities of the ministry proper.[37] But as views of inevitable cultural decay began to grip nineteenth-century American Protestantism, some editors began to consider journalism inferior to preaching. The editor of one Ohio newspaper said that "the work of a Christian minister" was far more important than the work of an editor.[38]

As Christian publications became less significant, selection of editors became more haphazard. Often those who could, preached, while those who could not, edited—and the latter knew that they were considered second-class Christians. One minister thrown into an editor's chair in Cincinnati wrote: "I had never seen a newspaper made up. . . . I was stunned by the cry of 'copy!' 'copy!'" That newspaper ceased publication when a follow-up editor took a vacation and never came back. The editor of the *Southern Christian Advocate* proclaimed that it was better to "wander through the earth on foot, preaching Christianity, than to be the editor of a religious newspaper."[39]

Sometimes it even seemed that a sense of "Whew! Glad I'm saved!" had replaced a strong sense of God's sovereignty over all areas of human life. The theological vision of social defeatism and separatism had some immediate practical consequences. With many Christian journalists hiding their light under a bushel, the newspaper field was wide open for the triumph of "yellow journalism" at the end of the nineteenth century, and the expulsion of God from the front page early in the twentieth.[40] By 1925, Christians often were voiceless, except in publications that largely preached to the choir.

The almost total dominance of major newspapers by non-Christians showed up in the way that news stories generally, and major news stories with obvious theological dimensions in particular, were covered. There were many examples of biased coverage, but one of the most striking involved coverage of a 1925 trial that divided believers in the biblical account of creation from those who had made their peace with materialism or pantheism or some combination of the two.[41]

JOURNALISTIC MONKEYS

Two faiths were in conflict at that Dayton, Tennessee, "monkey trial." The *New York Times*, greatly changed from the 1870s, editorialized for "faith, even of a grain of mustard seed, in the evolution of life. . . ." Realizing that there were only two ways upward from sin and misery—God's grace or man's evolution—a *Times* editorial stated that evolution offered the most hope: "If man has evolved, it is inconceivable that the process should stop and leave him in his present imperfect state. Specific creation has no such promise for man."[42]

That faith ran up against Christian faith in God's sovereignty and the hope offered by Christ's sacrifice. Tennessee legislators passed a law forbidding the teaching of evolution as scientific truth. The battle was joined when one young Dayton teacher, John T. Scopes, responded to an American Civil Liberties Union plea for someone to agree to be the defendant in a test case, with the ACLU paying all legal expenses. Clarence Darrow, the most famous lawyer of the era and an atheist, was hired to head the defense. William Jennings Bryan, thrice-defeated Democratic presidential candidate, former Secretary of State, and a fundamentalist Christian, became point man for the prosecution.

The issue and the superstars brought out the journalists. Over one hundred reporters were dispatched to the trial. They wired 165,000 words daily to their newspapers during the twelve days of extensive coverage in July 1925. In theory, trial coverage could have been an opportunity to illuminate the theological debate that lay behind the creation vs. evolution issue. But in practice, with few if any Christians among those reporters, the position established early on by columnist H. L. Mencken went apparently unchallenged: "On the one side was bigotry, ignorance, hatred, superstition, every sort of blackness that the human mind is capable of. On the other side was sense."[43]

Journalists from major city newspapers saw the story as one of evolutionist intelligence vs. creationist stupidity. Nunnally Johnson, who covered the trial for the *Brooklyn Eagle* and then became a noted Hollywood screenwriter, remembered years later, "For the newspapermen it was a lark on a monstrous scale. . . . Being admirably cultivated fellows, they were all of course evolutionists and looked down on the local fundamentalists." Such ridicule was not merely a function of geography or politics. Both liberal and conservative newspapers lambasted the creationists. Journalists constantly attacked the theology of the creationists, perhaps because it was something their cultures had only recently "outgrown."[44]

The *New York Times* even noted at one point "a certain unexpectedness in the behavior and talk of the Dayton people. The unexpectedness comes from the absence in these Dayton people of any notable dissimilarity from people elsewhere except in their belated clinging to a method of Scriptural interpretation that not long ago was more than common in both North and South." The *Times* writer in those two sentences understood that fundamentalist beliefs were far from bizarre. In fact, it was the newer method of scriptural interpretation that had been regarded as bizarre in Times Square as well as Tennessee only a short time before.[45]

The Christian exile from mainline journalism—the absence of salt—led to poor reporting. The evolutionists, without anyone to check them, wrote that Christians were trying to make one pro-evolution book "a book of evil tidings, to be studied in secret."[46] This was nonsense: Hundreds of pro-evolution writings were on sale in Dayton. Even a drugstore had a stack of materials representing all positions. John Butler, the legislator who introduced the anti-evolution bill, had a copy of Darwin's *The Origin of the Species* for his teenage children to read. He told reporters, "I am not opposed to teaching of evolution, but I don't think it ought to be taught in state-supported schools."[47]

The key issue, clearly, was not free speech, but parental control over school curricula. Even in Tennessee, Christian parents were already beginning to sense that their beliefs were being excluded from schools they were funding. William Jennings Bryan spoke for them when he said he "never advocated teaching the Bible in public schools," but believed "There is no reason why school children should not hear of Bible characters as well as other characters. In other words, there is no reason why the reading of the Bible should be excluded while the reading of books about other characters in history, like Confucius, should be permitted."[48]

Tennessee legislators saw their anti-evolution bill not as a way of putting Christian religion into the schools, but of forbidding proselytization for what they saw as a trendy but unproved evolutionary faith.

Tennessee Governor Peay opposed the uncritical acceptance of evolutionary material "that no science has established."[49] One anti-evolutionary organization called itself the Defenders of True Science versus Speculation, contending that evolution "is a theory not yet approved by science," particularly since species-transitional fossils ("missing links") had not been found. "Demonstrated truth," Bryan insisted, "has no terrors for Christianity"[50]

Journalists, instead of explaining that, wrote leads such as, "Tennessee today maintained its quarantine against learning." The battle was "rock-ribbed Tennessee" vs. "unfettered investigation by the human mind and the liberty of opinion of which the Constitution makers preached." Reporters regularly attacked Christian faith and "this superheated religious atmosphere, this pathetic search for the 'eternal truth.'"[51]

One journalist described Scopes, the teacher-defendant, as an imprisoned martyr, "the witch who is to be burned by Dayton." (Actually, Scopes did not spend a second in jail and was regularly invited to dinner by Dayton Christians.) If the creationists were to win, another wrote, "The dunce cap will be the crown of office, and the slopstick will be the sceptre of authority." Residents of Dayton were "the treewise monkeys" who "see no logic, speak no logic and hear no logic." When William Jennings Bryan Jr., an attorney, arrived for the trial, a columnist wrote, "Junior is bound to be a chip off the old blockhead. . . . Like father, like son, and we don't like either."[52]

Dayton jurors, who following the trial gave thoughtful accounts of the proceedings, were described in one New York headline: "Intelligence of Most of Lowest Grade." It seemed that "All twelve are Protestant churchgoers."[53]

There was not even accurate coverage of the debates between creationists and evolutionists. For instance, when Bryan debated Darrow's associate Dudley Malone on July 16, the court transcript shows strong and intelligent orations by both sides. Bryan, within Christian presuppositions, made a sophisticated and coherent argument. He stressed the evolutionary theory's lack of scientific proof and emphasized its inability to answer questions about how life began, how man began, how one species actually changes into another, and so on. He pointed out the irreconcilability of Darwinian doctrines of extra-species evolution with the biblical account of creation, original sin, and the reasons for Christ's coming.[54]

Malone stated the evolutionist position in a similarly cohesive way. Both sides apparently did well. But journalists wrote that Bryan's speech "was a grotesque performance and downright touching in its imbecility."[55] Bryan coverage by a variety of reporters was laden with sarcastic biblical allusions: "Dayton began to read a new book of revelations today. The wrath of Bryan fell at last. With whips of scorn . . . he sought to drive science from the temples of God and failed."[56] According to the *Chicago Tribune*'s news coverage, the debate proved that "the truth as applied to man's origin was not locked in a book in the days of Moses."[57]

Overall, most major newspaper reporters produced so many unobservant stories that it often seemed as if they were closing their eyes and not even seeing the trial at all. The ultimate in this came when one New York scribe, under a headline "Scopes Is Seen as New Galileo at Inquisition," wrote that the "sultry courtroom in Dayton, during a pause in the argument, became hazy and there evolved from the mists of past ages a new scene. The Tennessee judge disappeared and I racked my brain to recognize the robed dignitary on the bench. Yes, it was the grand inquisitor, the head of the inquisition at Rome. . . . I saw the Tennessee Fundamentalist public become a medieval mob thirsty for heretical blood. . . . [It was] 1616. The great Galileo was on trial."[58]

It seemed that most reporters in Dayton, even when they tried to be fair—some had no such intention—could not help seeing the atheistic side as plausible and the Christian view as "nonsensical." The life and beliefs of one of the best of the Scopes trial reporters, Raymond Clapper, shows the pattern. In 1912, ready to enter college, he was leading Presbyterian church meetings in Kansas. But after four years at the University of Kansas, he chose "a more reasonable belief." By 1923 Clapper and his wife had "discarded the orthodox teachings of our youth. We could not believe the Old Testament prophets, whose teachings no doubt fitted well the savage age in which they lived but suited our world no better than the Greek oracles. The story of Christ we thought was moving and beautiful but we could not accept the virgin birth or the resurrection."[59]

Before Clapper arrived in Dayton to cover the trial, his mind already was made up: He believed that "the whole case of fundamentalism [was] ridiculous." It was no surprise, then, when Clapper's stories argued that "Fundamentalist justice has plugged up the ears of this Tennessee mountain jury." Olive Clapper, his wife, argued that "Unbelievable as the trial was to intelligent people, it did have value because the end result was greater enlightenment of people on the subject of evolution." Clapper had done his best to provide that enlightenment.[60]

The Clapper story could be repeated many times: Journalists who were or had become opposed to the Bible wanted to teach readers the anti-Christian "truth" as they saw it. There was no one to counterbalance their emphases, because Christians no longer had much of a presence in American journalism. Yes, there were denominational magazines and church newsletters, but coverage of major events such as the Scopes trial was in the hands of those who might be ever watching but never seeing.[61]

Mainline news coverage in the United States is still in those hands.

NOTES

1. Paul Vitz, *Religion and Traditional Values in Public Textbooks* (Washington, D.C.: National Institute of Education, 1986). For comments on Vitz's study, see *Newsweek*, July 28, 1986, p. 20; *Saturday Evening Post*, July-August 1986, p. 16; *Christianity Today*, January 17, 1986, p. 49; *Christianity Today*, March 7, 1986, p. 15.
2. Edwin and Michael Emery, *The Press and America*, fifth edition (Englewood Cliffs, NJ: Prentice-Hall, 1984), pp. 109-138.
3. Roberta Moore, *Development of Protestant Journalism in the United States, 1743-1850* (unpublished doctoral dissertation, Syracuse University, 1968), p. 237.
4. Frank Luther Mott's *American Journalism*, revised edition (New York: Macmillan, 1950) has one paragraph on p. 206 about the "religious newspapers" of the 1801-1833 period. According to Mott, about one hundred such publications, scattered across the country, covered both secular events and church activities: The newspapers were "a phenomenon of the times" and "often competed successfully with the secular papers." Mott noted that "many of these papers were conducted with great vigor and ability."

Mott did not go into detail, but his brief mention was more than these newspapers have received in other journalism history textbooks written in the twentieth century, such as James M. Lee, *History of American Journalism* (Boston: Houghton Mifflin, 1917); George H. Payne, *History of Journalism in the United States* (New York: Appleton-Century-Crofts, 1920); or Sidney Kobre, *Development of American Journalism* (Dubuque, IA: Wm. C. Brown Co., 1969). A history written in the late nineteenth century, Frederic Hudson, *Journalism in the United States from 1690 to 1872* (New York: Harper & Brothers, 1873), is also unsympathetic to the Christian press, but at least provides some information. A monograph by Wesley Norton, *Religious Newspapers in the Old Northwest to 1861* (Athens, OH: Ohio University Press, 1977), and dissertations by Moore and Kenberry, provide useful records.
5. Howard Kenberry, *The Rise of Religious Journalism in the United States* (unpublished dissertation, University of Chicago, 1920), p. 35.
6. *New York Observer*, June 23, 1849, p. 98.

7. *Puritan Recorder*, October 21,1858; quoted in Hudson, p. 290. Willis had had no particular theological interests and did not attend church, "but spent my Sabbaths in roving about the fields and in reading newspapers."

8. *Boston Recorder*, January 3, 1816, p. 1.

9. Ibid., September 11, 1819, p. 147. (The *Recorder* produced four-page issues but numbered its pages consecutively throughout the year.)

10. Ibid., April 22, 1820, p. 57.

11. Ibid., December 23, 1817, p. 202; August 25,1826, p. 136. The *Recorder* is one of my favorite old newspapers; Chapters Four, Ten, and Eleven (on objectivity, sensationalism and crusading) provide more examples of *Recorder* news coverage.

12. Contents of the early publications could be almost as varied as those of newspapers. One early Christian magazine became a bit carried away in describing its variety: The *New England Magazine* contained, according to the editors, "Relations Wonderful, and Psalm, and Song,/Good Sense, Wit, Humour, Morals, all ding dong;/Poems and Speeches, Politicks, and News,/What Some will like, and other Some refuse;/Births, Deaths, and Dreams, and Apparitions, too . . . To Humour Him, and Her, and Me, and You" (Kenberry, p. 64).

13. *Presbyterian of the West*, December 30, 1858; *Northwestern Christian Advocate*, November 28, 1860; quoted in Norton, p. 2.

14. For details on Raymond, see *New York Times*. June 19, 1869, p. 4 (obituary); June 22, p. 1 (funeral); June 28, p. 8 (eulogy); also see Francis Brown, *Raymond of the Times* (New York: Norton, 1951), and Augustus Maverick, *Henry J. Raymond and the New York Press for Thirty Years* (Hartford: Hale, 1870).

15. See Emery and Emery, p. 215. When Raymond died in 1869 he was succeeded by his long-time partner George Jones in the business management of the *Times* and, after two short-lived appointments, by Louis Jennings as editor; both Jones and Jennings were Christians. When Jones turned down a $5 million bribe offered him by Boss Tweed, he said the Devil never again would offer him so high a price.

16. One pro-abortion article cited in the U.S. Supreme Court's *Roe v. Wade* decision suggests that newspaper stories contributed to a long-lasting abortion setback: See Cyril C. Means, "The Law of New York Concerning Abortion and the State of the Foetus, 1664-1968: A Case of Cessation of Constitutionality," *New York Law Forum*, Fall 1968, pp. 458-490.

17. *New York Times*, November 3,1870, p. 4.

18. Ibid., August 23, 1871, p. 6.

19. Ibid.

20. Ibid.

21. Ibid., August 27, p. 1. The young lady was later identified as Alice Mowlsby, a poor orphan who lived with her aunt in Patterson, New Jersey

22. Ibid., August 28,29,30, p. 8. A boy who had helped carry the trunk into the station tried to find a man and a mysterious lady who had delivered the trunk. Readers daily absorbed the strategy of the detective in charge, Inspector Walling, who "issued orders which practically put every policeman in the force upon the case."

23. Ibid., August 29, p. 8; August 30, p. 4.

24. Ibid., August 30, p. 8.

25. Ibid. What would be called today a "free press vs. fair trial" issue does emerge here: With one of its own reporters giving a firsthand account, the *Times* sometimes seemed to be convicting the abortionist in the press.

26. Ibid., December 8, 1871, p. 2. The *Times* did recommend passage of a bill "far-reaching enough to catch hold of all who assist, directly or indirectly, in the destruction of infant life," and gave its recommendation one additional populist thrust: "The people demand it." The New York legislature of 1872 passed tough new anti-abortion laws, with easier rules of evidence and a maximum penalty of twenty years imprisonment. Enforcement also was stepped up.

27. Ibid., November 3, 1870, p. 4.

28. The *New York Times* continued to run anti-abortion stories through the remainder of the century. Chapter Eleven has more discussion of the overall anti-abortion campaign.

29. *Central Christian Herald*, September 2, 1852; quoted in Norton, p. 32.
30. Quoted in Kenberry, p. 158.
31. See p. 208 of each *Recorder* volume during the 1820s for a list of such articles. See also *Recorder*, January 27, 1837, p. 14.
32. Emerson's address is published in many books, including Volume 5 of the *Harvard Classics*, ed. Charles Eliot (New York: Collier, 1937), pp. 25-42.
33. This chapter has room to mention only in passing the major theological and social developments; it does not attempt to be anything more than a quick overview. For general discussions of the period, see Perry Miller, *The Life of the Mind in America: From the Revolution to the Civil War* (New York: Harcourt, Brace and World, 1965), and Sydney E. Ahlstrom, *A Religious History of the American People* (New Haven: Yale University Press, 1972). For a discussion of Unitarianism and the public schools, see Samuel Blumenfeld, *Is Public Education Necessary?* (Boise: Paradigm, 1985). For a discussion of the impact of evolutionism, see appendices to Gary North, *The Dominion Covenant* (Tyler, TX: Institute for Christian Economics, 1982), pp. 245-454.
34. Abbott's books include *The Evolution of Christianity* (Boston: Houghton Mifflin, 1900); *The Other Room* (New York: Grosset, Dunlap, 1903); *Christianity and Social Problems* (New York: Houghton Mifflin, 1896); and *Reminiscences* (Boston: Houghton Mifflin, 1915).
35. This discussion of Christian trends is, again, just a quick overview. For further information and perspective, see George Marsden, *The Evangelical Mind and the New School Presbyterian Experience* (New Haven: Yale University Press, 1970); Timothy L. Smith, *Revivalism and Social Reform in Mid-Nineteenth-Century America* (Nashville: Abingdon Press, 1957); James E Findlay Jr., *Dwight L. Moody American Evangelist, 1837-1899* (Chicago: University of Chicago Press, 1969); John Woodbridge, Mark Noll and Nathan Hatch, *The Gospel in America* (Grand Rapids: Zondervan, 1979).
36. As historian George Marsden has noted in *Fundamentalism and American Culture* (London: Oxford University Press, 1980), the 1860-1900 period brought with it "a transition from a basically 'Calvinistic' tradition, which saw politics as a significant means to advance the kingdom, to a 'pietistic' view of political action as no more than a means to restrain evil." This movement led to what Marsden calls the "Great Reversal" early in the twentieth century, with social concerns becoming suspect among revivalist evangelicals. Meanwhile, the older Reformed concern for social action was transmuted into a "social gospel" clung to by many who no longer held to the biblical gospel.
37. See Abraham Kuyper, *Lectures on Calvinism* (Grand Rapids, MI: Eerdmans, 1983; first published in 1899). Also see Henry Van Til, *The Calvinistic Concept of Culture* (Grand Rapids: Baker, 1959), and John T McNeill, *The History and Character of Calvinism* (London: Oxford University Press, 1954). Primarily see John Calvin, *Institutes of the Christian Religion*, 1559 edition, trans. Ford Lewis Battles, ed. John I McNeill (Philadelphia: The Westminster Press, 1960).
38. Norton, p. 38.
39. Just as the *Boston Recorder* had been one of the first to see the entire society as a journalistic mission field, so it was one of the first to drop out under the twin pressures of Boston transcendentalism and the tendency to turn inwards. Circulation during the 1840s was stagnant at a time when non-Christian newspapers were soaring. A *Recorder* editorial in 1848 suggesting "encouraging prospects" for the newspaper was belied by both appearance and context. Type size was smaller, typography was muddy, and page size had decreased; those pages were filled with monthly, quarterly and annual reports of various church groups, indicating clearly that the *Recorder* had died as a newspaper and had become a public relations organ. In 1849 the *Recorder* officially merged with the *Puritan*, a ten-year-old newspaper. Examination of one advertisement in the last issue of the *Recorder*, though, makes the agreement seem more like a subscription list buyout than a merger. The little notice, placed by the *Recorder* itself, offered "the type and other printing materials which are now used in this office—the whole comprising all the fixtures of a weekly newspaper establishment" (*Recorder*, January 7, 1848, p. 2; May 4, 1849, p. 71).
40. An interesting test arose in 1899 and 1900, when international attention was focused on the battle in South Africa between Boers and British. Race was not an issue at the time, since

neither side spoke much of the black inhabitants; the issue was social Darwinist "progress," and to the *New York Times* the Boers seemed least likely to succeed, due to their fundamentalist religious beliefs. "Poor, hidebound, Bible reading, otherwise illiterate Boers," the *New York Times* sniffed. The Boers' religion, according to the *Times*, makes them a "very stubborn people . . . in a state of arrested development. They are not much different from the Dutch of this island two centuries ago. That is to say, they are simple minded, Bible reading, God-fearing people" with an "idiotic-heroic attitude" (August 24, 1899, p. 6; August 10, 1899, p. 6).

41. *New York Times*, July 26, 1925, Section II, p. 4. Leslie H. Allen, ed., *Bryan and Darrow at Dayton: The Record and Documents of the Bible Evolution Trial* (New York: Russell & Russell, 1925), p. 1, conveniently assembles materials against which press reports may be checked.

42. The importance of the Dayton trial, for both prosecution and defense, lay in the chance to debate the issues of the case. The judicial proceedings themselves were not of great interest. The case was open-and-shut, deliberately designed for conviction on obvious law-breaking so that the decision could be appealed to the United States Supreme Court for a ruling on the act's constitutionality. (Ironically, although Scopes was convicted, as planned by the ACLU, and although the anti-evolution law itself was upheld by the Tennessee Supreme Court, the Tennessee Supreme Court also overturned the conviction on a technicality involving the imposition of a $100 fine without jury approval.)

43. *Baltimore Sun*, July 9, 1925, p. 1. Mencken attacked the Dayton creationists (before he had set foot in the town) as "local primates . . . yokels . . . morons . . . half-wits." Mencken put aside his typical amusement with life to ride Paul Revere-like through the land with dire warnings about the trial: "Let no one mistake it for comedy, farcical though it may be in all its details. It serves notice on the country that Neanderthal man is organizing in these forlorn backwaters of the land, led a by a fanatic, rid of sense and devoid of conscience" (*Baltimore Sun*, July 18, 1925, p. 1).

   Mencken's intolerance was parallel to that of many anti-evolution spokesmen. Columbia University dean Henry H. Rusby demanded that universities not recognize degrees from universities that did not accept evolution. A leading liberal minister, Charles Francis Potter, argued that "educated and enlightened men ought not to rest until the possibility of such dense mental darkness is removed." The *New York Times* then editorialized against "the mental and moral infection which has been let loose upon the land. . . . (*New York Times*, July 12, 1925, section 1, p. 2; *Arkansas Gazette*, June 16, p. 2). Fundamentalists had some justification for believing that they were being told not "live and let live," but "your diseased religion does not deserve to exist."

44. Acid-tongued Westbrook Pegler, who covered the trial briefly, admired Mencken and imitated his coverage, but noted years later concerning the creationists, "They were intelligent people, including a fair proportion of college graduates. Nevertheless, the whole Blue Ridge country was ridiculed on religious grounds by an enormous claque of supercilious big town reporters. Such ridicule was not primarily a function of politics; it underlay the politics of liberal and conservative newspapers. The liberal *New York Times* editorialized that the creationist position represented a "breakdown of the reasoning powers. It is seeming evidence that the human mind can go into deliquescence without falling into stark lunacy" (July 13, p. 16). The conservative *Chicago Tribune* sneered at fundamentalists looking for "horns and forked tails and cloven hoofs" (July 19, p. 5).

45. *New York Times*, July 20, 1925, p. 14.

46. *Arkansas Gazette*, July 18, 1925, p. 5.

47. *Baltimore Sun*, July 10, 1925, p. 1. Also see *Atlanta Constitution*, July 9, p. 10.

48. *Arkansas Gazette*, July 12, p. 1. Also see *Arkansas Gazette*, June 23, p. 1, and June 28, p. 1; Washington Post, July 16, 1925, p. 6.

49. *Arkansas Gazette*, June 27, 1925, p. 1.

50. *Atlanta Constitution*, July 2, 1925, p. 1; July 8, 1925, p. 22.

51. *New York American*, July 18, 1925, p. 1; July 14, p. 1; *Arkansas Gazette* (*New York Times/Chicago Tribune* news service), July 16, 1925, p. 3.

52. *New York American*, July 13, 1925, p. 1; July 15, p. 4; July 16, p. 2; July 17, p. 2.

53. *New York American*, July 12, 1925, p. 1; see also *Arkansas Gazette*, July 11, p. 1.

54. See Allen, *loc. cit.*

55. *Baltimore Sun*, July 17, 1925, p. 1.

56. *Arkansas Gazette*, July 12, 1925, p. 1, July 13, p. 1; July 17, p. 3.

57. *Chicago Tribune*. See also *Arkansas Gazette*, July 14, p. 5.

58. *New York American*, July 14, 1925, p. 1. One more bizarre twist to the trial deserves mentioning: the last Bryan-Darrow confrontation arose unexpectedly on the final day of the trial. Many reporters were off swimming or carousing, with the result that other reporters, after telegraphing their own stories, hastily rewrote parts and sent them to the missing reporters' newspapers in order to cover for their friends. Scopes himself was asked by several reporters to write parts of the new articles; so journalistic coverage of the trial concluded with a bizarre touch: the defendant reporting on his own case under someone else's byline. See John T. Scopes and James Presley, *Center of the Storm: Memoirs of John T. Scopes* (New York: Holt, Rinehart and Winston, 1967), p. 183.

59. Olive Clapper, *One Lucky Woman* (Garden City, NY: Doubleday, 1961), pp. 34,51,109.

60. Ibid., p. 99.

61. The *Atlanta Constitution* editorialized about the trial coverage's potential effect: "Thousands of columns of newspaper debate have been published under Dayton date lines in the past two weeks, and from it all the cause of the religion of Jesus Christ has not been helped, but the world has been broadcast with the seeds of doubt and skepticism, and only the future can tell what the harvest will be . . . among the millions of people who congest the bumper ground between science and the Bible there may be thousands who will now find themselves drifting into the easy-going channels of agnosticism" (July 22, 1925, p. 6).

A Christian Journalism Revival?

[Chapter Twelve of *Prodigal Press*]

Technology provides the opportunity for a Christian comeback. Use of biblical sensationalism and crusading personalization will allow Christians to gain and keep an audience. But none of this will make much difference unless Christian communities view journalism as a vital calling and Christian journalists as ministers worthy of spiritual and economic support. Christian editors and reporters, after all. are like fish in a lake. Some Christian newspapers made mistakes in the nineteenth century, as indicated in Chapter One, but the lake itself was drying up fast.

The water level of Christian lakes appears to be rising. The environment for successful Christian publications earlier in American history was a Christian population willing to fight on social and political issues. Jolted by the atheism of many French revolutionaries and their American supporters, Christians resolved to publish rather than perish. Jolted in recent decades by similar revolutionary doctrines in modern wineskins, Christians are relearning what the *New York Times* proclaimed during its abortion campaign of the 1870s: "The evil that is tolerated is aggressive," and the good "must be aggressive too."

A recent statement of the Coalition on Revival (COR) typifies the trend. (COR's leadership group includes individuals such as Edith

Schaeffer, former *Christianity Today* editor Harold Lindsell, evangelists James Kennedy, Jack Van Impe and Tim LaHaye, and Southern Baptist Convention president Adrian Rogers.) The statement included admissions of sin such as, "We have neglected our God-ordained duties to be the world's salt, light, teacher, and example. . . . We, and our fathers, have settled for a sub-standard, false version of Christianity in our local churches and denominations. . . . We have allowed our churches to become irrelevant, powerless ghettos."[1]

The statement then asked for forgiveness by God, fellow Christians, and, significantly, non-Christians: "Forgive us for our failure to demonstrate to you biblical answers for your difficulties and problems in life. Forgive us for failing to occupy our proper position as servants in the affairs of law government, economics, business, education, media, the arts, medicine, and science as the Creator's salt and light to the world, so that those spheres of life might offer you more help, justice, hope, peace, and joy."

COR's Call to Action proclaimed several truths essential to the revival of Christian journalism: "We affirm that living under the total Lordship of Jesus Christ in every area of life is not optional for those who would call themselves Christians." Furthermore, we cannot be smiling all the time: COR stressed the "need for loving confrontation over matters of falsehood and unrighteousness in the Church and in the world." Regular confrontation, exhortation and rebuke are vital to the leading of biblically obedient lives and the transforming of culture.

The statement concluded with an affirmation "that all Bible-believing Christians must take a non-neutral stance in opposing, praying against, and speaking against social moral evils." Among those evils listed were abortion, infanticide and euthanasia; adultery and homosexuality; unjust treatment of the poor and disadvantaged; state usurpation of parental rights and God-given liberties; and atheism, moral relativism, and evolutionism taught as a monopoly viewpoint in public schools.

Other Christian organizations also are speaking out forcefully. Some within the church are offended by such efforts. Jesus, though, said to His followers, "Do not suppose that I have come to bring peace to the earth. I did not come to bring peace, but a sword" (Matthew 10:34). Christians may be sure of peace in Heaven and peace in our consciences, but peace in our worldly dealings is rare.

The sword brought by Christ is twofold, as commentator Matthew Henry pointed out: The sword of the Word eventually conquers (Revelation 19:21), but God's truth often provokes such a hostile reaction among non-Christians that they apply the sword to believers. This effect of the preaching of the gospel is not the fault of the gospel, but of those who do not receive it. Because of this backlash effect, it is a mistake to think Christianity preserves its followers from trouble in this world. Becoming a Christian is not the end of the battle, but the real beginning.

The battle record of some established Christian publications is not good. Some now are public relations vehicles for their organizations, denominations, or peculiar beliefs. Some seem devoted largely to keeping up appearances and smiles. Editors who try to wield the sword on controversial issues sometimes have found that readers and contributors have exceptionally thin skins. One editor who tried to renovate a dull and declining magazine complained, following his pressured resignation, that "readers sometimes expect a magazine to be something for the whole family, with everything positive. Readers don't seem willing to tolerate a few articles they don't like."

Some Christian publications are willing to wield a sword. *World* magazine (Box 2330, Asheville, NC 28802) covers hard news. *Twin Cities Christian (TCC)*, a biweekly newspaper published in Minneapolis with a circulation of eight thousand and considerable advertising, has had front-page coverage of issues that "soil the breakfast cloth," in the words of the nineteenth-century *New York Times*. For example, when the Supreme Court struck down claims by homosexuals that the Constitution protects sodomy, *TCC* did not shy away from front-page sentences about oral and anal sex. When members of a pro-life action group were arrested for distributing literature in front of a hospital where abortions are performed, *TCC* published a photograph and a sympathetic article.[2]

TCC's coverage of local controversies includes three elements. First, the newspaper throws a spotlight on anti-biblical activities. *TCC* gave front-page coverage to the sponsorship by a liberal church social services program of a program for sex offenders designed to help them "in the most important area of their lives, that of intimacy." To show what those nice words really meant, *TCC* had to quote charges from a responsible source that the program included use of explicit films portraying men and women masturbating to climax, having intercourse with animals, and engaging in a variety of homosexual and lesbian acts—the goal of the program apparently being not a consideration of right and wrong, but how-to training. The program concluded with a worship service featuring a pastor and his wife who were dressed as clowns. One clown wore huge glasses with obscene words written on the lenses.[3]

Second, *TCC* goes to bat for Christians facing discrimination. One headline stretching across the top of *TCC*'s front page read, "Christian Students Suspended." According to the story's lead, "They weren't selling drugs, skipping class, or damaging school property They didn't brawl in the halls or smoke in the bathroom. But last Thursday two Hopkins School seniors were suspended from classes." The students were "handing out religious literature. Their action violated a school board policy." The story explained that the students had deliberately handed out free copies of a Christian magazine before classes began in order to test the school board policy: "We need to fight for our rights," one student said.[4]

TCC has used biblically sensational headlines in coverage of stories involving such abridgment of First Amendment rights. "Bible-reading Grandma Kicked out of Mall" was the headline on a story of a grandmother talking with a young man about the Bible as they sat in a shopping mall rest area. "We were speaking quietly," she said. "When you're out in the world you're representing Jesus Christ, not only in your actions, but in how you're dressed and in how you talk. We were being careful not to offend anybody or to draw attention to ourselves. We were just talking one-on-one about the Lord." Then a security guard falsely accused the woman of selling religious literature, and escorted her off the mall property with orders not to return again.[5]

When the Bible-reading grandma protested and *TCC* investigated the incident, the mall management backed down, explaining that it was all a misunderstanding. "We had been picking up religious booklets that had been distributed in the mall, and when you were sitting discussing religious things with another person, we made an assumption that proved incorrect," the mall manager told the grandmother. "We apologize." She replied, "I'm not resentful, but people need to be warned about how our rights as Christians to worship God in public— even just reading a Bible—are being taken away from us." A loss of such rights can be more readily opposed when Christian journalists are present to blow the whistle.[6]

A third element of *TCC* coverage is also crucial: It will defend Christians who are suffering for Christ's sake, but it will also print critical evidence about Christians or Christian organizations engaged in unethical activity. The lead story in one issue concerned an evangelist accused of faking miracles at healing crusades for his own purposes. An editorial criticized a local Christian television organization for soliciting funds but not providing information on how the money was being spent. Other stories decried the fundraising tactics of some Christian organizations.[7]

Editor Doug Trouten defended his policy in a spirited editorial, "Why Write Bad Things About Good People?" He raised in print the questions that he had been asked: "When a ministry folds and its leaders leave town with its assets, why report it? When the leader of a ministry dependent on donations seems to live in unnecessary opulence, why tell the world? When an elected official strays from the Christian principles that were a part of campaign rhetoric, does somebody need to blow the whistle?"[8]

Trouten noted that "the Christian press often becomes a willing partner in efforts to cover up wrong-doing by religious leaders," but he argued that "this mentality runs contrary to Scriptural teaching. . . . Too often we are content to ignore unpleasant truths. Yet as Christians we worship a God of truth. We're not asked to follow our leaders blindly. The Bible says, 'I would not have you ignorant . . . ' and 'My people are destroyed for lack of knowledge.' We need to know about those who lead us."[9]

TCC's willingness to cover sensation and take tough stands is essential to the establishing of real Christian journalism (rather than public relations) and the resultant strengthening of the Body of Christ. More Christian publications should take lessons from *TCC*—or from a Kentucky editor of the 1840s, the original Cassius Clay. (Muhammed Ali was named after him, but showed his theology by making a change.)

The original Clay, born in 1810, was a Christian who published in Kentucky an anti-slavery newspaper. When pro-slavery partisans threatened to destroy Clay's printing press, he made a fort out of his three-story, red-brick newspaper office: Clay purchased two small brass cannon, loaded them to the muzzle with bullets, slugs, and nails, and stationed them at the entrance, while his friends stockpiled muskets and Mexican lances.

Those measures forestalled the attack. Then Clay took the fight to the opposition, going before hostile crowds to speak his piece. Once, facing his enemies, Clay held up a Bible and said, "To those who respect God's word, I appeal to this book." Then he held up a copy of the Constitution and said, "To those who respect our fundamental law I appeal to this document." Then he took out two pistols and his Bowie knife. He said, "To those who recognize only force . . ."[10]

Clay survived many fights and assassination attempts. Finally, he was seized by pro-slavery men and knifed. Gushing blood from a lung wound, Clay cried out, "I died in the defense of the liberties of the people," and then lost consciousness. He recovered, though, and helped to form the Republican Party during the 1850s. He had many political successes and personal adventures until he died in 1903, at age ninety-three.

The secret of Clay's strength may have been his belief in the power of God's law and personal faith. Clay saw even-handedness in the Bible: The rich should help the poor, and the poor should not envy or steal from the rich. Clay wrote, "Let true Christianity prevail, and earth will become the foreshadowing of Heaven." Clay also knew there is no such thing as neutrality in journalism. Knowing that all people, whether Christian or non-Christian, interpret the world through religious first principles, Clay openly acknowledged his beliefs and showed the willingness to fight for them.

The situation is a bit different now: In our daily business activities we can leave the Bowie knives home. Yet, the sword brought by Christ still flashes, and we need to be prepared to fight with our brains, pens, and computers. What keeps us from readiness to fight, often, is fear both obvious and subtle: Fear of ridicule and fear of audience are obvious problems; fear of distraction and, most crucially, fear of the Bible itself are the covert cripplers among Christians.

THE FOUR FEARS AND THEIR EFFECT UPON JOURNALISM

First, Christian journalists must not be afraid of boldly stating the Christian view of reality, which includes both material and spiritual dimensions. We must subdue our fear of what materialistic colleagues will think of us, not only because of the realization that Christ has come with a sword, but because the biblical emphasis on truth-telling is fundamental to Christian journalism.

Some materialists will be tolerant of religious belief as long as it is privatized and equated with subjectivity: If it makes you feel good, believe it. Some also argue that Heaven, if there is such a place, must be an equal opportunity employer. Christians, though, know that subjective feelings are ephemeral: Our friends need to gain an accurate picture of the cosmos and then act accordingly, or else they are lost.

The Bible always emphasizes reporting of what actually happened. Luke began his Gospel by writing, "Since I myself have carefully investigated everything from the beginning, it seemed good also to me to write an orderly account . . . so that you may know the certainty of the things you have been taught." Paul told the Corinthians that they should not believe in the doctrine of Christ's resurrection because it might be comforting for some: The important question was, did it happen? Paul insisted that either Christ rose from the dead, or Christian hope is in vain.

In short, when a Christian reports spiritual happenings as fact, not subjective impression, he will be ridiculed by some. That is the price to pay for worshiping the God who really is there, not just a psychologically soothing idol.

Second, Christian journalists must not be afraid of audience. We should not turn inwards, nor be willing to accept a journalistic strategy that churches might find pleasant but the world will ignore. We should not be afraid of picking from the best of the methods of journalism, while always evaluating all means and ends in the light of God's Word (2 Corinthians 10:5).

After all, the authors of the Gospels knew how to produce the same message but with different emphases for those with different backgrounds. Paul, in speaking to the Athenians, was willing to make contact with them by pointing out their worship of an unknown God (Acts 17). A successful Christian journalist must similarly attract attention in order to affect intentions.

Third, Christians must not fear that a new emphasis on journalism will distract from either concern for evangelism or the godly education of those already within the church. That concern is short-sighted, since both evangelism and education become more difficult when both non-

Christians and Christians are constantly being bombarded by messages on "non-religious" matters that assume materialism is true. Journalism is vital pre-evangelistic work, needed to prepare individuals to accept the reality of God's grace. Journalism also is post-justification work, helping those graced to construct godly lives.

Fourth, and most subtle of all, is the reluctance even among some Christians to acknowledge that all created things, including our own minds, are twisted by sin (Genesis 3:17–19; Romans 8:20–22). Our minds are not capable of creating a sound set of guidelines from either observation or pure reason. Our only hope lies in learning biblical principles of thought and conduct, and trusting the Holy Spirit to help us make the right practical applications.

The Bible teaches that thought independent of God's special revelation is untrustworthy at best and eventually suicidal. Only the Word of God can give us principles for establishing a life pleasing to God. This vital concept is hard to swallow in a society with strong belief in existentialist creativity: Individuals supposedly develop new ideas and ways of conduct *ex nihilo*, as if they were gods unto themselves. The Bible, though, stresses God as Creator and man as image-bearer. We cannot create virtue or virtuous ideas apart from God's thoughts.

Sometimes, in short, Christians confronted by tough problems are afraid of biblical truth. Why not abortion when there has been rape? Why not divorce when husband and wife fight? Why write a story that could lose the journalist his job? There are biblical answers to such questions, but they require hard analytical and practical work. Sometimes even Christians fear the Bible because it does not give comfortable answers.

A TWO-PRONGED STRATEGY

If the four fears are overcome, Christian journalists will be strong enough, and will be receiving sufficient community support, to ask another question: Where can I best serve God?

Some may now have a tendency to choose working at publications or media outlets owned and operated by Christians because those positions seem "safer," removed from contact with the world. A Christian journalistic revival, though, would mean that no place would be safe: Christian journalistic organizations would be aggressively reporting on the contrast between man's depravity and God's holiness, and non-Christian organizations would be prime mission fields.

Christian journalists sometimes seem tempted into arguments about whether explicitly Christian or secular media represent better alternatives for service. Such debates can be equivalent to Jesus' disciples squabbling about primacy on earth and seating arrangements in Heaven. As bad as many public schools are today, a toughminded, tenacious Christian teacher in the classroom can still be a Godsend to children. Similar considerations apply in journalism, where the influence of one person may be even more widespread.

Strong Christian publications and stations are vital, but salty Christians also are needed within today's influential, non-Christian media systems. As stories with overt theological dimensions continue to arise, and as the more subtle stories influenced by presuppositions cross newsroom desks, it is vital that there be Christian reporters and editors willing to speak up.

Christians in non-Christian media organizations can also serve as counselors and evangelists. Not only do the major media institutions have great power, but the individuals within them often have great problems. If we were to bring forward in time the series of mini-biographies in Chapter Three, we would see that many apparently secure contemporary journalists desperately need help. Smiling anchormen and women often are off-camera wrecks.

Christians who have thought through the nature of objectivity and sensationalism, and the ethical and legal problems of the field, can glorify God within such media outposts. Nor do well-prepared Christians necessarily have to choose between mealy-mouthedness and unemployment. As the discussions of objectivity and sensationalism in Chapters Four and Ten indicated, Christians do not have to *preach* in stories. Instead, Christians can work toward honest selection of details, fair and ample quotation of biblical Christian spokesmen, and examination of the spiritual/material interface.

Still, a Christian reporter should realize that even a small movement toward true objectivity might anger an atheistic editor. In such circumstances, firmness is essential. As soon as a worldview conflict becomes apparent, Christian journalists working for non-Christians have to decide which of two roads to potential success to follow: the way of the tough and talented Christian, or the path of the presuppositional sycophant. These two roads tend to divide early. A reporter who writes of funda- mentalists with appropriate sarcasm will be praised; a reporter who quotes not only Darwinian scientists but creation scientists will be ques- tioned. And yet, a skilled reporter will have some value to his editors even if he refuses to play the game. He may not receive fast promotions, but he will not necessarily be fired, for real talent is in short supply

The danger of slow career progress is clear. Yet, the prayer that Christ gives us as a model includes the sentence, "Give us today our daily bread" (Matthew 6:11). The sentence is not, "Give us today our daily steak." Nor is it, "Give us today our daily starvation." We need bread: Good, healthy sustenance, both material and spiritual. If a Christian's career is not as visibly spectacular—at least in the short run—as that of a person who is crafty and corrupt, that is a relatively small cross to bear.

Christians working for unsympathetic employers can make some practical intellectual and financial preparations while they are on the job. A Christian journalist must know that a news organization is not a home. We are wayfarers and sojourners here on this earth generally, and in newspapers or broadcast stations specifically. If God's providence has put the Christian in a high-paying job, he must immediately calculate what he needs to live on, not what he is temporarily able to live on. Any extra money is a special gift from God and should not be squandered: Some of that money might support the journalist if he is forced to resign. Furthermore, the goal should always be to develop skills that will allow the Christian to become his own boss, if the possibility arises. For, in the long run, Christian journalists will need Christian publications.

In that long run, it is clear that only news organizations owned and staffed by Christians will be able to practice journalism consistent with strong biblical faith. Only through independence can Christians make sure that the Bible is taken seriously in journalism. Therefore, Christian entre- preneurs who start new publications now and have the talent and dedica- tion to make a go of them are worthy of double honor. Support for such individuals is as important as support for those who preach within a church.

CONCLUSION

Joshua in his old age told the Israelites, "Choose for yourselves this day whom you will serve." The Israelites then promised that they would obey God, for they had learned that "It was the Lord our God himself who brought us and our forefathers up out of Egypt, from that land of slavery, and performed those great signs before our eyes. He protected us on our entire journey and among all the nations through which we traveled." The education of the Israelites, through God's grace, had enabled them to see events as they really occurred, with both material and spiritual dimensions.

Throughout the Bible, God's spokesmen and reporters constantly tried to explain to their listeners and readers the reality of His involvement in human history. Moses told the Israelites (Deuteronomy 29): "Your eyes have seen all that the Lord did in Egypt to Pharaoh, to all his officials and to all his land. With your own eyes you saw those great trials, those miraculous signs and great wonders. But to this day the Lord has not given you a mind that understands or eyes that see or ears that hear." Seeing was not believing; reporters had to provide context, and then pray for God's grace on eyes and ears. Psalm 78 reported "the praiseworthy deeds of the Lord," and Stephen testified before the Sanhedrin to God's continued working in human history (Acts 7).

Christian journalism, as history's first draft, should follow the Bible in depicting God's grace and man's sinfulness. Non-Christian journalism has led to attempts to make people happy, either by suggesting that things are right (the position of some non-Christian conservatives) or that man by his egotistical efforts can make all things right (the position of some liberals). Christians, though, know that things are not right, due to original sin, and will be made right only through Christ: "He is before all things, and in him all things hold together" (Colossians 1:17).

"Be strong and courageous," God commands Joshua repeatedly. Avoidance of the four fears, through the strength and courage that only God can give, is vital for Christian journalists.

If Christians are willing to cover all aspects of life, to soil the breakfast table, to deal honestly with evil, to avoid intellectual trendiness, to meet communication demands of a fast-paced marketplace, to hit hard in a compassionate way that does not libel individuals—then we have done as much as we can, and we can pray with clear consciences for God to grant us success.

If Christians are willing to report faithfully that God is sovereign, that Satan is active but under control, that man pursues evil by nature but can be transformed, and that God does answer prayers in the way that is best for our growth in grace—then, with God's grace, Christians will have the most insightful and exciting news publications and programs in the United States.

Gloria in Excelsis Deo.

NOTES

1. *A Manifesto for the Christian Church: Declaration and Covenant*, July 4, 1986 (Mountain View, CA: Coalition on Revival, 1986).
2. *Twin Cities Christian*, July 3, 1986, p. 1. [Note from 1995: This biweekly, still edited by Doug Trouten, is now called the *Minnesota Christian Chronicle*, and it is still a fine newspaper.] *World*, edited by Joel Belz, has this mailing address: Box 2330, Asheville, NC 28002.
3. Ibid., February 15, 1983, p. 1.
4. Ibid., April 12, 1984, p. 1.
5. Ibid., April 24, 1986, p. 3.
6. *Twin Cities Christian* also has reported the more severe intrusions on religious liberty that prevail in other countries. One front-page story, "Christian Woman Interrogated by KGB at Moscow Airport," told of a woman who "will never forget Mother's Day 1985. On that day she was arrested at Moscow airport, interrogated for more than six hours, strip-searched and later expelled from the Soviet Union. Her crime? Wanting to give gifts to Russian Christians—Bibles, copies of the Sermon on the Mount, Christian music tapes and clothing" (July 4, 1985, p. 1).
7. Ibid., May 8, 1986, p. 1; August 29, 1985, p. 18.
8. Ibid., May 9, 1985, p. 18.
9. Ibid.
10. See Clay's autobiography, *The Life of Cassius Marcellus Clay* (Cincinnati: J. Fletcher Brennan and Co. 1886), and an essay he wrote in 1845: *Appeal of Cassius M. Clay to Kentucky and the World* (Boston: Macomber and Pratt, 1845). My thanks to the University of Kentucky library for allowing me access to several rare biographies.

INDEX